FORT SUPPLY

INDIAN TERRITORY

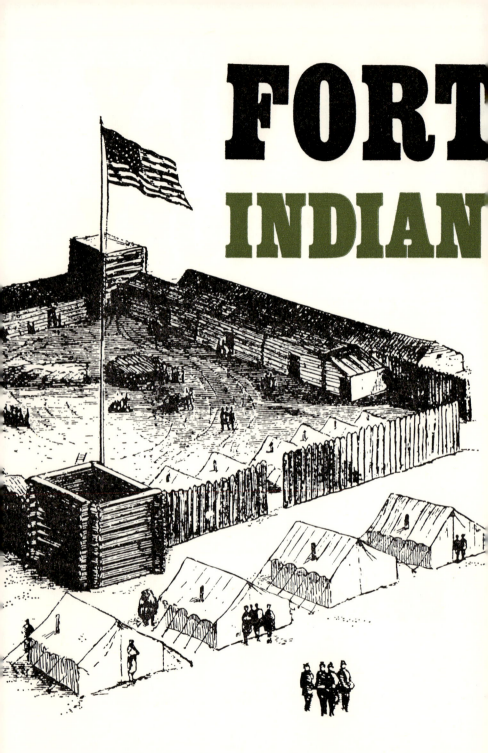

FORT

INDIAN

SUPPLY

TERRITORY

FRONTIER OUTPOST
ON THE PLAINS

Robert C. Carriker

University of Oklahoma Press

Norman

INTERNATIONAL STANDARD BOOK NUMBER: 0–8061–0929–7

LIBRARY OF CONGRESS CATALOG CARD NUMBER: 71–123345

COPYRIGHT 1970 BY THE UNIVERSITY OF OKLAHOMA PRESS, PUBLISH-
ING DIVISION OF THE UNIVERSITY. COMPOSED AND PRINTED AT NOR-
MAN, OKLAHOMA, U.S.A., BY THE UNIVERSITY OF OKLAHOMA PRESS.
FIRST EDITION.

TO

Thomas B. Carriker, my father

Thomas H. Carriker, my brother

Thomas A. Carriker, my son

Preface

Not long after my arrival in Norman, Oklahoma, in the summer of 1963, I first came across mention of Fort Supply. In the University of Oklahoma Western History Collections I discovered the Walter S. Campbell Collection. Many of the interests of Professor Campbell (who often wrote under the pseudonym Stanley Vestal) soon became my own. Indians, Dodge City, the Santa Fe Trail, and dozens of other western topics spiced the correspondence, manuscripts, and research papers that make up the collection. In the voluminous papers the materials about one military station, Fort Supply, which was established in northwestern Indian Territory in the post–Civil War years, particularly attracted my interest.

Some weeks after my initial contact with accounts of the post I went to the Oklahoma Panhandle to visit a friend. My route, northwest from Norman, passed through Supply, Oklahoma, and the scattered buildings of the old fort, which is now the Western State Mental Hospital. The next few days, which I spent on Beaver River exploring an area often scouted by troopers from Fort Supply in the early days, left me with an abiding interest in the post and the region.

Although I did some research on Fort Supply during the next three years, visiting the area four more times, I was never able to get a clear picture of events at the post. When at last the opportunity came to study the post records in the National Archives, I accepted the challenge with great anticipation. I was not disappointed. To my amazement there were four times more records on Fort Supply than there were on its famous neighbor, Fort Dodge, Kansas, and upon scrutiny they turned out to be some of the best-kept records in the Old Army Military Division.

After more than fifteen hundred pertinent documents were pulled from the post records, the history of an important camp began to take form. Connecting these documents with other sources in the National Archives—books, articles, and newspapers—I began to learn the forgotten story of Fort Supply. In the first ten years of the post's existence, from 1868 to 1878, its personnel were involved in three Indian uprisings and yet found time to protect the Cheyennes and Arapahoes from depredations by other Indian tribes, white stock thieves, and whisky traders from Kansas and New Mexico. In the decade of the 1880's, Fort Supply troops provided protection for the emerging cattle industry of western Indian Territory by guarding the Old Caldwell and Dodge City trails and later by clearing the leased ranges of the Cheyenne-Arapaho Reservation and the Cherokee Outlet.

As the frontier continued to diminish after 1890, Fort Supply performed its last role in history by serving as headquarters for the opening of the Cherokee Outlet to settlement, in September, 1893. For roughly twenty-five years Fort Supply played a meaningful part in the lives of three important elements of Southern Plains history: the red man, the cowboy, and the sodbuster. It seemed a story worth pursuing.

Many persons assisted me in this study, among them Forrest D. Monahan, Jr., of Midwestern University, Wichita Falls, Texas; Joseph Snell, of the Kansas Historical Society; Mrs. Alice Timmons, of the Phillips Collection, University of Oklahoma Library; and Mrs. Faye B. Crain, of the Panhandle-Plains Historical Society. Others have made contributions so significant that the project might never have been completed without their co-operation. Arrell M. Gibson, curator of the

University of Oklahoma Western History Collections, carefully read the entire manuscript with a professional eye and saved me from several errors. Jack D. Haley, assistant curator of the University of Oklahoma Western History Collections, has worked with me since my first encounter with materials about Fort Supply and has constantly offered good advice, research leads, and friendship. Donald J. Berthrong, of the University of Oklahoma, took time from his duties as chairman of the Department of History to guide me through the history of the difficult years of the 1870's and greatly enhanced the value of my work by directing me in the use of the records of the Office of Indian Affairs in the National Archives. Mrs. Sara Jackson, of the National Archives, steered my researches with unfailing skill and good humor.

A special word of gratitude is due the University of Oklahoma for financial assistance through the National Science Foundation Science Faculty Fellowship, which made possible my research in the National Archives, and the Jesuit Research Council of Gonzaga University, which made possible a grant to prepare the manuscript for publication. Mr. and Mrs. William Zimmerer, of Arlington, Virginia, very dear friends, opened their home to me for the month I spent in Washington, D.C., and made my stay enjoyable. Mrs. Lonnie Demaray typed the manuscript with exceptional accuracy and speed, assisted several times by Mrs. Ginny Moeller.

My wife, Eleanor, proved herself patient and self-sacrificing, besides being a first-class proofreader of the many revisions this manuscript has undergone. Any mistakes, of course, are my own.

Robert C. Carriker

Spokane, Washington
January 10, 1970

Contents

Preface   *page*   *vii*

I   Camp Supply in the Winter Campaign, 1868   3

II   Indian Unrest at Camp Supply, 1869–70   30

III   Indians, Whites, and Whisky, 1871–73   56

IV   Camp Supply in the Indian Territory
Expedition, 1874–75   85

V   Indians, Whites, and Thievery, 1875–79   107

VI   Soldier and Citizen at Fort Supply   137

VII   Cattle, Reservations, and Trails, 1880–89   156

VIII   Cattle, the Outlet, and Leases, 1880–92   182

IX   Opening the Outlet and Closing the Post, 1893–94   201

Bibliography   221

Index   234

Illustrations

Camp Supply in 1869   *following page* 112
Issue of Rations to Indians at Camp Supply, 1870
Teamster's Cabin, Erected about 1869
Ground Plan of Camp Supply, 1870
Guardhouse at Fort Supply
Hospital Building at Fort Supply
Major General Philip H. Sheridan
The Opera House
The Lee and Reynolds Shop
Barracks on the North Side of Fort Supply
Ground Plan of Fort Supply, 1886
Cavalry Inspection, about 1890

Maps

The Southern Plains Frontier, 1867–75   *page*   6
Fort Supply Area, 1868–94   41
Deep Creek Trail Refinement, 1887   176
Military Districts for Opening the Cherokee Outlet   206

FORT SUPPLY

INDIAN TERRITORY

Chapter I

Camp Supply in the Winter Campaign
1868

Camp Supply was established in 1868 as an operational base for the United States Army in its extended campaign to control the Southern Plains. The years following the Civil War saw this region ripped by savage warfare. Relentlessly pushed by white intruders, warriors from the Plains tribes mounted violent raids along the frontiers of Colorado, Kansas, and Texas. Wagon trains were attacked and burned, horses and mules stolen, settlers and miners killed. Torture, murder, and pillage became the fate of numerous pioneers.

It cost the United States forty million dollars and countless lives to contain the Plains Indians after the 1864 Sand Creek Massacre.[1] The energy of eight thousand troops was expended until October, 1865, when a peace commission met with the hostiles. The Treaty of the Little Arkansas River brought temporary peace as Cheyennes and Arapahoes, Kiowa-Apaches, and Kiowas and Comanches accepted reservations.

The truce, however, succumbed in the early months of 1866. Texas' control of its public lands nullified the proposed reservation for the Kiowas and Comanches, and Kansas similarly refused Cheyenne settlement along its southern border. Before long, Cheyenne Dog Soldiers, the warrior society conspicuously absent from the Little Arkansas meetings, were suspected of hostilities. In spite of the efforts of Agent Edward W. Wynkoop to bring them into the treaty fold, the Dog Soldiers remained at large, harassing wagon trains and livestock herds. Those Chey-

[1] *Sen. Exec. Doc. No. 13*, 40 Cong., 1 sess., 2.

ennes committed by the treaty became restless, and farther south the Kiowas, led by Satanta and Lone Wolf, raided through a defense-poor Texas undergoing federal Reconstruction. The fires of Indian raids once again swept the Southern Plains, charring frontier settlements.

Governor Samuel J. Crawford of Kansas journeyed to Washington and urged greater federal protection. A peace commission was sent to counsel with the hostiles, and this meeting resulted in the Medicine Lodge Treaty. The Kiowas, Comanches, and Apaches of the Plains pledged themselves to a reservation of 3,000,000 acres between the Washita and Red rivers and the ninety-eighth and one hundredth meridians.[2] A week later, on October 28, 1867, the Cheyennes and Arapahoes came to terms. More than two thousand Cheyennes received presents, fresh supplies of clothing, blankets, and ammunition, and the government's promise to provide twenty thousand dollars annually for their benefit over a period of twenty-five years. The Indians also retained the privilege of hunting buffalo south of the Arkansas River. In return the Cheyennes agreed not to impede railroad construction or restrain overland transportation, never to molest the whites, and to move to a new 4,300,000-acre reservation bounded by the thirty-seventh parallel and the Cimarron and Arkansas rivers.[3]

Unfortunately, the Medicine Lodge Treaty was no more suc-

[2] Charles J. Kappler (ed.), *Indian Affairs: Laws and Treaties*, II, 984–89. The Kiowa-Comanche Reservation began at a point where the Washita River crosses the ninety-eighth meridian; thence up the Washita River to a point thirty miles, by river, west of Fort Cobb; thence due west to the North Fork of Red River; thence down said North Fork to the main Red River; thence down said river to its intersection with the ninety-eighth meridian; thence north, on said meridian line to the place of beginning.

[3] *Ibid.*; Donald J. Berthrong, *The Southern Cheyennes*, 297–98. The Cheyenne and Arapaho Reservation began at the point where the Arkansas River crosses the thirty-seventh parallel of north latitude; thence west on that parallel to the Cimarron River; down the Cimarron to the Arkansas River; up the Arkansas River to the place of beginning.

cessful than the Treaty of the Little Arkansas River. Early in 1868, with scarcely an interruption for the winter months, the Texas frontier was overrun by war parties. Kiowas under Lone Wolf ravaged Texas in January and February, and Comanche warriors were equally active.[4]

By late May, 1868, the Cheyennes had entered the new hostilities. Warriors from that tribe burned Council Grove, Kansas, and by the middle of August rampaging war parties were streaking through the Saline and Solomon valleys and onto the eastern Colorado frontier. Depredations on settlers and the overland traffic continued through September on the Cimarron crossing and the Santa Fe Trail.[5]

Appeals to the War Department for better protection led to eventual military action. Post–Civil War military structure divided the United States into divisions, departments, and districts, commanded respectively by lieutenant generals, major generals, and brigadier generals. The Great Plains, stretching from the Río Grande to the northernmost border of the United States and eastward from the Rocky Mountains to the ninety-eighth meridian, was designated the Division of the Missouri, commanded by Lieutenant General William T. Sherman. Boundaries of the departments within this division frequently changed, but in general the Southern Plains were administered by the Department of the Missouri, while the Departments of the Platte and Dakota controlled the Northern Plains.

General Sherman named Major General Philip H. Sheridan

---

[4] William H. Leckie, *Military Conquest of the Southern Plains*, 65; Philip McCusker to W. B. Hazen, Dec. 22, 1868, in the Sherman-Sheridan Papers, typescript in the Carl Coke Rister Collection, 117, University of Oklahoma Library. (The Sherman-Sheridan Papers will hereinafter be cited as the S-S Papers.)

[5] U. S. Army, Military Div. of Mo., *Record of Engagements with Hostile Indians within the Military Division of the Missouri, from 1868 to 1882*, 8; Berthrong, *Southern Cheyennes*, 303–307. "In sixty days that summer they killed 117 settlers and took 7 women into captivity." Oliver H. Knight, *Following the Indian Wars*, 71; *Annual Report of the Secretary of War for the Year 1868*, 13–16.

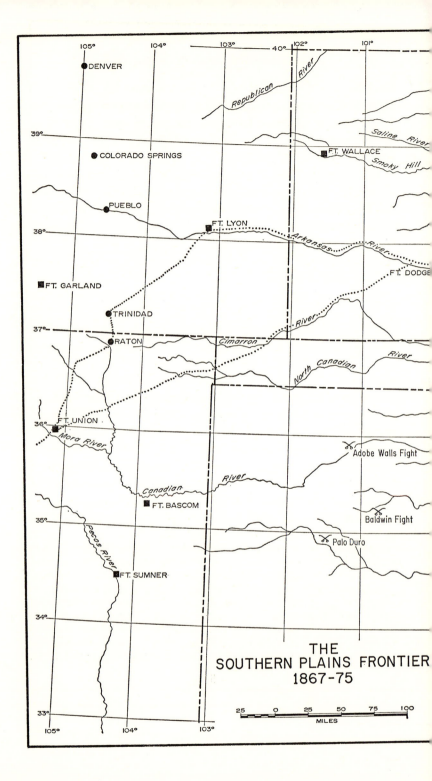

THE
SOUTHERN PLAINS FRONTIER
1867-75

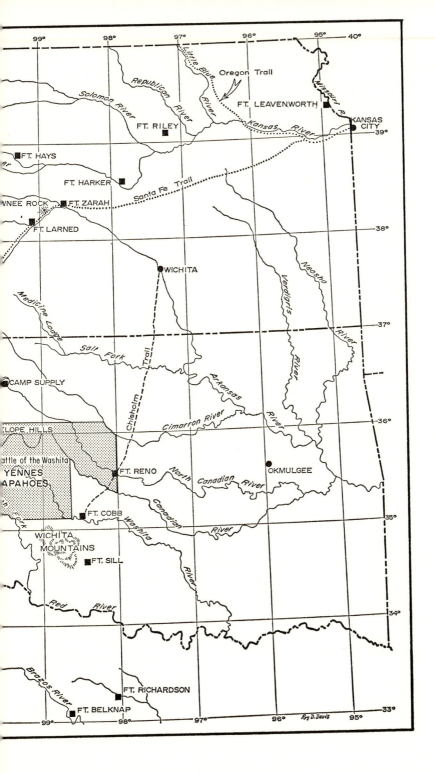

commander of the Department of the Missouri, and the latter assumed his duties on March 2, 1868. At that time the Department of the Missouri included the state of Missouri, plus the military districts of Kansas, Upper Arkansas, Indian Territory, and New Mexico, totaling about 150,000 square miles. To control Indian hostilities that by March, 1868, were of monumental proportions, Sheridan was allowed 1,200 cavalry and 1,400 infantry at twenty-four frontier posts. Central and southern Kansas was dotted with Forts Leavenworth, Riley, Dodge, Harker, Hays, Zarah, Larned, and Wallace and a camp near Fort Hays. In Colorado Territory, Forts Lyon, Reynolds, and Garland formed a western frontier with Forts Bascom, Bayard, Craig, Cummings, McRae, Selden, Stanton, Union, and Wingate in New Mexico Territory. South of Kansas, Forts Gibson and Arbuckle stood in Indian country, and Fort Smith in Arkansas was associated with the Indian Territory posts.[6]

As commander of the troubled department, Sheridan was eager to co-operate with his superior in bringing the Indian problem to a conclusion. Following his spring, 1868, inspection of Forts Hays and Dodge, the department commander meditated on his problem. Containing warlike Indians was difficult under the best of circumstances, but protecting outlying settlements with an undermanned and widespread command was virtually impossible owing to the warfare technique of Southern Plains tribes.

The Indians moved about the plains in small parties, making swift strikes against settlements and commerce. Riding twenty-four hours nonstop after an attack, the roving red men could put one hundred miles between themselves and their pursuers. Frontier troops had little success in making contact with so mobile an enemy. Moreover, the semiarid, treeless expanse on which the Indians lived hampered punitive expeditions. The

[6] Philip H. Sheridan, *Personal Memoirs*, II, 297; Carl Coke Rister, *Border Command*, 42–43.

climate, the soldiers' ignorance of survival techniques on the plains, and the tremendous problems of supply made extended campaigns seem impossible.

In winter, however, the tribesmen camped in the protected river valleys of southwestern Indian Territory and generally were quiet until spring. With this fact in mind, Sheridan developed an attack plan which would make the most effective use of his limited military resources. If his troops were used defensively for the remainder of the summer, he reasoned, once winter approached the Indians and their grass-fed ponies would not be as active and could be dealt with decisively.[7] Weakened ponies and a contracted winter campground were made to order for the movement he planned. An extensive and deftly prepared campaign would force the Indians onto their proper reservations, at the same time showing that the winter season offered them no respite from pursuit. The lesson would be clear: security could come only in obedience to the treaty.

Sherman agreed with Sheridan that Indians who rejected prior agreements should be reminded of their obligations. Eight hundred persons had died in Indian raids since June, 1862. Twice since October, 1865, the Indians had cast off treaty obligations and taken up the lance. Sherman determined that they would do so no more.

On August 21, 1868, Sherman telegraphed the War and Interior departments that he had ordered General Sheridan to drive the Indians "south of the Kansas line and in pursuing to kill if necessary." The same day Sheridan informed Kansas Governor Crawford that he would order all Indians to return to their reservations. Those who refused would be attacked. In September, Sherman advised Secretary of War John M. Schofield of

[7] Report of F. M. Gibson, as published in Melbourne C. Chandler (comp.), *Of Garry Owen in Glory: The History of the Seventh United States Cavalry Regiment*, 13; Sheridan, *Personal Memoirs*, II, 297; William T. Sherman to A. C. Hunt, Oct. 22, 1868, Headquarters of the Army, Letters Received, Records of the War Dept., in Donald J. Berthrong Collection, University of Oklahoma Library.

9

his intentions, reporting that red men had continued their aggressions, refused peace, and virtually demanded war. He would give them enough war "to satisfy their hearts' content."[8] Between the time Sheridan requested authority for a winter campaign and his receipt of that authority, Indians were met several times in combat. The future location of Camp Supply was directly affected by one of those incidents. Brigadier General Alfred Sully commanded the District of the Upper Arkansas, directly subordinate to General Sheridan. Upon receiving intelligence that Cheyenne families and stock were assembled near the Cimarron River in Indian Territory, Sheridan ordered Sully and a force of more than five hundred men south of the Arkansas to attack them.

On the afternoon of September 7, 1868, nine troops of the Seventh Cavalry, under Major Joel H. Elliott (or Elliot), and one company of the Third Infantry, led by Captain John H. Page, followed Sully across the Arkansas two miles west of Fort Dodge. After riding about thirty miles, from dusk until nearly 3:00 A.M., the troops rested. At 7:00 A.M. they returned to their saddles and rode to Goose Creek, Kansas, arriving about 2:00 P.M. on the eighth. Indian trails were checked at this point, and later the troops moved south on Goose Creek for the night.[9] The next day Elliott and four troops of cavalry followed the few visible Indian trails, while the remainder of the force moved eight miles south to await developments. A messenger from Elliott arrived during the night bringing news of Indians, and

[8] Sherman to J. R. Townsend, Aug. 22, 1868; Sherman to John A. Schofield, Sept. 26, 1868, Office of the Adjutant General, Letters Received, Records of the War Dept., in Donald J. Berthrong Collection, University of Oklahoma Library. (Hereinafter these records will be cited as AGO, Letters Received, OU.)

[9] E. S. Godfrey, "Some Reminiscences, Including an Account of General Sully's Expedition against the Southern Plains Indians," *Cavalry Journal*, Vol. XXXVI (July, 1927), 421–22; George H. Shirk, "Campaigning with Sheridan: A Farrier's Diary," *Chronicles of Oklahoma*, Vol. XXXVII (Spring, 1959), 74; Alfred Sully to C. McKeever, Sept. 16, 1868, AGO, Letters Received, OU.

reveille brought the troops to their feet. On September 10, Elliott rejoined the main command thirteen miles south and west of camp, and proceeded down the Cimarron. Four hours later the advance scouts, John Smith, Ben Clark, and Amos Chapman, were attacked, but emerged from the scrape unhurt. Shortly afterward, Elliott's vanguard countered an attack, killing two Indians. The troops spent the night within one mile of the confluence of the Cimarron River and Crooked Creek.[10]

Camp was broken early the next morning, and just as the rear guard was forming, a party of Indians entered camp at full gallop and carried off two men of F Troop, Seventh Cavalry. Private Louis Curran, one of the captives, lost his life in the rescue attempt, but his comrade was successfully recovered. The Indians, encouraged by this near success and the capture of four horses, harassed Elliott's column for the next ten miles. About two hundred Cheyenne Dog Soldiers, fully armed and supplied, attacked under bugle-call orders but were driven off with a loss of eight warriors. At the site of a deserted Indian village, six miles from Beaver River, the Indians again struck Elliott's column in great force but were repulsed with heavy casualties. The final surprise raid, at 2:00 A.M., was ineffectual. [11]

Sully's line of march continued at dawn on the twelfth. About midday, sixteen miles out, at the approach to Beaver River, the Indians made another stand. Eight troops of cavalry and one company of infantry dismounted to drive the Indians from their stronghold in the surrounding sandhills. An intense general action continued for two hours, and when the Indians withdrew, with about twelve dead, Sully continued fifteen miles down Beaver River.[12]

---

[10] *Ibid.*; Record of Troop G, Seventh Cavalry, for Sept., 1868, as published in Chandler, *Of Garry Owen*, 26–27.

[11] *Ibid.*; Shirk, "Campaigning with Sheridan," *loc. cit.*, 74–75.

[12] *Ibid.*; Medical History of Fort Supply, Vol. 166, 1, Records of the War Dept., National Archives, Washington, D.C.

On the morning of September 13 camp was broken early, and troops crossed the ridge dividing Beaver River from Wolf Creek, struck Wolf Creek, and marched southeastward for two miles. Confused by the false trails laid down for him, Sully rode blindly into a trap. A large body of Cheyennes, Arapahoes, Kiowas, and Comanches held the sand hills on all sides of a pass and almost succeeded in capturing the supply train. Holding the infantry in the rear to protect the wagons, Sully ordered half the cavalry to move against the sand hills on foot. Heavy resistance cost the life of Private Cyrus McCorbitt, but in the end the Indians were dislodged. Later it would be discovered that the Indian village was but a short distance beyond and that had the entire cavalry force been used the Washita Campaign might never have been necessary. The weary command camped on the North Canadian River, barely one-half mile from the future Camp Supply.[13]

Convinced that the Indian families had gone south to the Wichita Mountains, Sully decided to return to Fort Dodge. Twenty miles were made in that direction on the fourteenth, though with continual harassment by the Indians, and on the following day's march the troops crossed the Cimarron at the head of the Salt Plains, bringing the command thirty-two miles closer to the Arkansas. The main command remained in camp at Bluff Creek on the sixteenth, while the sick and wounded went on to Dodge. The next day General Sully left Major Elliott in command and proceeded to Fort Dodge, arriving late in the day.[14]

Although something less than effective, Sully's expedition had scouted 255 miles, much of it in uncharted Indian Territory, had creditably engaged the Indians, and counted twenty to thirty warriors dead, with troop casualties held to three killed and six wounded. The expedition also demonstrated the need

13 *Ibid.*; Gibson, Report, in Chandler, *Of Garry Owen*, 11.
14 *Ibid.*

for a much stronger force if the Indians were to be dealt a telling blow.[15]

Some weeks after this campaign Sully was commissioned to set up a base inside Indian Territory for use by a large attack force.[16] Recalling his September 13 and 14 engagements near the confluence of Beaver River and Wolf Creek, Sully selected that area for his base camp. In addition to his own recollections of the site Sully also relied on the judgments of Major Elliott, Captain Page, and the scout John Smith. All four men would return to the area with the field command in November, 1868.

On October 9, 1868, Sheridan received authority from his superiors for the winter campaign.[17] The difficulties and hardships which troops were sure to encounter caused several experienced officers and frontiersmen to discourage the project, but Sheridan continued preparations. He was confident that the soldiers, better fed and clothed than the Indians, had the advantage. To make sure the soldiers maintained that advantage was Sully's duty. Large amounts of supplies began to accumulate at Forts Dodge and Lyon, some of which would later be transferred to Sully's depot. Three months of subsistence was also sent to Fort Arbuckle, the post from which Sheridan expected his command to draw rations when they moved into southern Indian Territory.[18]

By the end of October most of these arrangements had been completed. Directions were then given to the commander at

[15] Berthrong, *Southern Cheyennes*, 320. General Sheridan in his Annual Report listed seventeen to twenty-two Indians killed and two troopers killed and one wounded. *Report of Secretary of War, 1868*, 18.

[16] Arrangements had already been made for the establishment of a supply base "at a point one hundred and ten miles (110) south of Dodge," by October 10, 1868. P. H. Sheridan to Sherman, Oct. 10, 1868, AGO, Letters Received, OU.

[17] *House Exec. Doc. No. 1*, 41 Cong., 2 sess., 44.

[18] Sheridan, *Personal Memoirs*, II, 310; Sheridan to Samuel J. Crawford, Oct. 9, 1868, AGO, Letters Received, OU; 400,000 rations were sent to Fort Dodge, 300,000 rations to Fort Lyon, and 300,000 rations to Fort Arbuckle from Fort Leavenworth, via Fort Gibson. *House Exec. Doc. 1*, 41 Cong., 2 sess., 45.

Fort Bascom, New Mexico Territory, to organize a column and march eastward, while Major Eugene A. Carr received orders to move southeastward from Fort Lyon, Colorado Territory. Sully, in command of a third column, would lead the main force to the supply post at Beaver River and Wolf Creek. In a projected six-month campaign the Indians were to be struck a hard blow and forced onto their reservations. Sheridan's plan of operations was

> to let the small column from Bascom, consisting of six companies of the 3rd Cavalry, two companies of the 37th Infantry, and four mountain howitzers, aggregating five hundred and sixty-three men, operate along the main Canadian—establishing a depot at Monument Creek, and remaining out as long as it could be supplied—at least until sometime in January; the column of General Carr to unite with a small force under General Penrose—then out, composed of one company of the 7th and four small companies of the 10th Cavalry—establishing a depot on the headwaters of the North Canadian, and operate south, towards the Antelope Hills and headwaters of Red River. These columns were really beaters in, and were not expected to accomplish much. The main column, from Camp Supply, was expected to strike the Indians either on the headwaters of the Washita or still further south on the Sweetwater and other branches of the Red River.[19]

When Major Eugene A. Carr reported that his late October engagement on the Republican River had sent the Cheyennes and Arapahoes south, the final defensive movement had been completed. On November 1, 1868, General Sheridan issued final orders to his commanders, and the offensive maneuvers began. In the meantime, during September and October, Sheridan and Sherman had arranged for General William B. Hazen to accommodate all peaceful Kiowas, Comanches, and Kiowa-

---

[19] Sheridan to Sherman, Nov. 1, 1869 (copy), Ben Clark Collection, University of Oklahoma Library.

Apaches at Fort Cobb.[20] Those Indians still remaining outside their reservations henceforth were considered hostile, and in the ensuing expedition no quarter would be given.

On November 5 another strike force, the Nineteenth Kansas Volunteer Cavalry of twelve hundred men, organized in late October, 1868, in Topeka, departed in two groups for the supply camp on the Beaver. Companies D and G proceeded by rail to Fort Hays and there joined Sully's supply trains en route to Indian Territory by way of Fort Dodge. The remaining ten companies marched south from Topeka, heading for the depot listed only as "100 miles south of the Arkansas River." Colonel Andrew W. Evans left Fort Bascom on November 18, and Major Carr departed Fort Lyon on December 2.[21]

On November 12 the Seventh Cavalry abandoned its position six miles east of Dodge City on the Arkansas River and marched five miles to Mulberry Creek, where it joined General Sully, the infantry, and the supply train. There Sully, as commander of the District of the Upper Arkansas, assumed responsibility for the combined force now totaling eleven hundred men.[22]

Marching due south, the command moved in four closely formed parallel columns. The usual order of march, as docu-

---

[20] Leckie, *Military Conquest*, 90–91; Marvin E. Kroeker, "William B. Hazen: A Military Career in the Frontier West, 1855–80" (Unpublished Ph.D. dissertation, University of Oklahoma, 1966), 130–39.

[21] *House Exec. Doc. No. 1*, 41 Cong., 2 sess., 44; De B. Randolph Keim, *Sheridan's Troopers on the Borders*, 101. The Nineteenth Kansas Volunteer Cavalry was authorized by Sheridan on October 9, 1868, and was ordered to be in the field November 1, 1868. Sheridan, *Personal Memoirs*, II, 308; David L. Spotts, *Campaigning with Custer*, 13; Andrew W. Evans to Assistant Adjutant General, District of New Mexico, Report of the Canadian River Expedition, Jan. 23, 1869, S-S Papers, 165; Report of Eugene A. Carr, Commanding Expedition from Fort Lyon, Operations of the Command during the Late Campaign against Hostile Indians, Apr. 7, 1869, S-S Papers, 243.

[22] Gibson, Report, in Chandler, *Of Garry Owen*, 14; Shirk, "Campaigning with Sheridan," *loc. cit.*, 83–84; George A. Custer, *My Life on the Plains*, 210; Keim, *Sheridan's Troopers*, 101; Sheridan, *Personal Memoirs*, II, 308.

mented by Colonel George A. Custer of the Seventh Cavalry, was as follows:

> . . . the four hundred wagons of the supply train and those belonging to the troops formed in equal columns; in advance of the wagons at a proper distance rode the advance guard of cavalry; a corresponding cavalry force formed the rear guard. The remainder of the cavalry was divided into two equal parts, and these parts again divided into three equal detachments; these six detachments were disposed of along the flanks of the column, three on a side, maintaining a distance between themselves and the train of from a quarter to half a mile, while each of them had flanking parties thrown out opposite the train.[23]

The force maintained steady marches. It covered twenty miles on November 13 and eighteen miles the next day, crossing Cavalry Creek and camping on Bear Creek. On the fifteenth snow and chilling winds slowed the column, which advanced only eleven miles, to the Cimarron River. On the following day the command marched eighteen miles south and then completed nine more miles south-southwest to Beaver River. During the afternoon guides discovered the trail of an Indian party estimated at from 100 to 150 warriors. Custer requested permission to backtrack to the undefended village and strike while the warriors were absent, but Sully refused.[24]

Another trail was struck on November 17, but it was found to be the Sully trail from the previous September. Sixteen miles were covered that day as the troops moved east of Beaver River. On November 18 a fifteen-mile march brought the full command to Wolf Creek at its confluence with the Beaver. General Field Orders No. 8, Headquarters, District of the Upper Arkansas, named the spot Camp Supply.[25]

[23] Custer, *My Life on the Plains*, 211.

[24] *Ibid.*; Shirk, "Campaigning with Sheridan," *loc. cit.*, 83; Record of Troop G, Seventh Cavalry, for month of Nov., 1868, in Chandler, *Of Garry Owen*, 27.

[25] *Ibid.*; Post Returns, Camp Supply, Nov., 1868, Records of the War Dept.,

The next few days were spent building a post. Stockades to check surprise raids were erected, and industrious soldiers constructed a blockhouse and a storehouse and dug wells. The cavalrymen worked with the infantry in erecting winter quarters "as comfortable as circumstances and appliances would permit," but for their part they were content "with the ordinary camp discomforts, for being but 'birds of passage' " they knew their stay would be short. Building crews laughingly referred to the name Camp Supply as a "misnomer, for while there was a partial supply of everything, there was not an adequate supply of anything."[26] The "comfortable quarters," when completed, were pits four and one-half feet deep, walled with cottonwood logs extending above the ground about three feet and covered with logs, straw, and earth.

In the meantime, Sheridan had left Fort Hays on November 15 to accompany the main column in the field. After a brief stopover at Fort Dodge, Sheridan with his staff, escort, and *New York Herald* correspondent De B. Randolph Keim departed on the eighteenth and arrived at Camp Supply on the afternoon of November 21.[27] Sheridan later explained:

> I deemed it best to go in person, as the campaign was an experimental one—campaigns at such a season having been deemed impractical and reckless by old and experienced frontiersmen, and I did not like to expose troops to great hazard without being present myself to judge of their hardships and privations.[28]

National Archives, Washington, D. C. The North Fork of the Canadian River is formed where Beaver River and Wolf Creek meet at the site of Camp Supply. Keim, *Sheridan's Troopers*, 120; *New York Herald* (Dec. 12, 1868).

[26] Gibson, Report, in Chandler, *Of Garry Owen*, 14.

[27] Post Returns, Fort Dodge, Kansas, Nov., 1868, Records of the War Dept., National Archives, Washington, D. C.; Keim, *Sheridan's Troopers*, 89–100; Sheridan to Sherman, Nov. 23, 1868, S-S Papers, 57. Sheridan's escort consisted of Troop C, Tenth Cavalry, Forsyth's Scouts, now under command of Lieutenant Silas Pepoon, and two troops of the Nineteenth Kansas Volunteer Cavalry, added at Bluff Creek on November 18. Sheridan, *Personal Memoirs*, II, 310–12.

[28] *House Exec. Doc. No. 1*, 41 Cong., 2 sess., 45.

The department commander found the site of Camp Supply to his liking. "There is plenty of wood, water and grass at the point, and it is in the very heart of Indian Country. The distance from Dodge is (105) one hundred and five miles and [Fort] Cobb about (100) one hundred, it is thirty-five miles from the Antelope Hills."[29]

While at Fort Dodge on November 17, Sheridan learned that two companies of the Kansas Volunteers were just ahead of his party, and the next day they were added to the escort. When he arrived at Camp Supply, Sheridan felt confident that the main command from Topeka would arrive presently. On the other hand, he had just braved five days of snow and sleet on the trail, and since the weather was turning colder, he decided on the immediate march of the invasion force. He ordered Colonel Custer to move the next day and strike the encamped Indians wherever he might find them. Accordingly, at daybreak on November 23, 1868, eleven troops of the Seventh Cavalry marched south from Camp Supply. A foot of fresh-blown snow covered the ground.[30]

The next afternoon, concerned over the whereabouts of the Kansas Volunteers, Sheridan ordered a reconnaissance of the area. Scouts ranged as far as fourteen miles from camp but found no sign of the missing cavalry. The following afternoon a lookout alerted the camp to an approaching party of volunteers led by Captain A. J. Piley. The men reported near starvation and freezing cold and said that the remaining companies were hopelessly lost on the Cimarron. The next day volunteers, scouts, and a train of supply wagons began a search for them. A second party of Kansas troops, under Colonel Horace L. Moore, reached Camp Supply on November 28, but the final

[29] Sheridan to Sherman, Nov. 23, 1868, AGO, Letters Received, OU; *New York Herald* (Dec. 26, 1868). The actual distance from Dodge to Supply at this time was closer to 113 miles.

[30] Sheridan, *Personal Memoirs*, II, 311–12; Keim, *Sheridan's Troopers*, 102-- 103; Shirk, "Campaigning with Sheridan," *loc. cit.*, 84.

group of six hundred men, led by Colonel Samuel J. Crawford and Major R. W. Jenkins, did not arrive until December 1.[31]

With the arrival of the first group of Kansas Volunteers Sheridan felt it safe to send wagons and messengers to Fort Dodge. A train of 250 wagons, commanded by Major Henry Inman, snaked its way north with orders to draw from the stockpile at the fort. Guarded by companies of the Nineteenth Kansas Volunteers, the heavily loaded wagons returned to Supply on December 5, after twelve days on the trail. In addition to supplies, Inman brought news. Correspondent Keim detailed the events for New York readers on December 6, 1868:

> Arriving at Mulberry Creek the Major found a piece of pantaloons covered with blood, a coat filled with bullet holes and other signs of a fight. Reaching the ravine near by a pack of thirty wolves started up. A number of letters were now found strewn around, one of which was a dispatch from your correspondent, dated at Bluff Creek, November 18, 1868. On the morning of November 19, 1868, before leaving Bluff Creek, General Sheridan sent two couriers to Fort Dodge with dispatches. It would appear these couriers fell into an ambuscade while crossing Mulberry Creek, which vicinity is much broken by ravines covered with underbrush. On his return Major Inman, after diligent search, found fragments of the bodies. One skull was broken as if struck by a tomahawk. The fight was evidently a desperate one. The route of the couriers could be traced for a mile by empty cartridge shells. A tree was discovered with the head of a spear sticking in it and full of bullet holes. It is probable the couriers took position here after they had lost their horses. The remains of the men, such as could be found, were gathered together and

[31] Up to this time United States policy had been to keep all non-Indians out of the Indian Territory. Few men in Crawford's command had ever crossed the boundaries of Indian country. James A. Hadley, "The Kansas Cavalry and the Conquest of the Plains Indians," *Collections of the Kansas State Historical Society*, Vol. X (1908), 435; Lonnie J. White, "Winter Campaigning with Sheridan and Custer," *Journal of the West*, Vol. VI (Jan., 1967), 73–76.

buried. The names of the men were [Bill] Davis and [Nate] Marshall.[32]

The loss of these scouts was sorely felt, and they were not the only casualties. Before Marshall and Davis were killed, two young messengers were captured alive in the brush off Beaver River, and their bodies were discovered with throats cut, scalped, and stripped. Indians were not frequently sighted, but it was obvious that they were close to Camp Supply. It seemed to the soldiers that silent Indians were peering over the nearby sand hills as they transformed a former Indian campsite for a dozen buffalo hunts into a military base.

The snowstorm that accompanied Sheridan to Supply temporarily suspended work on the fort. Sun and a clear sky on November 25, however, enabled the troops to resume construction. Infantry wood choppers felled cottonwood trees a mile away, while mounted guards watched for Indians. Drag teams under heavy cavalry guard pulled the logs to assembly crews. Notched logs were put into position in the blockhouse, and the outpost gained strength with each insertion of a timber. Reporter Keim observed that the post in its finished condition on December 4, 1868, was

> of sufficient strength to be defended by a small force against any number of warriors that may undertake to attack it.... The north and west fronts consist of a stockade; the east and south are made up of warehouses for stores. At the northeast and southwest angles are platforms sweeping all sides of the fort, and at

---

[32] Post Returns, Fort Dodge, Nov., 1868; *New York Herald* (Dec. 26, 1868). R. M. Wright of Dodge City, Kansas, had a completely different account. Nate Marshall and Bill Davis, he asserts, were returning from Camp Supply with dispatches and had ridden to within twenty miles of Fort Dodge when they spotted a band of Cheyennes and Arapahoes. Marshall was well known by the Indians and versed in their ways. He showed himself to them with signs of peace, but he and Davis were struck down. R. M. Wright, "Personal Reminiscences of Frontier Life in Southwest Kansas," *Collections of the Kansas State Historical Society*, Vol. VII (1902), 70–71.

the northwest and southeast angles are block houses with loopholes. From all points the rifles of the troops have . . . range of at least 800 yards.[33]

A *Harper's Weekly* correspondent who visited Camp Supply proclaimed it to be,

> without doubt, one of the most defensible works of its kind on the Plains. The store-houses and quarters of the soldiers are constructed of heavy timber, cut in the vicinity of the post, and are loopholed for musketry; the stockade is ten feet high, and the blockhouses are also ten feet in height, with a parapet of four feet, from which an additional fire can be brought to bear on all points of approach. The soldiers quarters are so constructed that they can fire over the roofs of the buildings (which form lunettes at the angles), while an additional fire is delivered from the loopholes inside. [34]

Garrison duty was performed by three companies of the Third Infantry, one company of the Thirty-eighth Infantry, and detachments of the Tenth Cavalry and Nineteenth Kansas Volunteer Cavalry. Because these regiments had camped separately as far as one mile from headquarters, one day was spent concentrating the camp into a smaller compass. Troops moved toward the stockade and winterized their tents against icy blasts by fitting them with cottonwood frames. Construction parties then resumed the building of permanent infantry quarters. On December 1 a field hospital was established, consisting of four hospital tents arranged as two wards with a double chimney of stone between them. The picture the post presented, wrote Keim, "reminded us more of the first steps to the establishment of a pioneer settlement, than the work of the less peaceful pursuit of war."[35]

[33] *New York Herald* (Dec. 26, 1868).

[34] *Harper's Weekly Magazine*, Vol. XIII (Feb. 27, 1869), 140.

[35] Keim, *Sheridan's Troopers*, 105–106; Medical History of Fort Supply, *loc. cit.*, Vol. 166, 2.

Daily life at the wilderness post began at 4:00 A.M. with roll call. Sheridan ordered an early reveille to give the men time to arm and prepare for the possibility of a dawn attack by Indians. Breakfast was prepared after sunup, with stable call or work report an hour later. While the infantry attended to garrison duties, cavalry horses were grazed under heavy guard. Dinner was served at noon, after which the infantry returned to post business and the cavalry once more grazed their animals. Retreat sounded at sunset, and taps closed the day at 9:00 P.M. Lookouts were posted in daylight hours and replaced at night by sentries ordered to fire upon anyone who approached without waiting to challenge.

The work was strenuous, the weather unseasonably mild, and the food fresh and fit for hardy men. Game abounded near the camp. The immediate vicinity yielded grouse, ducks, wild turkeys, elk, antelope, deer, bears, buffaloes, rabbits, and squirrels, in addition to a wide assortment of wild fruits and berries. Hunters daily brought in enough meat to feed one thousand men. Turkey hunting was particularly exciting to the enlisted men. The discovery of a roost was the signal for such promiscuous firing that the lives of man and beast were endangered. One old scout testified, "I've a bin a fittin Injuns an' other critters all my life, an' I never seed sich a time. I was a shootin of turkies one minit an a doggin bullets the other minit, an yit no blood spilt. All I got to say, it was lucky for the men ef it wasn't for the turkies."[36]

General Sheridan and his officers found jack-rabbit hunting more to their liking. The general's staghound, Cynch, and another officer's hound, the fleet Juno, chased many a hare across the plains, much to the delight of the pursuing horsemen.

Thursday, November 26, 1868, Thanksgiving, was the first holiday at Camp Supply. It was appropriately celebrated with

[36] *Ibid.*; Spotts, *Campaigning with Custer*, 68.

a dinner almost entirely produced from the area. Keim listed the following bill of fare:

Soup—Wild Turkey.
Broiled—Wild Turkey, Buffalo Tongue.
Roast—Buffalo Hump, Wild Turkey, Saddle of Vension, Red Deer, Common Deer, Antelope, Rabbit.
Entrees—Rabbit Pies, Wings of Grouse, breaded, Turkey Giblets.
Broiled—Quails, Pinnatted Grouse.
Vegetables (imported)—Canned Tomatoes, Lima Beans, Dessicated Potatoes.
Bread—"Hard Tack," plain and toasted, Army Biscuits.
Des[s]ert (imported)—Rice Pudding, Pies, and Tarts.
Wines and Liquors—Champagne, "Pinetop Whisky," Ale.

"Camp life on the Canadian, isolated entirely from the world as we were, was found a happy episode, away from the noise and bustle of human strife, and full of interesting incidents and days of ease and amusement," Keim commented.[37]

About ten o'clock on the morning of Saturday, November 29, California Joe, chief scout for Custer, surprised the officers at Camp Supply with a hasty entrance. When California Joe drew up at Sheridan's tent, it had been only thirty-six hours since he and Joe Corbin had left Custer on the night of November 27. After a few words with the scout Sheridan read aloud the dispatches from the Seventh Cavalry.[38]

Word spread quickly through the post that Custer had destroyed Black Kettle's Cheyenne camp on the Washita River. The victory was complete, but grim signs indicated that Major Elliott and fifteen troopers had been trapped, for they had not rejoined the main command. Sheridan immediately sent a telegram relating the known details of the event to Major General W. A. Nichols, assistant adjutant general, Military Division

---

[37] Keim, *Sheridan's Troopers*, 108–109.
[38] *Ibid.*; Sheridan, *Personal Memoirs*, II, 312, 320.

of the Missouri, at St. Louis. A congratulatory order to Custer and his men was issued the same day.[39]

Two hours after breakfast on December 1, word circulated that the Seventh Cavalry was only about ten miles from the post and would arrive early that morning. General Sheridan, his staff, officers, and the garrison of Camp Supply formed outside the stockade to review the heroes. The Kansas Volunteers were given no place in the review, but were allowed to witness the parade.

About 10:00 A.M. the Osage scouts under Hard Rope and Little Beaver broke into view from the southwest hills. Dressed in war paint and finery, they rode in circles, firing their weapons and chanting war songs. They were closely followed by California Joe, pipe in mouth, riding his familiar mule, leading Lieutenant Silas Pepoon's sharpshooters. Next came the Seventh Cavalry band, playing, as might be expected, "Garry Owen," the regimental song. Huddled between the band and the first company of sharpshooters were the widows and orphans of the Black Kettle band, many riding their own ponies. David Spotts, an observer from the Kansas Volunteers, commented that they were the best dressed participants in the parade. At the head of his troops rode Colonel Custer, dressed in fringed buckskin shirt and leggings. Troop after troop followed the colonel in precision marching. The train and guard brought up the rear.[40]

The conquerors moved across the parade grounds and up the Beaver about half a mile and there went into camp. Among his trophies Custer had a white Indian-style lodge, which was unloaded and erected by several of the captive women. At this point the weary troopers rested while the Kansas cavalry re-

[39] Sheridan to Nichols, Nov. 29, 1868, S-S Papers, 69; General Field Orders No. 6, Headquarters, Dept. of Mo., Nov. 29, 1869, S-S Papers, 67.

[40] Spotts, *Campaigning with Custer*, 65–66; Keim, *Sheridan's Troopers*, 122; Custer, *My Life on the Plains*, 268; Sheridan to Nichols, Dec. 23, 1868, S-S Papers, 71–73; Shirk, "Campaigning with Sheridan," *loc. cit.*, 86–87; Hadley, "The Kansas Cavalry," *loc. cit.*, 442.

assembled their equipment and command for a new expedition. That evening Camp Supply was treated to an Osage scalp dance in honor of the victory. Displaying the scalps of Black Kettle and others, the young men jumped and danced while companions chanted a song of triumph. Keim remembered that "during almost the entire night, long after the officers and men, assembled to witness the occasion had departed, the Indian drum and the shout of warriors could be heard, borne upon the still air."[41]

December 3 was a day of great sadness at the post. On that day Captain Louis M. Hamilton, the grandson of Alexander Hamilton, and two other casualties of the battle on the Washita were buried at Camp Supply. The Seventh Cavalry, aided by the Camp Supply garrison, attended the flag-draped coffins as they were taken to graves on a little knoll. General Sheridan and Colonel Custer served as pallbearers to their fellow officer.[42]

Intense questioning of the captives revealed the possibility of other villages below the Black Kettle camp. While the members of the Seventh Cavalry rested, Sheridan used the time to plan a return to the Washita battlefield and points south in hopes of striking another blow at the Indians.

On December 7 three hundred wagons and about sixteen hundred men departed Camp Supply, bound for southwestern Indian Territory. Loaded with thirty days' supplies, tents, cooking utensils, and baggage, the train moved slowly down Wolf Creek. Although Sheridan accompanied the expedition, Custer was in command of the task force. Severe storms on the previous two days had not dampened the spirit of the troops.[43]

[41] *Sheridan's Troopers*, 123–24; *New York Herald* (Dec. 26, 1868).

[42] *Ibid.*; Custer, *My Life on the Plains*, 269–70; Shirk, "Campaigning with Sheridan," *loc. cit.*, 87.

[43] Keim, *Sheridan's Troopers*, 128; Spotts, *Campaigning with Custer*, 72; Post Returns, Camp Supply, Dec., 1868; Sherman to Sheridan, Dec. 7, 9, 1868, AGO, Letters Received, OU; Custer to J. S. Crosby, Dec. 22, 1868, S-S Papers, 94; Sheridan, *Personal Memoirs*, II, 324; Custer, *My Life on the Plains*, 274.

Two hundred men of the infantry and cavalry remained behind to garrison Camp Supply.[44] Although the main force had departed, the necessity for the supply depot was undiminished. Actually, the importance of the post increased as the line of supply and communication extended another one hundred miles south. Each mile that separated the troopers from their provisions made it more difficult to supply them.

As early as November 22, 1868, General Sheridan had decided that a small force would remain at Camp Supply even after the present struggle had ceased. The wealth of natural resources at the post—water, game, and winter forage—made it ideal for the accommodation of troops. Other advantages were its strategic position as a base from which to oversee the Cheyenne and Arapaho Reservation and its proximity to the favorite resorts of the Indian during the winter months.[45]

Captain John H. Page of the Third Infantry assumed command of the post and quickly went about the business of securing additional commissary supplies. On December 8, Major Inman, escorted by a detachment of the Nineteenth Kansas Regiment and a company of the Fifth Infantry, left Supply with 180 empty wagons, 53 Indian captives from the Washita, and 115 sick and wounded of the Seventh Cavalry, bound for Fort Dodge. The captives and the sick made travel necessarily slow. Two days out of Supply a blinding snowstorm struck the train, causing death and injury to many of the animals. A. L. Runyon, a member of the Kansas Volunteer Cavalry, wrote that "Uncle Sam must have lost several thousand dollars in

---

[44] On December 6, 1868, General Sheridan designated Companies B, E, F, Third Infantry, Company K, Fifth Infantry, and Company G, Thirty-Eighth Infantry, as the post garrison. Troop C, Tenth Cavalry, and Companies M and E, Nineteenth Kansas Volunteer Cavalry, were attached as escort for supply trains to Fort Dodge. Keim, *Sheridan's Troopers*, 127; Post Returns, Camp Supply, Dec., 1868.

[45] *New York Herald* (Dec. 12, 1868); Keim pronounced Camp Supply "the most important centre of operations in the present war" on December 4, 1868.

horse and mule flesh alone, that day as there were between 20 and 30 killed. Indian hunting is a very expensive business." The contingent reached Fort Dodge on December 14, and it took four days to load 250 wagons before the return trip to Supply. Another trip to Dodge later in December to fill 270 empty wagons was necessary before the required amount of subsistence was on hand at Supply.[46]

In the meantime, the main column, now assembled near Fort Cobb, was relying upon stores that had already been taken to Gibson. As the campaign drew to a close, the need for provisions from Camp Supply declined. Trips to Fort Dodge gradually diminished in number, and by January, 1869, only eleven wagons forded the Arkansas moving south to Indian Territory.[47]

Custer's command, meanwhile, proceeded south to the Washita. There the bodies of Major Elliott and his troopers were recovered and the abandoned Indian villages inspected. An encampment of Kiowas was found on December 17, but they were spared from attack owing to the intercession of General William B. Hazen, who was in charge of the peaceful Indians. In late December, after much discussion and coercion of the Kiowa chiefs Satanta and Lone Wolf, the Kiowas reluctantly joined the Comanches at Fort Cobb. In the following month the Kiowas, Kiowa-Apaches, and Comanches moved to their Medicine Lodge reservation near the newly established Camp Wichita (soon to be Fort Sill).

At the same time Lieutenant Colonel Andrew W. Evans had moved up the Canadian from Fort Bascom to Monument Creek, where he established a depot. Turning south, he attacked a party of hostile Comanches on Christmas Day, 1868, killing

[46] A. L. Runyon to Editor of *Manhattan* (Kansas) *Standard*, dated Fort Dodge, Kansas, Dec. 19, 1868, published Jan. 2, 1869, "A. L. Runyon's Letters, from The Nineteenth Kansas Regiment," *Kansas Historical Quarterly*, Vol. IX (Feb., 1940), 68–69; Post Returns, Fort Dodge, Dec., 1868.

[47] Medical History of Fort Dodge, Record for Jan., 1869, Records of the War Dept., in Walter S. Campbell Collection, University of Oklahoma Library.

as many as twenty-five. On December 30 scouts from Evans' column made contact with Sheridan at Fort Cobb, and upon his instructions the command started their return to Fort Bascom on January 3, 1869.[48]

After leaving Fort Lyon on December 2, Major Eugene A. Carr spent three weeks attempting to engage the Indians before joining an earlier expedition under General William H. Penrose. Cold weather and the long march took their toll of men and horses, and "Buffalo Bill" Cody, one of Penrose's scouts, was dispatched to Camp Supply on December 29 in hopes of learning the direction of the winter campaign. Cody's efforts were of no help, for although Captain Page gave him a sealed letter for Carr, a statement of supplies on hand, a map, and other information, as well as thirty private letters, all were lost before he returned to the camp on January 12, 1869. Carr decided to give up the struggle and headed back to Fort Lyon on January 8.[49]

The movements of Evans and Carr helped force the Comanches into surrender, leaving the Cheyennes and Arapahoes on the eastern edge of the Staked Plains, where there was no game. Starvation and the loss of supplies at the Washita finally turned them to peace. The Arapahoes under Little Raven surrendered at Fort Sill in January, 1869.

The Cheyennes were more reluctant to come in, however; and Colonel Custer was ordered to move against them. Sheridan sent Custer and the combined forces of the Seventh Cavalry and the Kansas Volunteer Cavalry to the mouth of Salt Creek on the North Fork of Red River. Sheridan proposed to establish a new supply depot at that point, which was more easily accessible from Camp Supply than Fort Arbuckle. In order to

[48] Leckie, *Military Conquest*, 114–17; Carl Coke Rister, "Colonel A. W. Evans' Christmas Day Indian Fight (1868)," *Chronicles of Oklahoma*, Vol. XVI (Sept., 1938), 275–86; Evans, *Report*, S-S Papers, 154–93.

[49] Carr, *Report*, S-S Papers, 253–55; *Record of Engagements*, 17.

make arrangements with Camp Supply for the new field depot, Sheridan journeyed from Fort Sill to Camp Supply in seven days, arriving unexpectedly on the afternoon of March 1. Sheridan intended to meet Custer on Red River with the supplies, but a message from President-elect Ulysses S. Grant changed those plans. At Camp Supply on March 2, Sheridan received a telegram from Grant summoning him to Washington. Arrangements were made for wagons to join Custer at the meeting spot, and Sheridan left the post on March 3, bound for Washington by way of Fort Dodge.[50]

Custer cornered the Cheyennes on March 15, 1869, recovered two white women captives, and obtained from Little Robe a renewal of his promise to go into reservation at Camp Supply. Apparently the Indians had been confused about the location of their reservation and had understood their reporting station to be Fort Cobb (actually General Sheridan had told them to go to Fort Cobb, but only until a certain time, after which they must go to Camp Supply). General Hazen intended to gather about one thousand Cheyennes and Arapahoes and then direct them to the Medicine Lodge reservation near Camp Supply.[51]

Custer's troopers returned to Camp Supply on March 28, 1869. Remaining there only until March 30, the men proceeded to Fort Hays by way of Fort Dodge with three Indians who had been taken prisoner at the March 15 meeting.[52] The winter campaign of 1868 ended on April 1, 1869, when Colonel Custer and his men crossed from Indian Territory into Kansas.

[50] Sheridan, *Personal Memoirs*, II, 344–46; Keim, *Sheridan's Troopers*, 304; Shirk, "Campaigning with Sheridan," *loc. cit.*, 100; Berthrong, *Southern Cheyennes*, 335–38.

[51] Sheridan, *Personal Memoirs*, II, 345; Berthrong, *Southern Cheyennes*, 339.

[52] Spotts, *Campaigning with Custer*, 172–73; Custer, *My Life on the Plains*, 376.

Chapter II

Indian Unrest at Camp Supply
1869–70

Following their capitulation to Colonel Custer on March 15, 1869, the Cheyennes retreated south toward Fort Sill. There, on April 7, they joined the Arapahoes who had arrived five days earlier. General Hazen hoped to collect the Cheyennes and Arapahoes at Fort Sill and from there send them to Camp Supply.[1] On April 19, however, Red Moon broke from the Cheyenne camp with 30 lodges, leaving only 46 lodges, under Little Robe and Minimic, to move north on April 26. A total of 170 Arapaho lodges plus the remaining Cheyennes were expected at Camp Supply between May 5 and May 15, 1869.[2]

Few Cheyennes followed the Arapahoes to Camp Supply. Hunting parties crossed the Texas boundary between the Washita and Canadian rivers, and there the Dog Soldiers of Tall Bull and White Horse withdrew to go north and join the Sioux. Their efforts to escape were futile, for Tall Bull and his band were methodically tracked down and defeated by Major Eugene A. Carr on the Republican River in May. The survivors eventually surrendered at Camp Supply in mid-September.[3]

[1] Berthrong, *Southern Cheyennes*, 339; B. H. Grierson to Assistant Adjutant General, Dept. of Mo., Apr. 7, 1869, S-S Papers, 273–74. (Hereinafter, Assistant Adjutant General will be abbreviated AAG.)

[2] Henry Alvord to AAG, Dept. of Mo., Apr. 24, 1869, S-S Papers, 262; Post Returns, Camp Supply, May, 1869; S. L. Woodward to AAG, Dept. of Mo., Apr. 26, 1869, Upper Arkansas Agency, Letters Received, Records of the Office of Indian Affairs, National Archives, Washington, D.C.

[3] Berthrong, *Southern Cheyennes*, 340–44; Medical History of Fort Supply, Vol. 166, 5; *House Exec. Doc. No. 1*, 41 Cong., 2 sess., 50; Sheridan to Schofield, Sept. 7, 1869, S-S Papers, 63; M. H. Kidd to AAG, Dept. of Mo., Sept. 18, 1869,

Caring for recently defeated Indians was a challenge for any officer. On April 24, 1869, Lieutenant Colonel Anderson D. Nelson, with six troops of the Tenth Cavalry, was ordered to Camp Supply, where he was directed to provide for the Indians who had already arrived. Eventually, when the Cheyennes and Arapahoes had reached full strength, he was to conduct them to the Medicine Lodge reservation. Colonel Nelson reached Camp Supply on May 26 and went into camp with his detachment six hundred yards from the infantry quarters.[4]

At that time there were 1,300 Arapahoes in 257 lodges within one mile of Camp Supply. Only 50 Cheyennes, faithful to the promise of Little Robe to come to Camp Supply, reached the post before the end of May. Eighty more Cheyennes under Lean Bear straggled in on June 2, and still more lodges were three days from the post. Medicine Arrow and 29 others visited Camp Supply on June 20 to view the treatment of the early arrivals. The following day Medicine Arrow was allowed to return to his band. Nelson hoped that he would bring in his band of 65 lodges.[5]

As temporary superintendent of the Cheyennes and Arapahoes, Colonel Nelson issued rations, held council with the Arapahoes, and guarded against any renewal of hostilities by the Cheyennes. When Brinton Darlington arrived at Camp Supply in July as agent for the Upper Arkansas Agency,[6] Nelson re-

Fort Supply, Letters Sent, Vol. 25, Records of the War Dept., National Archives, Washington, D.C.

[4] Schofield to Sheridan, Apr. 24, 1869, S-S Papers, 268; Schofield to AAG, Military Div. of Mo., May 19, 1869, Military Div. of Mo., Letters Received, Records of the War Dept. in Donald J. Berthrong Collection, University of Oklahoma Library; Nelson to AAG, Dept. of Mo., May 29, 1869, Fort Supply, Letters Sent, Vol. 25.

[5] John H. Page to AAG, Dept. of Mo., May 19, 1869, Fort Supply, Letters Sent, Vol. 24; Nelson to AAG, Dept. of Mo., May 29, June 2, 22, Fort Supply, Letters Sent, Vol. 25; Post Returns, Fort Dodge, June, 1869.

[6] The Upper Arkansas Agency was created in 1855, and after 1861 was responsible to the Colorado Superintendency. In 1866 the agency was assigned

linquished his authority over the Indians.[7] Later Darlington built two log cabins and dug a well at Pond Creek, a tributary of the Salt Fork of the Arkansas, but the Indians would not acknowledge the agency headquarters and refused his invitations.[8]

Nelson was bound by an agreement with the Indians to issue rations every five days from Camp Supply, and he faithfully fulfilled his promise. Feeding over fifteen hundred Indians was a trying task for a post whose garrison seldom exceeded two hundred men. At length the magnitude of the assignment caused the Army Commissary Department to place Captain Seth Bonney in charge of issuing rations to the Indians within the temporary reservation.[9] Bonney assumed his duties on July 16.

The ration was one pound of beef for each person every day (twice each month a ration of twelve ounces of pork or bacon was substituted for the beef), eight ounces each of flour

---

to the Central Superintendency, which, by the time Darlington arrived Camp Supply, was headquartered at Lawrence, Kansas. Upper Arkansas Agency was officially renamed the Cheyenne and Arapaho Agency in 1874. Edward E. Hill, *Preliminary Inventory of the Records of the Bureau of Indian Affairs*, II, 298–301.

[7] Nelson in his capacity as temporary superintendent of the Cheyennes and Arapahoes turned the care of these Indians over to Darlington. In October, however, Nelson as commander of Camp Supply claimed the sole control of the Indians until placed on their reservation, and the day following withdrew that claim, acknowledging that duty properly belonged to the agent. Brinton Darlington to A. G. Farnham, Sept. 6, 1869, Darlington to Enoch Hoag, Oct. 11, 1869, Central Superintendency, Field Office Files, Letters Received, Records of the Office of Indian Affairs, National Archives, Washington, D. C.; Darlington to Hoag, Oct. 17, 1869, Central Superintendency, Field Office Files, Letters Sent, Records of the Office of Indian Affairs, National Archives, Washington, D. C. (Hereinafter Field Office Files will be abbreviated FOF.)

[8] Berthrong, *Southern Cheyennes*, 346; Seth Bonney to W. A. Elderkin, Aug. 7, 1869, Camp Supply Letter Book, 16, Camp Supply Collection, University of Oklahoma Library.

[9] Memorandum of M. R. Morgan, Office of Chief Commissary of Subsistence, Dept. of Mo., June 14, 15, 1869, Camp Supply, Letters Received, Box 1, Records of the War Dept., National Archives, Washington, D. C.

and ground corn, and four pounds of salt for each one hundred rations. The first time that live Texas steers were turned over to the Indians, a melee erupted. The Indians slaughtered several hundred steers in the same manner they hunted buffalo. They charged the steers on horseback, lanced them with spears, or shot them with arrows. Before long dead animals littered the trail from Supply to the Indian camp. Scarcely one of them was touched for food, however; the still-plentiful buffaloes were more to the Indians' taste.[10]

The necessity of providing fifteen hundred rations every ten days quickly resulted in shortages. Supplies remained limited, but even the anticipated arrival of Medicine Arrow's large band did not concern General M. R. Morgan, Bonney's superior in the Commissary Department. In a short time the department was heavily indebted to the quartermaster of Camp Supply, the result of heavy borrowing.

Storehouses were desperately needed, but in that problem as well Bonney received no help. Military work details were unavailable to him, and the Indians considered the work demeaning. Moreover, the Indians would not come to Supply for the rations, and Bonney had to have the provisions hauled three to seven miles and deposited. When at last warehouses were built and filled and cattle deliveries regularized, the responsibilities became somewhat lighter. Perhaps the strain had already been too much, however, for on January 7, 1870, Bonney was relieved of his post following a touch of "lunacy," when he assaulted one of the commissary employees and then attempted suicide by strychnine.[11] Lieutenant Silas Pepoon replaced Bonney and performed the subsistence chores until he, in turn, was relieved by Captain H. I. Ripley. Rationing the Cheyennes and

10 Wright, "Personal Reminiscences," *loc. cit.*, 71.
11 Bonney to Morgan, July 20, 30, Aug. 14, Sept. 1, 1869, Camp Supply Letter Book, 3, 21, 36; Nelson to AAG, Dept. of Mo., Jan. 8, 1870, Fort Supply, Letters Sent, Vol. 24.

Arapahoes at Camp Supply continued until the commissary duty was assumed by Agent Darlington on July 1, 1870.[12]

Since Colonel Nelson's orders explicitly stated that Camp Supply would not remain an Upper Arkansas Indian agency, he informed the Cheyennes and Arapahoes that they would soon be moved to the Medicine Lodge reservation. Indians at the post refused to leave Camp Supply, however, and in the protests the Arapahoes took the leadership. In council with their chiefs Nelson came to realize that the Indians had never understood the Medicine Lodge boundaries. They had envisioned a reservation of twenty to thirty miles surrounding Camp Supply, running up Beaver River and Wolf Creek and down the North Canadian River for possibly one hundred miles.[13]

Having many times traveled the country in which the government intended to settle them, the Indians knew that the streams were salty and that the ground in some areas assumed a snow-like character. Moreover, the Arapahoes feared their Osage neighbors. Guide Ben Clark and even Colonel Nelson agreed that the Medicine Lodge reservation had some decided drawbacks. The conflict was a serious one, for as Nelson was aware, a contented Arapaho tribe was the key to success with surrounding bands.[14]

Nelson favored keeping the Cheyenne and Arapaho Agency at Camp Supply. Darlington's Pond Creek establishment he found totally unacceptable, and in this view he was supported by Bonney. "The Indians are all quite well satisfied with the arrangement [at Camp Supply]," wrote Bonney, "but all the

[12] Martha Buntin, "Difficulties Encountered in Issuing Cheyenne and Arapaho Subsistence, 1861–70," *Chronicles of Oklahoma*, Vol. XIII (Mar., 1935), 45.

[13] Nelson to AAG, Dept. of Mo., May 29, 1869, Fort Supply, Letters Sent, Vol. 25. The actual Medicine Lodge reservation, as noted in note 3, Chapter I, was almost totally within the Cherokee Outlet, bounded by the thirty-seventh parallel and the Cimarron and Arkansas rivers.

[14] Nelson to Schofield, June 11, 1869, in *ibid.*

Cavalry in the Department cannot drive them to where Agent Darlington is (at Pond Creek) in my opinion, for they would scatter to the four winds."[15]

In an effort to obtain more information on the area in dispute, on July 2, 1869, Nelson ordered Lieutenant Pepoon to reconnoiter the Cheyenne and Arapaho Reservation. Accompanied by twenty-six enlisted men of the Tenth Cavalry and five Arapaho guides, Pepoon set out on a mission to select a suitable site for the possible location of a military post and Indian agency.

During his eighteen-day, 400-mile scout the lieutenant inspected several sites. At a point on the North Canadian River, 105 miles southeast of Camp Supply and 20 miles from the crossing of the Fort Sill to Fort Harker road, Pepoon found a good location for a post, with level bottom land, plenty of timber, and a pure spring. The junction of Hackberry and Skeleton creeks in the Black Bear River vicinity was also noted as an excellent location for a post. Rich soil, nearby stone for a quarry, and salt-free creeks promised adequate accommodations for a large body of troops.

Pond Creek, the temporary residence of Agent Darlington, was also inspected. A careful examination of the region revealed that the grass was drying up and that the soil was sandy and alluvial. Twenty-four miles north of Pond Creek, at the juncture of Bluff Creek and Fall Creek, a fourth possible site was found. An area of at least four thousand fertile acres was complemented by a variety of timber with good water resources. Small waterfalls on Fall Creek were potential sites for mills.

The Bluff Creek site was Lieutenant Pepoon's first choice for the combined post and agency. He reported that if that position was too far to one side of the reservation, however, the Black Bear country or the area about the North Fork of the Canadian would also be acceptable.[16]

---

[15] Bonney to Elderkin, Aug. 7, 1869, Camp Supply Letter Book, 16.
[16] Silas Pepoon to L. H. Orleman, July 22, 1869, S-S Papers, 338–42.

Nelson submitted Pepoon's report to his superior, General John M. Schofield, with some comments of his own: "I am yet of the opinion that Camp Supply is the place for the new Post, and the next point is the one mentioned by Lieutenant Pepoon, on the North Fork of the Canadian." One of his arguments for the Camp Supply site was the fact that the Indians were very reluctant to move east of Supply and that they would be greatly opposed to being moved from the area. Captain Bonney agreed that "if the Post is to be far removed from here . . . it will require all the Cavalry force in the Department to induce them to 'go in' for rations."[17]

When on August 10, 1869, a special Indian commission arrived at Camp Supply to meet with Cheyenne and Arapaho chiefs, a compromise was reached, by which it was agreed that the agency would be located away from Camp Supply, but not at Pond Creek. The tribes were to stay at Camp Supply for the remainder of 1869 and would move to the yet unselected site of the new agency in the spring of 1870.[18]

Thousands of miles away, on the same day on which the Camp Supply conference was held, President Grant, acting on recommendations of Eli S. Parker, commissioner of Indian affairs, proclaimed the new Cheyenne and Arapaho Reservation. The reservation was bounded on the north by the Cherokee Outlet, on the east by the Cimarron River and ninety-eighth meridian, on the south by the Kiowa-Comanche Medicine Lodge reservation, and on the west by the one hundredth meridian.[19] The Cheyennes and Arapahoes thus received title to a

17 Nelson to Schofield, July 24, 1869, *ibid.*, 337; Bonney to Morgan, Aug. 6, 1869, Camp Supply Letter Book, 17.

18 Felix R. Brunot to Eli S. Parker, Aug. 10, 1869, Report of Council Held with Cheyenne and Arapaho, Aug. 10, 1869, Central Superintendency, Letters Received, Records of the Office of Indian Affairs, National Archives, Washington, D.C.

19 Kappler, *Indian Affairs*, I, 839–41; *Annual Report of the Commissioner of Indian Affairs for the Year 1882*, 269–70.

new reservation by executive order and a new agency location by agreement with the Indian commission.

The decision to move the agency away from the military post was not without its critics. General Sheridan joined with Colonel Nelson in defense of Camp Supply:

> The Indians evidently want to remain at Camp Supply or vicinity. It is a most excellent place for them, also a good place for the troops. . . . The point selected by the Agent [at Pond Creek] is too far East, and will never be satisfactory to the Indians. The second point on the North Canadian, selected by Lieutenant Pepoon, is off the reservation, and not half as good as that of Camp Supply.[20]

The removal of the tribes from Camp Supply, Nelson believed, might precipitate a general uprising. Medicine Arrow had seemed peaceable enough at the conference with the Indian commission, but Nelson suspected that Medicine Arrow's band, which was lingering on the nearby plains, was only watching for an opportune moment to strike the post:

> The younger men of the Cheyenne exhibit occasionally little impertinencies and insolence which indicates anything rather than a friendly footing and the elders of the tribe convey they have great difficulty in managing them.
>
> I am prepared to see their young men set the whole tribe by the ears and force them on the war path before the setting in of winter and in connection with this I believe that the presence of five hundred Cavalry here kept in readiness for the field is almost an absolute necessity. . . . I am now constantly on the alert for the uneasiness manifested in the Cheyenne camp and a mere spark may at any time set this whole region ablaze.[21]

General Schofield did not share Colonel Nelson's fears of an

[20] Sheridan to Commissioner of Indian Affairs, Aug. 22, 1869, S-S Papers, 343.
[21] Nelson to AAG, Dept. of Mo., Aug. 14, 1869, Fort Supply, Letters Sent, Vol. 25.

outbreak. He reported that three additional companies of infantry could be made available from Forts Dodge and Larned but commented that for the present the 340-man force at Camp Supply appeared to be sufficient.[22]

Darlington, who had been at Supply for the meetings with the Indian commission, left the post on August 22, bound for his Pond Creek camp. General Schofield ordered military protection for Darlington and his five ox-drawn wagons of stores, and once the train had arrived at the temporary agency, Lieutenant Myron J. Amick and twenty men of the Tenth Cavalry were to take charge of all public property until it could be transferred in the spring. Much to the satisfaction of the Arapaho chiefs, Darlington's quarters were constantly exposed to plunder by Osage hunting parties, and Lieutenant Amick was forced to remain at Pond Creek throughout October.[23]

In early September, 1869, Agent Darlington tramped the new Cheyenne and Arapaho Reservation in search of a suitable location for his agency. Accompanied by W. A. Rankin, a trader of sorts, Darlington found a spot about 125 miles southeast of Camp Supply on the North Fork of the Canadian.[24]

His selection made, Darlington insisted that the agency be moved immediately. The agent knew that his nemesis, Colonel Nelson, had assumed command of Camp Supply on August 21 but that, because of urgent duty in Nevada, he had returned temporary command of the post to Captain John H. Page, who had in turn been replaced by Major Milo H. Kidd upon his arrival from Fort Sill on September 13. Prompt action on the new agency was imperative, Darlington explained to his

[22] Schofield to AAG, Dept. of Mo., Aug. 24, 1869, S-S Papers, 344-45.

[23] Hazen to AAG, Dept. of Mo., Aug. 9, 1869 (copy), Camp Supply, Letters Received, Box 1; Nelson to AAG, Dept. of Mo., Oct. 8, 1869, Fort Supply, Letters Sent, Vol. 24.

[24] Darlington to Hoag, Sept. 17, 1869 (copy), Central Superintendency, FOF, Letters Received; Bonney to Elderkin, Sept. 18, 1869, Camp Supply Letter Book, 58.

superior, because "I have learned that Col. A. D. Nelson will supersede Major Kidd in a short time, and I cannot anticipate so hearty a cooperation with his administration as I can of Major Kidd."[25] The request for immediate removal of the agency was denied, and Darlington could only wait for spring.

At Camp Supply, much of the fall of 1869 was spent constructing post buildings. Recruits had boosted the garrison numbers to nearly six hundred men, now housed in five new barracks. Each set of quarters consisted of rough logs placed upright to form a stockade nine feet high, ninety feet long, and eighteen feet wide, which was covered with logs and a layer of earth one foot thick. The space between the logs was chinked with timber or daubed with mud to insulate the barracks against the ever-present winds. Married soldiers and officers had similar quarters of smaller dimensions with attached kitchens. The earth roofs and floors made the quarters damp, and toadstools and mushrooms sprang up nightly, to be cut down each day.

The location of Camp Supply was conducive to rapid construction. Beaver River and Wolf Creek virtually surrounded the sandy bottom on which the post was planted. Although the streams flooded the post more than once, the waterways held many natural resources. Good brick clay and sand could be found along the banks of Wolf Creek, and several tributaries contained high-quality gypsum for plaster. Limestone fit for building purposes was not far away, and game abounded close to the camp. A post hospital, stables, corrals, and storehouses arose, and it was not long before the camp assumed an air of permanence.

The Arapahoes, now numbering about thirteen hundred, remained about Camp Supply. A peaceful and friendly group,

[25] Darlington to Hoag, Sept. 24, 1869, Central Superintendency, FOF, Letters Received; Post Returns, Camp Supply, Aug.-Oct., 1869; Kidd to AAG, Dept. of Mo., Sept. 17, 1869, Fort Supply, Letters Sent, Vol. 25. Colonel Nelson resumed command of Camp Supply on October 3, 1869.

they visited the post almost daily. Efforts were made to discourage the visits, which the post officers feared were potentially dangerous. A post order of September 23, 1869, directed that all bartering with the Indians cease and prohibited the Indians from visiting camp quarters. When the trading moved to the Indians' camps the next month, it was further ordered that no enlisted men or citizens could enter the Indian district without permission. It was not easy to halt all fraternization. An order of November 10 read: "All persons under military control are hereby prohibited from horse or mule racing with Indians."[26]

The Cheyennes, contemptuous of the friendly attitude of the Arapahoes, drew their rations in small bands and then quickly returned to their camp. They appeared to have accepted the situation, however. In September, 1869, 130 survivors of Tall Bull's band approached Camp Supply and, followed by Medicine Arrow's band, quietly slipped onto the reservation. Still later the Dog Soldiers under Bull Bear arrived and even camped within sight of the post.[27]

The winter months at Camp Supply were no less active than the milder seasons. One project of great interest to the post was the establishment of a fixed trail from the camp to Fort Dodge. As early as mid-May, 1869, Lieutenant I. Wallace and ten men of the Third Infantry had traveled the route, taking odometer readings and making itinerary reports of the terrain. Acting on their reports, Ben Clark, the post guide, selected a more direct wagon route from Supply to Dodge than either the old "Custer Trail" or the "Sully Trail." In early November officers at Camp Supply proudly reported that the old route had been shortened by some twenty miles.[28]

[26] Medical History of Fort Supply, Vol. 166, 4–7.

[27] Berthrong, *Southern Cheyennes*, 349, 351.

[28] Post Returns, Fort Dodge, May, 1869; Special Orders No. 142, Headquarters, Camp Supply, Oct. 14, 1869 (copy), Ben Clark Collection, University of Oklahoma Library; Nelson to AAG, Dept. of Mo., Nov. 7, 1869, Camp Supply, Letters Received, Box 1.

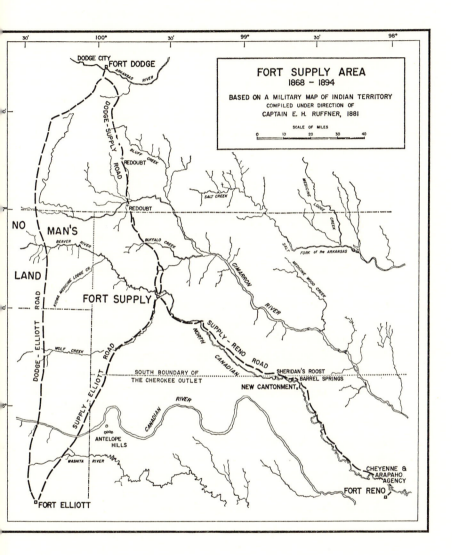

FORT SUPPLY AREA
1868 – 1894

BASED ON A MILITARY MAP OF INDIAN TERRITORY
COMPILED UNDER DIRECTION OF
CAPTAIN E. H. RUFFNER, 1881

SCALE OF MILES
0   10   20   30   40

DODGE CITY
FORT DODGE
ARKANSAS RIVER

DODGE-SUPPLY ROAD

BLUFF CREEK
REDOUBT

SALT CREEK

MEDICINE LODGE CREEK

REDOUBT

NO   MAN'S

BEAVER   RIVER

BUFFALO CREEK

SALT FORK of the ARKANSAS

LAND

MEDICINE LODGE CR.

VERDIGRIS MEDICINE LODGE CR.

MEDICINE WOOD CREEK

CIMARRON

FORT SUPPLY

RIVER

DODGE - ELLIOTT ROAD

WOLF CREEK

SUPPLY - RENO ROAD

NORTH CANADIAN

SUPPLY - ELLIOTT ROAD

SOUTH BOUNDARY OF
THE CHEROKEE OUTLET

SHERIDAN'S ROOST
BARREL SPRINGS
NEW CANTONMENT

RIVER

CANADIAN   RIVER

ANTELOPE
HILLS

WASHITA   RIVER

CHEYENNE &
ARAPAHO
AGENCY

FORT RENO

FORT ELLIOTT

A new threat to peace on the frontier rose in early 1870. On the night of January 8, Cheyenne and Arapaho camps within fifty miles of the post were struck by horse thieves, who made off with 269 head of stock. The Cheyennes sent a party of young warriors in pursuit, but they were forced by their promise to Little Robe to halt the chase at the Arkansas River. Young Arapaho scouts continued to search for the thieves, on one occasion traveling as far north as Fort Hays, Kansas. At last, in mid-February, 1870, a company of cavalry from Camp Supply persuaded the youths to return to their winter campgrounds. Later the Cheyennes discovered that the thieves were Kaw raiders, who had peddled the stolen stock to whites at Council Grove, Kansas.[29]

During the winter Kiowa braves, recently returned from raids in Texas, put in an appearance at Camp Supply. Satanta, leader of the war party, was no stranger to the camp, for he had visited the post in May, 1869, before launching the forays into Texas. Kickingbird, another Kiowa chief, visited Camp Supply in early January, 1870, and was welcomed by being locked in the guardhouse for several hours. On January 14, Satanta tried to create bad relations between the reservation Cheyennes and the whites by diverting or destroying a cattle herd en route from Texas to the agency. Three hundred Kiowas and Comanches surrounded the herd of Jacob Hershfield about forty miles south of Camp Supply and held Hershfield and his sixteen riders at bay. After robbing the men and wagons of coffee, tobacco, sugar, knives, ammunition, and money, Satanta prepared to kill the whites, who were saved only through the intercession of Kickingbird and a Caddo Indian in Hershfield's crew. Satanta relented but said that in the future he would kill every drover and soldier he could, "as he was no more the friend of the white

[29] Nelson to AAG, Dept. of Mo., Jan. 10, 15, 1870, C. Van Horn to Nelson, Jan. 15, 1870 (copy), in Nelson to Commanding Officer, Fort Dodge, Jan. 16, 1870, Nelson to AAG, Dept. of Mo., Jan. 29, 1870, Fort Supply, Letters Sent, Vol. 24.

man." After five hours Hershfield and his men were permitted to leave. Before they could gather their herd, however, Satanta's warriors stampeded the cattle and slaughtered 271 head. The crew reached Camp Supply the next day richer in experience but poorer by nearly seven thousand dollars' worth of stock.[30]

Major Kidd and four troops of the Tenth Cavalry immediately set out after the raiders and after a surprise attack succeeded in chasing the Kiowas south. Colonel Nelson feared that the raid was the beginning of extensive new hostilities. Eager to whip Satanta's band in the winter months, as the Cheyennes had been beaten the year before, Nelson pressed his superiors to authorize an eight-week campaign. A force able to meet up to fifteen hundred warriors was requested. When Kiowas in full war costume could be seen from the Camp Supply gates, Nelson's demands seemed credible, but later reliable intelligence persuaded his superior that Major Kidd's expedition had successfully cleared the area of hostiles and that the post was no longer threatened.[31]

Nelson later admitted that there had been satisfying aspects to the episode. At the first hint of trouble the Cheyenne and Arapaho chiefs had offered to fight with the army against the Kiowas and Comanches—an offer rejected by higher authority —and in addition Bull Bear's Dog Soldiers had refused Satanta's invitation to join in the raids.[32]

One direct result of the confrontation with the Kiowas was the establishment of a mail station at Bear Creek, Kansas, a campsite on the Dodge–Supply road which mail and freight details had found particularly favorable. On February 3, 1870,

[30] Affidavit of Jacob Hershfield in Nelson to AAG, Dept. of Mo., Jan. 15, 1870, in *ibid.*

[31] Nelson to AAG, Dept. of Mo., Jan. 15, 16, 22, 1870, in *ibid.*; John Pope to Nelson, Jan. 17, 1870, Camp Supply, Letters Received, Box 1.

[32] Medical History of Fort Supply, Vol. 166, 8; Nelson to AAG, Dept. of Mo., Jan. 22, 23, 1870, Fort Supply, Letters Sent, Vol. 24.

a force under Captain George F. Raulston left Camp Supply to build a temporary station at Bear Creek. After it was completed, a small detachment was stationed there to protect the increasing traffic on the Dodge–Supply road.[33]

At about the same time the presence of whisky in the Indian camps became a problem for the troops at Fort Supply. In September, 1869, Samuel Parker, the post hay contractor, was discovered to be doubling as a whisky runner, trading his potent wares to the Indians for horses. The following month, at the request of officers at Camp Supply, a "whisky ranch" on Bluff Creek in Kansas was raided and destroyed by troops from Fort Dodge. "Whisky ranch" was the contemporary term for an inn that bootlegged liquor or ran games, and in some areas such establishments were nearly as numerous as cattle ranches. In a final effort to curtail the liquor traffic, it was ordered that all public and private wagon trains were to be stopped and searched for illegal liquor at Bear Creek Mail Station. "Loafers and vagabonds" were also to be held unless they had the written permission of the commanding officer of either Fort Dodge or Fort Hays to enter the Indian Territory.[34]

Another problem was illegal sales of arms and ammunition to the Indians. W. A. Rankin, a licensed trader in Indian Territory, frequently brought gunpowder, lead, and percussion caps to Medicine Arrow's band. Despite the alleged support of Rankin by Kansas Congressman Sidney Clark, Darlington ordered Rankin off the reservation. Colonel Nelson backed Darlington's action, but it was not until the spring of 1870 that the trader was removed.[35]

[33] AAG, Dept. of Mo., to Nelson, Jan. 16, 1870, Camp Supply, Letters Received, Box 1.

[34] Commanding Officer, Fort Larned, to AAG, Dept. of Mo., Sept. 9, 1870 (copy), in *ibid.*; Nelson to George F. Raulston, Feb. 10, 1870, Fort Supply, Letters Sent, Vol. 24.

[35] Nelson to AAG, Dept. of Mo., Jan. 22, 28, Apr. 23, 1870, Fort Supply, Letters Sent, Vol. 24; Berthrong, *Southern Cheyennes*, 252.

Spring, 1870, was also a busy time at Camp Supply. In March, Enoch Hoag, superintendent of Indian affairs, scheduled a council at Camp Supply with the Cheyennes and Arapahoes. Meeting the Indians on March 21, he urged them to accept their new agency, but little was accomplished. The Indians' earnest plea for the release of the prisoners taken by Major Carr during the Republican River campaign of May, 1869, was received with some sympathy.[36]

As the time grew near to shift the Cheyenne and Arapaho Agency south, the Cheyennes became more reluctant to leave. On April 23, Nelson alerted the commanding officer at Fort Dodge that the bands under Medicine Arrow and Bull Bear might make a break for the north, and that, if so, they would probably cross the Arkansas somewhere above his post. On the same day, Company E, Third Infantry, Lieutenant Joseph Hale commanding, left Camp Supply on detached service to the new Cheyenne and Arapaho Agency, bearing orders to protect supplies being shipped to the new headquarters. Hale expected to remain at the agency only until June 1, but warlike activity in the region delayed his return. Colonel Nelson, in turn, encouraged the Department of the Missouri to increase the number of troops at the agency, for its remote location made protection difficult from Camp Supply.[37]

On May 3, Darlington began his journey down the North Fork of the Canadian to the site of the new agency. He was followed the next day by nearly all the Arapaho lodges and by all the Cheyennes who had been staying at Camp Supply.[38] Because of the uninviting location of the agency, however, the

---

[36] Hoag to Parker, Oct. 8, 1870, *Annual Report of the Commissioner of Indian Affairs for the Year 1870*, 254.

[37] Nelson to AAG, Dept. of Mo., Apr. 23, May 7, 1870, Fort Supply, Letters Sent, Vol. 24; Nelson to Commanding Officer, Fort Dodge, Apr. 23, 1870, Fort Supply, Letters Sent, Vol. 24.

[38] Nelson to AAG, Dept. of Mo., May 7, 1870, Fort Supply, Letters Sent, Vol. 24.

Indians camped some distance away. By late May it was reported that only twelve to fifteen lodges of both tribes had remained with Darlington. Nelson wrote to General John Pope: "It was a mistake, I think, to move the agency at this time, very few if any of the Indians of either tribe were in favor of the moving it to its present location, . . . [and] they were opposed to it, it might be said, to a man."[39]

Relocating the agency complicated the responsibilities of Colonel Nelson. A shortage of wagons at the post doubled the number of delivery trips to the new agency, and the Indian wards, once comfortably camped under the watchful eye of Camp Supply troops, were now widely separated. Arapahoes camped in the vicinity of the new agency, but the Cheyennes steadfastly refused to join them. Bull Bear's and Medicine Arrow's bands maintained camps eighty miles up the Beaver, slowly moving north, while the remaining Cheyenne lodges clustered near the Washita, at the Kiowa and Comanche Sun Dance.

The Kiowa Medicine Lodge was held in May, 1870, and lasted for ten days. Delegations of Kiowas, Kiowa-Apaches, Comanches, and Cheyennes freely discussed the question of war or peace. When the war pipe was passed, only one Cheyenne chief, Whirlwind, a man without influence, accepted it. The grand council then broke up, and the warriors spread out. Little Heart, with a party of Kiowas and Kiowa-Apaches, headed for Camp Supply. White Horse and his gathering of Kiowas and Comanches went to Fort Sill. Satanta and Kickingbird took their bands into Texas. Cheyennes under Little Robe and Big Horse went peacefully to the new agency, but the uncommitted main band went to the headwaters of the Washita to hunt buffalo.[40]

[39] Nelson to Pope, May 28, 1870, in *ibid.*

[40] J. A. Covington, Report, n.d., Central Superintendency, FOF, Letters Received.

Little Robe warned Colonel Nelson of the impending outburst with secret messages from the Sun Dance. Preparations were quickly made to put the post in readiness. It was ordered that in case of an attack all the cavalry would be sent to the field and that an infantry company would move in to hold the exposed cavalry camp against a frontal assault. Horses were grazed at the post from 8:00 A.M. to noon and from 4:30 P.M. to near sunset, with each armed trooper responsible for his own mount. Four horses of each troop were held in stable, saddled and ready to move. Because the infantry quarters were about six hundred yards from the cavalry camp, the commanding officer of the cavalry battalion was to call his troops into the field at his own discretion.[41]

Kiowa and Apache forces soon appeared near Camp Supply. During a fierce electrical storm on the night of May 28, Little Heart fatally shot a Mexican servant named Monroe while he slept in his tent. The only clue was the report of a clerk in the Indian commissary building that in a flash of lightning he had had a momentary glimpse of a huddled, blanketed figure peering through his window.[42]

At daybreak the post interpreter, Dick Curtis, who lived about five miles from the post, reported that two of his horses had been stolen during the night. Ben Clark and a companion followed the thieves' trail one mile beyond Curtis' garden and found several unshod pony tracks which joined the trail where it crossed the Beaver. Moccasin tracks on the soft banks were unmistakable signs. Three miles farther Clark spotted two mounted Indians but ignored their taunts and returned to the post, where he reported on his reconnaissance. That evening Captain Nicholas Nolan and fifty men of the Tenth Cavalry

[41] Nelson to AAG, Dept. of Mo., May 6, 7, 1870, Fort Supply, Letters Sent, Vol. 24; Nelson to AAG, Dept. of Mo., June 12, 1870, Fort Supply, Letters Sent, Vol. 26.

[42] Nelson to AAG, Dept. of Mo., May 29, 1870, Fort Supply, Letters Sent, Vol. 24.

proceeded thirty miles up Beaver River to seek out the Indians. "I apprehend we may consider the Indian war opened in this region," wrote Colonel Nelson.[43]

As Captain Nolan and his troops moved north in a futile effort to track the thieves, the Kiowas and Kiowa-Apaches wandered southeast of the post. On May 29, forty miles from Camp Supply, these warriors attacked a train of thirteen wagons loaded with Indian subsistence stores for the new agency. In the engagement one teamster was killed and the wagonmaster, Charles F. Tracy, lost fifty-eight mules. It was not until early on the morning of May 30 that two men were able to slip from the besieged train and take news of the ambush to Supply. Colonel Nelson dispatched two troops of the Tenth Cavalry under Captain Louis H. Carpenter to the rescue.[44]

Captain Carpenter set out under orders to save the wagons, send them back to Supply with one troop as escort, and with the other troop locate Lieutenant Mason M. Maxon, who was still on the road with an escort and four wagons from the Cheyenne and Arapaho Agency. Upon reaching the embattled teamsters, Captain Carpenter found that Lieutenant Maxon had arrived a few hours earlier. Conditions were critical for the train. Nelson later reported: "It was clear that the Indians intended to attack them, and it does not appear that they were deterred from this intention by the reinforcement of the Lieut. and his party." The timely arrival of Captain Carpenter dispersed nearly three hundred warriors. Two days later the combined train reached Camp Supply.[45]

[43] Captain Nolan returned to post on May 30, having failed to catch the Indians. Post Returns, Camp Supply, May, 1870; *Record of Engagements*, 27; Nelson to Hoag, June 18, 1870, Nelson to Pope, July 2, 1870, Fort Supply, Letters Sent, Vol. 26.

[44] Nelson to AAG, Dept. of Mo., May 29, 1870, Fort Supply, Letters Sent, Vol. 24; Darlington to Hoag, Sept. 1, 1870, *Report of the Commissioner of Indian Affairs, 1870*, 255.

[45] Nelson to AAG, Dept. of Mo., June 4, 1870, Fort Supply, Letters Sent, Vol. 26.

On May 30 marauding Kiowa braves continued the offensive, killing a lone teamster barely three miles from Camp Supply. A sergeant and ten men found the arrow-riddled, scalped, mutilated body of the man, stripped of everything but his shirt. Later that day Captain George W. Armes arrived at the post, followed five hours later by the army paymaster and his escort. Both parties had sighted a band of Indians on the Dodge–Supply road within sixty miles of the post. In each case the Indians had approached peacefully, shaken hands, and asked for tobacco, backing away only when the escorts drew close. The Indians, it was said, were leading a mule, possibly that of the dead teamster, plus Dick Curtis' two horses. They also carried two fresh scalp locks.[46]

Later that evening Major Milo H. Kidd, with Lieutenant L. H. Coleman and fifty enlisted men of the Tenth Cavalry, left Camp Supply to patrol the Dodge–Supply road. Still later Lieutenant Robert G. Smithers with twenty-five men of the Tenth Cavalry took the field to meet a wagon train that was reported south of Fort Dodge and lacking a sufficient escort. Lieutenant Smithers passed Major Kidd's patrol on the road north and on the morning of May 31 met the train near the Cimarron. The reinforcements arrived just three hours after a band of Kiowas had begun keeping watch on the small train. Smithers led the convoy safely into Camp Supply on June 1.[47]

The Kiowas who had been turned away from the wagon train by Lieutenant Smithers angrily proceeded to Bear Creek Mail Station, forty-five miles south of Fort Dodge. Calling themselves Arapahoes, forty or fifty of them approached the station, which was guarded by Sergeant James Murray and four privates of the Third Infantry out of Camp Supply. The Indians

[46] Nelson to Hoag, June 18, 1870, Nelson to AAG, Dept. of Mo., June 2, Sept. 23, 1870, in *ibid.*

[47] Nelson to AAG, Dept. of Mo., June 4, 1870, in *ibid.*; Medical History of Fort Supply, Vol. 166, 8.

accepted some food, and at length all but seven drifted away. Sergeant Murray ordered two of the men to guard the weapons in the house and the other two to watch the stock in the stable. Suddenly shots echoed from the house, and when Murray rushed in he found both men dead—one shot in the heart, the other through the head. The Indians, turning on Murray, who was armed only with an ax, attacked him with bows and arrows, hitting him six times in the arms and once in the forehead. Dashing outside, the Indians were confronted by the last two soldiers, who were armed only with pitchforks. The uneven contest would have ended quickly but for the dramatic appearance of Major Kidd and his command bearing down on the station. The Indians quickly mounted their ponies and escaped. Kidd left several men behind to hold the station and led the rest of the column to Fort Dodge. Sergeant Murray recovered from his multiple wounds.[48]

After many raids on civilian and mail-station herds, on the morning of June 1, Indians made an attempt on Camp Supply stock. Darting from the cover of nearby sand hills, the Indians seized two government horses and a mule and a horse belonging to a civilian as they were grazing five hundred yards from the post. While the raiders were passing within a hundred yards of the civilian and his companions, however, they were so heavily fired upon that they released the stock. Lieutenant Myron Amick and twenty men followed the warriors for fifteen miles, but the swift Indian ponies outran their pursuers.

When Lieutenant Smithers arrived at Camp Supply on June 1 with the rescued supply train, he also brought word of a train of thirty-two wagons south of the Arkansas without sufficient protection. Accordingly, on June 2, Lieutenant John A. Boda-

---

[48] Nelson to AAG, Dept. of Mo., June 4, June 18, Sept. 23, 1870, Fort Supply, Letters Sent, Vol. 26; Nelson to Pope, June 6, 1870 (copy), Fort Supply, Letters Received, Box 6, Records of the War Dept., National Archives, Washington, D.C.

mer left Camp Supply with twenty-five men to meet and escort the train. Two days later Lieutenant William Davis and twenty enlisted men escorted the train which Lieutenant Smithers had brought in on its return to Dodge.[49]

Colonel Nelson blamed the Cheyennes for the raids. Suspecting that Big Mouth was among the hostiles camped in seventy lodges about forty miles east of Supply, Nelson ordered his detachment at the agency, under Lieutenant Joseph Hale, to inform the Indians that none of them would be permitted to visit Camp Supply and that sentries had been ordered to fire at Indians on sight. Further, all friendly Indians must report to the agency, where a count would be made every day or two, and any individuals known or even thought to have been on the warpath would be arrested. Nelson concluded: "All such [arrested] Indians should be executed as there can be little doubt of their participation in the outrages recently committed in this region."[50]

Rebuffed in their earlier efforts to capture stock at Camp Supply, the Cheyennes made dashes for post animals on the afternoon of June 6, at midnight the same day, and again at 3:30 A.M. the following morning. No government stock was captured, but two civilians lost thirteen mules and one horse. Each attempt brought the Indians closer to the post.[51]

By June 9, Cheyenne war parties had located themselves on the north end of the Dodge–Supply road. In three separate encounters a party of officers, the mail detachment, and Lieutenant Bodamer and an escort who were accompanying a long ox train from Dodge were attacked. The officers, led by Captain John H. Page, succeeded in beating off the attackers, as did the mail party, and two Indians were killed. The train escorted by

---

[49] Nelson to AAG, Dept. of Mo., June 4, 1870, Fort Supply, Letters Sent, Vol. 26.

[50] Nelson to Joseph Hale, June 7, 1870, Nelson to Pope, June 18, 1870, in *ibid.*

[51] Nelson to AAG, Dept. of Mo., Sept. 23, 1870, in *ibid.*

Lieutenant Bodamer was forced to corral to protect itself from flanking movements. When the Indians relaxed their siege at nightfall, Lieutenant Bodamer dispatched Private Will Edmonson of the Tenth Cavalry to Camp Supply for relief. Edmonson narrowly escaped capture by the Indians in his break through their lines and managed to reach Supply at 11:00 P.M. The next morning Captain Nolan went to Bodamer's relief, and the train arrived at the post at noon on June 11. Lieutenant Bodamer reported three Indians killed and ten wounded.[52]

More than once in June, 1870, Indians sent word to Colonel Nelson of their determination to destroy Camp Supply. On June 11 the Kiowas, reinforced by several bands of Comanches, launched a full-scale attack on the post. Two hundred Indians charged across the west side of the Tenth Cavalry camp at 3:30 P.M., capturing two diseased horses and a pony belonging to Lieutenant Maxon. Captain Nolan, commanding the Tenth Cavalry troops, quickly ordered his command to counterattack. The chase had proceeded five miles up the Beaver when Lieutenant Amick withdrew Troop I from Nolan's command to support a small picket party stranded at Dick Curtis' home. A reserve band of Indians saw the move and attacked Lieutenant Amick's group, cutting them off. The Indians' greater numbers temporarily placed Troop I at a severe disadvantage, but Captain George Raulston with Troop A soon moved in, and the Indians withdrew.

Colonel Nelson, meanwhile, took a position about a half-mile from the cavalry camp atop a hill from which he could direct his entire command. Through a spyglass he saw great numbers of Indians on the Beaver River slopes directly ahead of Captain Nolan. Lieutenant Maxon and eighteen men were ordered to march rapidly along the ridge above the Beaver to the highest point, about two miles off, and then turn right to aid Nolan.

[52] Nelson to AAG, Dept. of Mo., June 12, 1870, in *ibid.*; *Record of Engagements*, 28.

Lieutenant Maxon had gone only a thousand yards when his detachment was itself met by a large body of dismounted Indians. Heavy fighting broke out, and Lieutenant Smithers and the reserve cavalry, followed closely by Lieutenant J. P. Davis and a Third Infantry howitzer crew, were sent to join Lieutenant Maxon. Before they arrived, however, Amick and Maxon put the Indians to flight in sharp encounters, at a cost to the Indians of six dead and many wounded. The cavalry loss of the combined engagement consisted of two wounded horses.[53]

The country surrounding Camp Supply was filled with Indians, and the brave resistance of the Camp Supply garrison against a direct attack did not deter raids. On June 13 a herder employed by the beef contractor was set upon by ten Indians. The man barely escaped with his life. The following night Indians took positions in the sand hills and fired shots into the post, but without doing any damage. On June 16, Captain Nolan, escorting an empty wagon train to Dodge, encountered four woodchoppers north of the camp and warned them of the danger. When he returned two days later, he found the bodies of three of the woodsmen.[54]

Then, as suddenly as the raids began, they ended. Lieutenant Hale, who had remained at the Cheyenne and Arapaho Agency throughout these events, reported that all the Arapahoes and thirty-odd lodges of Cheyennes were at the agency. It was his opinion that for the most part the Cheyennes and Arapahoes had refrained from violence during the past month and that the Kiowa chief Little Heart was most likely the leader of the hostilities.[55]

During September trains of one to twelve wagons cautiously

[53] Nicholas Nolan to Post Adjutant, Camp Supply, June 11, 1870, Dept. of Mo., Letters Received, Records of the War Dept., National Archives, Washington, D. C.

[54] Nelson to Pope, June 25, 1870, Nelson to AAG, Dept. of Mo., Sept. 23, 1870, Fort Supply, Letters Sent, Vol. 26.

[55] Nelson to Pope, July 2, 30, 1870, in *ibid.*

made the journey to the agency on the North Fork of the Canadian without incident. In all, 700,000 rations, originally sent to Camp Supply during the time it was the agency, were transferred to the new location. Beef continued to be unacceptable to the Indians, and the fall buffalo hunt brought the Cheyennes and Arapahoes back to the vicinity of Camp Supply. Nelson approved the winter campsites near his post, for he need not transport rations to the agency. Besides, the commander announced, "I have always maintained that the present location of the agency was a wanton piece of cruelty to the Indians, and every day strengthens the conclusion."[56]

Meeting with the Arapahoes in September, while they were on their hunt, Colonel Nelson listened to complaints that involved more than just the location of the agency. The Arapaho chiefs were angry that they were treated not better but probably worse than the tribes who had plundered all summer. The case of Little Heart was particularly annoying. His boasts that he had killed the Mexican servant Monroe at Camp Supply, the teamster on May 30, and the two soldiers at Bear Creek Mail Station were common knowledge. Yet he was well received at Fort Sill and drew regular winter rations. Moreover, those Cheyennes who had been on the warpath were rationed at their agency with as little hesitation as were the Arapahoes.[57]

The agency site, the general treatment of the Arapahoes, and the usual dissatisfaction with the quality of the rations were not the only complaints the Indians had. Dr. William Nicholas, making a tour of Indian agencies in November, 1870, for the Associated Executive Committee of the Society of Friends, listed four additional annoyances to the tribes: they were weak because the government had disarmed them; they did not want to be confined to a small reservation; they did not like to be

---

[56] Nelson to Pope, Sept. 2, 1870, in *ibid*.

[57] Nelson to AAG, Dept. of Mo., Sept. 16, 23, 1870, in *ibid*.

prohibited from going to Camp Supply; and, finally, they did not want railroads through their country.[58]

Thus, when the year 1870 ended, Camp Supply was a cantonment of rude structures in a land teeming with discontented and only temporarily pacified Indians. As the winter snows fell on the post for the third year, the topic of conversation centered on the words of Big Jake, the principal Cheyenne chief in the region, who had threatened to go on the warpath in the spring. It would be war, he promised, "the like of which has not been seen on this frontier for some years."[59]

[58] *Ibid.*; William Nicholson, "A Tour of Indian Agencies in Kansas and the Indian Territory in 1870," *Kansas Historical Quarterly*, Vol. III (Nov., 1934), 346–48.

[59] Nelson to AAG, Dept. of Mo., Nov. 18, 1870, Fort Supply, Letters Sent, Vol. 26.

Chapter III

Indians, Whites, and Whisky
1871–73

Dᴜʀɪɴɢ the winter of 1870–71 many officers at Camp Supply shared in the fears of an Indian outbreak in the spring. Colonel Nelson dutifully informed his superior, General John H. Pope, of Big Jake's threat, as well as what Nelson considered to be mismanagement at the Cheyenne and Arapaho Agency. Pope recorded the complaints and explained to Eli S. Parker, commissioner of Indian affairs, that military authorities could not correct agency abuses but could only disperse troops along lines of transportation and protect exposed frontier settlements if hostilities began. It was hoped that the officials dealing with Indian affairs would check the Indians' restiveness before April 1.[1]

The interest of Nelson and Pope was not welcomed by officials of the Central Superintendency. Darlington refuted Nelson's charges, insisting that they were based on incomplete knowledge. As for the threat of an outbreak, the agent stated that he considered Big Jake a reliable and influential leader of peace among the Cheyennes, not a warmonger. Warfare was not imminent, in his opinion, "when the grass grew green."[2]

Nevertheless, as the winter months turned into spring, military observers continued to fear the worst. Lieutenant Colonel John W. Davidson, who replaced Colonel Nelson as command-

[1] Pope to Parker, Jan. 4, 1871, Central Superintendency, Letters Received.

[2] Hoag to Parker, Jan. 9, 1871, Central Superintendency, FOF, Letters Sent; Darlington to Hoag, Feb. 11, 1871, Central Superintendency, FOF, Letters Received.

ing officer at Camp Supply on February 5, 1871, also foresaw trouble brewing in winter camps on the Washita, where Cheyenne chiefs were conferring with the Kiowas, Comanches, and Kiowa-Apaches. Reports by officers, traders, and scouts throughout February and March noted that the bands were more interested in fattening war ponies than in killing buffalo.[3] Little Raven and the Arapahoes, camped on the Cimarron halfway between Camp Supply and the agency, were thought not to be inclined to join the hostiles should an outbreak occur. As for the other bands, Captain William B. Kennedy reported, "I would state that I know of no officer or citizen at Camp Supply, I. T., at the time of my leaving there [February 19, 1871] who was not fully convinced of the hostile intent of the Indians mentioned."[4]

With Indian unrest apparent to the military if not to the Indian officials, Colonel Davidson took measures to reinforce the line of communication with Fort Dodge, ninety-three miles away. On his journey down the Dodge–Supply road to take command of Camp Supply, Davidson erected a new defensive earthworks at a point on Upper Bear Creek thirty-three miles south of Dodge. Bear Creek Mail Station, farther down the road, approximately halfway between Fort Dodge and Camp Supply, was inspected and found to be in a not very defensible condition but was retained for the time being.

After reaching Camp Supply, Colonel Davidson decided that for the safety of the mail and supply trains on the Dodge–Supply road more protection was needed than the small station at Bear Creek and the new redoubt north of it. Captain John H. Page was therefore dispatched on February 12, 1871, with one company of the Third Infantry, to build Cimarron Redoubt,

[3] John Davidson to AAG, Dept. of Mo., Feb. 11, 1871, Fort Supply, Letters Sent, Vol. 26; T. R. Curtis to E. W. Wynkoop, Mar. 4, 1871 (copy), Upper Arkansas Agency, Letters Received.

[4] W. B. Kennedy to AAG, Dept. of Mo., Mar. 2, 1871 (copy), Central Superintendency, Letters Received.

thirty-eight miles north of Camp Supply. A week later Captain Robert P. Hughes took two additional companies of infantry to complete the job. Located on the banks of the Cimarron River, the third station on the Dodge–Supply road consisted of Sibley tents and a sod breastworks supporting gunny sacks filled with sand. The redoubt was built on the principle of a permanent "fortification in miniature, with bastions, flanks, curtains, and ditch." A detachment of one officer and twenty-five men, relieved each month, was stationed there to aid wagons through five miles of nearly impassable bottom on the Cimarron River.[5]

Collaterally, Captain Joseph B. Rife and a company of the Sixth Infantry moved out of Camp Supply on February 25, 1871, to reinforce the construction of Upper Bear Creek Station, begun by Davidson on his trip south to Camp Supply. This cantonment, located higher up on a stream, was formed into a stockade fifty feet square, built of burlap bags filled with dirt. Walls ten feet thick at the base held bastions at diagonally opposite corners. The western wall served as one side of the enclosed mule corral, while the eastern side contained quarters for the men. The earth-covered roofs were a few feet lower than the walls, forming a good defensive position in case of attack.[6]

With the road to Dodge secure, Davidson turned his attention to other matters. Many four-day scouting trips near Beaver River and Wolf Creek in early March served to acquaint the post garrison with the region, keep the commanding officer informed of the location of potentially hostile tribes, and at the same time allow troops to investigate the haunts of renegade traders.

On March 26, after creditable information was received

---

[5] Davidson to AAG, Dept. of Mo., Sept. 20, 1871, Fort Supply, Letters Sent, Vol. 27; Frances M. A. Roe, *Army Letters from an Officer's Wife, 1871–88*, 86.

[6] Davidson to AAG, Dept. of Mo., Feb. 10, 1871, Fort Supply, Letters Sent, Vol. 26; Richard T. Jacobs, "Military Reminiscences of Captain Richard T. Jacobs," *Chronicles of Oklahoma*, Vol. II (Mar., 1924), 30–31.

about the anticipated outbreak, a more extensive scout was begun from Camp Supply. The primary duty of Captain Nicholas Nolan and his squadron of Tenth Cavalry was to patrol the Beaver River area between Camp Supply and the Santa Fe Trail crossing near Round Mound, in order to prevent the Kiowas, Comanches, Cheyennes, and Arapahoes from leaving their reservations and going north. Captain Nolan was directed to pursue northward any Indians detected on the trail and return them to their reservation.

Commanding 4 officers and 120 men, Captain Nolan left on a seventeen-day march north and west 235 miles to the Santa Fe crossing. During the several weeks they were on the trail the troopers encountered severe rains, heavy snows, and cold north winds. Moreover, the grass had been eaten by buffaloes, and for a 70-mile burned-off stretch south of Round Mound no wood was obtainable. Water was so poor as to be harmful to men and animals, and ponds marked on the maps were found to be dry or nonexistent. After an equally arduous return journey, the party reached Camp Supply on May 3. No trails, camps, or signs of Indians were discovered during the entire patrol.[7]

Captain Nolan's reconnaissance was the first extensive patrol into the present Oklahoma Panhandle. Nolan made his own trail from the Beaver to the Santa Fe Trail and reported on the nature of the country, using the itinerary of his march to sketch a more realistic map of wood, water, grass, and buffaloes to be expected west of the one hundredth meridian. Further, Nolan's scouting trip indicated that whisky traders suspected of infiltrating the area were not following Beaver River to Indian bands near Camp Supply.

Rumors were heard of increased whisky traffic with the Indians, however. The Lee and Reynolds Company, the official

[7] Davidson to Nolan, Mar. 25, Apr. 15, 28, May 2, 1871, Fort Supply, Letters Sent, Vol. 27; Nolan to Post Adjutant, Camp Supply, May 4, 1871, Fort Supply, Letters Received, Box 2.

post traders at Camp Supply and frequent visitors to the Indian camps, had reported trade irregularities early in February, 1871. In May violations became so frequent that liquor-inspection details were placed on the Dodge–Supply road, with indifferent success. Yet the military kept after the smugglers, most of whom were from Kansas. In spite of the vigilance of the patrols, the army was hampered by legal technicalities. Until June, 1871, officers were under orders not to pursue or arrest Indians with contraband. Moreover, there were few if any United States marshals in Indian Territory. It was suspected that travelers, and even government guides and interpreters, secreted small quantities of liquor for sale to Indians. The ultimate complication was that Indians refused to expose the culprits in or out of court.[8]

Much to everyone's relief, the expected uprising failed to materialize. Captain Jeremiah S. Schindel at the Cheyenne and Arapaho Agency was unconvinced that trouble would not begin and believed that an attack was being contemplated on Atlantic and Pacific Railroad surveyors working nearby. It was the prevailing opinion that Cheyenne and Kiowa warriors would be searching out victims before the end of March. Captain Charles D. Viele and a company of the Tenth Cavalry escorting the surveyors were alerted, but the anticipated attack did not come. Colonel Davidson considered that the April 6, 1871, announcement to Little Raven and Little Robe that they, together with five or six other chiefs, would visit the Great White Father in Washington, had had a tranquilizing effect on the two tribes.[9]

[8] Lee and Reynolds Company to Joseph B. Rife, Feb. 14, 1871, Fort Supply, Letters Received, Box 2; Davidson to AAG, Dept. of Mo., Oct. 2, 1871, Fort Supply, Letters Sent, Vol. 27; Parker to W. W. Belknap, June 21, 1871, Commissioner of Indian Affairs, Letters Sent, Vol. 102, Records of the Dept. of the Interior, National Archives, Washington, D. C.; Darlington to Hoag, June 23, Aug. 7, 1871, Central Superintendency, FOF, Letters Received.

[9] Jeremiah S. Shindel to Davidson, Mar. 22, 1871, Central Superintendency, Letters Received; Davidson to Charles D. Viele, Mar. 30, 1871, Davidson to AAG,

Once the Cheyenne and Arapaho chiefs had departed for Washington, Davidson relaxed his vigil. As it turned out, however, not all the tribesmen felt peaceably inclined that summer. The desire of the Cheyennes and Arapahoes to raid their historic enemies the Colorado Utes remained strong. Left Hand, a war chief of the Arapahoes, had, in fact, petitioned Darlington in February, 1871, for permission to go on such a raid. Because the agent did not want to offend the chief with a direct refusal, he had promised to refer the request to higher authority. Left Hand waited a reasonable length of time and then left the reservation with fifty braves. He was returned through the temperate intercession of Yellow Bear, and the peace was not broken.[10] But the Cheyennes were also determined on a try for the Utes, and in May, 1871, a band of three hundred Dog Soldiers under Grey Beard attempted an expedition.

About the same time Captain William B. Kennedy and a troop of the Tenth Cavalry left Camp Supply on a routine scout between Beaver River and Round Mound. As they neared San Francisco Creek, about 125 miles west of the post, Kennedy sighted a large band of Indians moving north. Upon confrontation it turned out to be Grey Beard's band, and at a parley a promise was extracted from the Indians to return peacefully to their camps on the Canadian and the Washita. Colonel Davidson was advised of these events, and Captain Nolan with two additional troops was sent to Kennedy's assistance. On their arrival they found that the Indians had kept their word, and Nolan returned to post, satisfied that the Cheyennes were not headed for the Colorado frontier.[11]

Dept. of Mo., Sept. 20, Apr. 28, 1871, Davidson to Ed Guerrier, Apr. 6, 1871, Fort Supply, Letters Sent, Vol. 27.

[10] John Murphy, "Reminiscences of the Washita Campaign and of the Darlington Indian Agency," *Chronicles of Oklahoma*, Vol. I (June, 1923), 271; Darlington to Hoag, Feb. 9, 1871, Central Superintendency, FOF, Letters Received.

[11] Medical History of Fort Supply, Vol. 166, 12; Darlington to Hoag, Aug.

Even as this band of Cheyennes drew near Camp Supply, the Kiowas were moving north. Agent Darlington, concerned about the effect that warlike tribe might have on the Cheyennes, appealed for military support to force the Kiowas back to their reservation. Scouting reports through mid-July placed the Arapahoes fourteen miles south of Camp Supply on the North Fork of the Canadian and the combined camp of the Cheyennes and Kiowa-Apaches eight miles north of the post on Wolf Creek. The Kiowas, Comanches, and some displaced Mescalero Apaches were thought to be eighty miles south of Camp Supply on tributaries of the Washita. From that point these tribes were sending agitators into the Cheyenne camp.[12]

Reinforcements were necessary before Camp Supply could move against the Kiowas, and a request was made to the commanding officer at Fort Dodge for a temporary detachment of cavalry. Captain Tullius C. Tupper's troop of the Sixth Cavalry arrived on July 25 and was joined with Captain Nolan's force of the Tenth Cavalry from Camp Supply. Together they would go to the Cheyennes' camp, from there crossing to the southern line of the reservation, then west along the Canadian until they reached the headwaters of the Washita. All the Kiowas in the area were to be driven out. Marching on July 28, Nolan followed his plan, forcing the Kiowas to retreat south. There was no bloodshed, and Colonel Davidson later commented that "the moral effect of the promptness with which troops were sent for and appeared had saved a campaign." Within two days all the Kiowas and their cohorts had withdrawn, and the Cheyennes moved across the Canadian to camp south of Camp Supply.[13]

26, 1871, *Annual Report of the Commissioner of Indian Affairs for the Year 1871*, 472; Davidson to Nolan, May 15, 1871, Fort Supply, Letters Sent, Vol. 27.

[12] Davidson to AAG, Dept. of Mo., July 10, 21, 1871, Fort Supply, Letters Sent, Vol. 27; Darlington to Davidson, July 7, 1871, Central Superintendency, Letters Received; Darlington to Hoag, July 15, 1871, Central Superintendency, FOF, Letters Received.

The remaining summer weeks of 1871 were spent patrolling the Dodge–Supply road for illegal traders and escorting railroad survey crews. Captain Viele protected one survey crew into September, and Captain Nolan escorted another from August 24 to September 29, from one hundred miles east of Camp Supply, through the Antelope Hills, and on to Fort Bascom, New Mexico Territory.[14]

September and October brought the Cheyennes and Arapahoes closer to Camp Supply, and all remained quiet near the post. Sixty Arapahoes under Heaps of Birds made another attempt to strike the Utes but were dissuaded by Colonel Davidson. Only the rumor of Kiowas in the area upset the tranquillity of Camp Supply, and the post ended the year much as it had entered it—with rumors of a spring outbreak.[15]

As it entered its fourth year on the Southern Plains, Camp Supply had lost its temporary look. Six sets of troop barracks had replaced the original mud huts, and seventeen officers' quarters, a commanding officer's building, a guardhouse, and two warehouses were recent additions to the post. In close proximity were the already established stables, bakery, hospital, adjutant's office, and quartermaster corral, helping to add a permanent character to the establishment. With few exceptions, building walls at the post were of picket construction—upright cottonwood logs covered with canvas.

Always aware of its responsibility as a supply depot, Camp Supply kept in readiness 800,000 pounds of grain and forage for animals and one year's supply of subsistence stores for six

---

[13] Davidson to AAG, Dept. of Mo., July 26, 31, 1871, Fort Supply, Letters Sent, Vol. 27.

[14] Medical History of Fort Supply, Vol. 166, 13, 14; Davidson to AAG, Dept. of Mo., Aug. 24, 28, Sept. 20, 1871, in *ibid.*

[15] Davidson to AAG, Dept. of Mo., Dec. 15, 20, 1871, Davidson to Darlington, Dec. 26, 1871, Fort Supply, Letters Sent, Vol. 27; Davidson to AAG, Dept. of Mo., Jan. 16, 1872, Fort Supply, Letters Sent, Vol. 28; John F. Williams to Davidson, Jan. 2, 1872, Camp Supply, Letters Received, Box 2.

companies of soldiers. Transporting these provisions to Indian country was a long haul, often beginning in St. Louis, Missouri. From Fort Leavenworth, Kansas, stores were shipped by the Kansas Pacific Railroad 453 miles to Hays City, Kansas, and thence by wagon to Camp Supply, 166 miles by way of Dodge City. The extension of the Atchison, Topeka and Santa Fe Railroad to Fort Larned, Kansas, and to Dodge City in 1872 cut the wagon mileage in half. Surveys of the Atlantic and Pacific Railroad up the Canadian River valley gave rise to hopes of even closer railroad connections.

For the time being, however, Camp Supply was an isolated post with only one wagon road north to Fort Dodge, and one road south, 196 miles to Fort Sill, by way of the Cheyenne and Arapaho Agency. Post subsistence required that wood, beef, and vegetables must be furnished by outside contractors.[16] Oddly enough, although Camp Supply had more garrison strength and a larger physical plant than most trans-Mississippi military establishments and required its men to perform important and hazardous duty, the camp officially remained only a temporary supply station.

Cheyenne and Arapaho bands hunted separately for buffalo through the winter of 1871–72. The Arapahoes moved from the North Canadian to the Cimarron, but the Cheyennes remained fifteen miles from Camp Supply on Beaver River. On January 4, 1872, the long-forecast trouble arrived, but at the instigation of white civilians rather than Indians.

Little Raven, an Arapaho chief, reported to Colonel Davidson that white men were erecting cabins just across the Kansas state line and were peddling whisky to Indians. Because of the confusion surrounding the Indian intercourse laws, Colonel Davidson submitted the problem to his superiors and on Jan-

[16] Medical History of Fort Supply, Vol. 166, 14; Davidson to AAG, Dept. of Mo., Feb. 16, 1872, Fort Supply, Letters Sent, Vol. 28.

uary 23 received authority from the Department of the Missouri to destroy the cabins.[17]

Throughout February and March, patrols and scouts from Camp Supply hunted renegade Kansan traders from the north and New Mexico whisky runners from the southwest. Captain William Kennedy and his squadron of the Tenth Cavalry left Camp Supply on February 3 to seal off the New Mexico traffic but returned without success. On February 4, Colonel Davidson led a detachment to break up the northern whisky trade, but he too returned empty-handed. A ten-day scout in mid-March, led by Captain Orlando H. Moore with the Sixth Infantry and Tenth Cavalry, traveled one hundred miles only to return with the same discouraging results. The traders were able to give the military the slip by moving from place to place in light two-horse wagons, often taking refuge among the Indians. When on one occasion the cavalry went to the Cheyenne camps to make arrests, the Indians' fears that another Sand Creek Massacre was about to take place forced the troops to back away. It was not until the first week of April that Captain Viele and a company of the Tenth Cavalry successfully captured three wagons loaded with New Mexican whisky twenty miles west of the Antelope Hills.[18] Temporarily the illicit traffic slowed.

In spite of the Indians' resentment over military actions that curbed illegal tradings, the Cheyennes and Arapahoes appeared to remain peaceful. One incident that occurred in late April greatly pleased Davidson. Several Lee and Reynolds teamsters were frightened from their wagons, which were loaded with freight, by the sight of approaching Cheyennes on the road

[17] Davidson to AAG, Dept. of Mo., Jan. 4, 1872, Fort Supply, Letters Sent, Vol. 28; AAG, Dept. of Mo., to Davidson, Jan. 15, 1872, Camp Supply, Letters Received, Box 2.

[18] Miles to Hoag, Aug. 28, 1872, *Annual Report of the Commissioner of Indian Affairs for the Year 1872*, 251; Davidson to AAG, Dept. of Mo., Feb. 9, 1872, Davidson to Orlando H. Moore, Mar. 13, 1872, Fort Supply, Letters Sent, Vol. 28.

forty miles south of Camp Supply. Yet when Captain Viele was sent to retrieve the wagons, which he assumed would be empty, he found them undisturbed. Loose mules had even been tied to bushes. "I have taken measures," wrote Davidson, "to learn the indications among the Arapahoes, Cheyennes and Kiowa tribes of Indians, and am well assured, that hostilities are not impending, and that the indications of a friendly and peaceful relation are good."[19]

Colonel Davidson's prediction, while basically correct, did not take into account the roving bands of Kiowa warriors, who had come to the area bent on capturing mounts. Captain Orlando H. Moore left Camp Supply on May 12 commanding four companies of the Sixth Infantry on the first leg of a journey to Fort Hays by way of Fort Dodge. In addition to his regimental equipment Moore borrowed sixty-two mules, eight wagons, and one ambulance from the camp. When the party stopped to make camp at Bear Creek Station, thirty-nine mule teams plus the escort company's horses were put out to graze two hundred yards from camp under a seven-man guard. Suddenly eight Indians, under cover of bluffs and ravines, swept around a hill and onto the creek bank. Yelling and firing shots, they succeeded in stampeding 125 mules and horses. The pickets in camp opened fire, and the guards on the other side, caught in the middle, had to duck both soldiers' and Indians' bullets.

Moore immediately dispatched an officer and twenty men on the remaining horses to try to recover the stolen animals. They followed the Indians' trail, joined by the tracks of fifteen more riders, for some miles until the trail was erased by that of a buffalo herd. Fortunately for Moore, a Mexican train soon arrived and pulled the stranded wagons to Fort Dodge.[20]

[19] Davidson to AAG, Dept. of Mo., Apr. 26, 1872, Fort Supply, Letters Sent, Vol. 28.

[20] Moore to AAG, Dept. of Mo., May 17, 1872 (copy), Central Superintendency, Letters Received; Medical History of Fort Supply, Vol. 166, 17; William Fetterer to Editor, *Winners of the West*, Vol. II (May, 1925), 3.

The loss of forty-six of its mules severely crippled the transportation facilities of Camp Supply. Colonel Davidson, rightfully angry about the episode, suggested to his superiors that Captain Moore had been negligent. In a letter of May 19, 1872, Davidson remarked that he passed through Bear Creek Station, moving in the opposite direction, only a few hours before the attack and had observed few security precautions—he had seen Indians loitering around Captain Moore's camp. Moreover, he complained, if Captain Moore, who admitted that he suspected that the Kiowas had headed for Antelope Hills, had immediately informed Camp Supply of the incident, the mules could probably have been recovered, since the Kiowa trail passed less than twenty-five miles west of that post. Despite determined efforts of scouts and friendly Indians, by January, 1873, only fifty of the stolen mules had been recovered.[21]

On May 22 rebellious Cheyenne warriors, using the Kiowa attack as a veil, murdered two couriers of the Sixth Cavalry eight miles north of the Cimarron crossing. The Indians took the soldiers' horses, arms, and equipment.[22] Frequent scouts of the area were begun in an effort to prevent a recurrence of the attacks of May and June, 1870.

The tense situation with the Indians was only one of the problems Davidson had to face. It was believed that the location of Camp Supply, situated between two streams, was unhealthy, and in late May an attempt was made to relocate the post. For several months Davidson had felt that the 125-mile distance between Camp Supply and the Cheyenne and Arapaho Agency was unnecessarily dangerous, but, assuming that Camp Supply would be abandoned shortly, he had not pressed the

[21] Davidson to AAG, Dept. of Mo., May 19, 1872, Fort Supply, Letters Sent, Vol. 28; Davidson to AAG, Dept. of Mo., Jan. 8, 1873, Lawrie Tatum to Davidson, Dec. 23, 1872, Camp Supply, Letters Received, Box 2.

[22] Private Alexander Christopher was immediately killed, and Private Henry Weusserman died of injuries at Camp Supply on June 1. Davidson to AAG, Dept. of Mo., June 3, 23, 1872, Fort Supply, Letters Sent, Vol. 28.

issue to his superiors. When word was received in January, 1872, that the Department of the Missouri had no immediate plans for closing the post, Colonel Davidson began looking for a new site.

With fifty mounted men the post commander conducted a reconnaissance of the surrounding area. Covering the territory eighty miles west and thirty-five miles east of the post, he selected several potential sites. When the final choice was made, the most suitable location turned out to be within half a mile of the existing establishment. Davidson's recommendation was to construct all new post buildings on the higher ground, using the older post structures as stables, shops, mechanic houses, and corrals. The camp would thus remain in Indian country (although the problem of its distance from the agency would not be solved), and the existing system of roads and mail stations would not be lost.[23] The only advantage gained by the move, it seemed, was that the camp would be in a more healthful location.

Davidson's superiors did not believe that the proposed relocation of the post a mere half-mile away was necessary or desirable and ordered him to abandon the idea, especially in view of the Indian troubles in his vicinity. The orders did not reach the post until Captain George B. Head had left to examine still other sites that had been suggested by scouts and traders. Upon investigation both Cedar Bluff, on the south bank of the North Fork of the Canadian, eighteen miles from the post, and Osage Springs, on the north bank of the same river, thirty-six miles from Camp Supply, proved to be unacceptable. In the end it was decided that the present site, when extended half a mile, was the best location in the region.[24] General Sully's original choice of a site for the post had been a good one.

---

[23] AAG, Dept. of Mo., to Davidson, Jan. 15, 1872, Camp Supply, Letters Received, Box 2; Davidson to AAG, Dept. of Mo., May 19, 28, 1872, in *ibid.*

[24] AAG, Dept. of Mo., to Davidson, May 29, 1872, Camp Supply, Letters

Colonel Davidson, who had held only fifty-six cavalry troops at Camp Supply, began taking a more serious view of the Indian raids on June 3, when the Kiowas struck near the camp, running off the post beef contractor's herd. Up to that point it was not known whether the Cheyennes were involved in the hostilities. When questioned by Davidson on June 23, Cheyennes admitted murdering the Sixth Cavalry messengers. Until then one dying courier's identification of his attackers as Kiowas had led the military to place the blame for all the depredations on the Kiowas. Fearing a general outbreak, Davidson asked for and received from Fort Dodge another troop of the Sixth Cavalry.

Convinced that the Kiowas were on the warpath, with one group bound for northern Texas and another party of two hundred warriors operating between Fort Dodge and Camp Supply, Davidson concerned himself with the intentions of the Cheyennes and Arapahoes.[25] Grey Beard's band had returned twenty-five of the mules stolen from Captain Moore, but the colonel considered the act only a gesture intended to remove suspicion from the Cheyennes.[26] When Little Raven promised peace in his tribe and lent an Indian escort to Camp Supply cavalrymen on patrol in a dangerous area, it appeared that the Arapahoes had no plans to join the Kiowas in making war.[27] The Camp Supply garrison went into defensive formation and awaited the Cheyennes' decision.

Under orders from General Pope, Colonel Davidson was

Received, Box 2; George B. Head to Post Adjutant, Camp Supply, May 30, 1872, Davidson to AAG, Dept. of Mo., Oct. 9, 1872, Fort Supply, Letters Sent, Vol. 28.

[25] Davidson to AAG, Dept. of Mo., May 22, 29, June 3, 6, 1872, Fort Supply, Letters Sent, Vol. 28.

[26] Apparently these mules were recovered by the Cheyennes after a buffalo herd stampeded the Kiowa booty. Tatum to Davidson, Dec. 23, 1872, Camp Supply, Letters Received, Box 2.

[27] Davidson to AAG, Dept. of Mo., May 29, June 3, 1872, Fort Supply, Letters Sent, Vol. 28.

charged with the safety of all trains between Camp Supply and Fort Dodge. In the discharge of this duty he placed troops from Camp Supply on constant patrol of the Dodge–Supply road, near which Kiowa warriors were known to be concentrated. The Kiowas were particularly interested in the fortifications at Upper Bear Creek and the Cimarron crossing. Indian scouts were repeatedly seen spying on the redoubts. On the night of June 3 three Indians rode to within four hundred yards of Cimarron Redoubt, dismounted, crept to the walls under cover of the bank, and were scaling the parapet before they were discovered and driven off by the sentry. Such incidents led the commanders to install howitzers, increase the garrison, strengthen the stockades, and add sentry dogs to the guard posts.[28]

All mail, supply, and contractors' trains were given escorts on the Dodge–Supply road. The general policy required of each escort was

> two marches daily of the train, one in the early morning of eight to ten miles, and one in the evening of the same distance. You will require the train to corral at all camps, and on the appearance of hostile Indians. During the march you will cause flankers to be thrown out to give timely warning. And always camp the train with pickets posted upon commanding points. And do the same on breaking camp.[29]

In addition, patrols of one officer and at least twenty men operated between Camp Supply and the Arkansas River; the region to the north was scouted by Fort Dodge. From June to August, 1872, Captains Kennedy, Viele, Kelley, Walsh, and Head and Lieutenant Harper were constantly in the field, looking for signs of Indians. In most instances the command was under orders to

[28] Davidson to AAG, Dept. of Mo., June 6, 13, 1872, in *ibid*. The Indians reacted to the use of dogs by spreading poisoned meat about the station.

[29] Post Adjutant, Camp Supply, to V. A. Goddard, June 15, 1872, in *ibid*.

march up Beaver Creek on what is known as the Sully Trail camping on Beaver the first day. On the second you will proceed via Buffalo Springs to the head of the series of ponds on which the Redoubt at the Cimarron is located camping there. On the third day you will march to Bear Creek Station, camping at that place. On the fourth to Bluff Creek where you will remain one day.

Then on your return you will camp at Bear Creek, at the Cimarron, at what is known as Buffalo Ponds on the main road and from thence to the Post.[30]

The increased military activity in the area north of Camp Supply was for the most part successful in keeping the Indians in check. Late in June the Cheyennes moved closer to the agency, indicating their peaceful intentions. The Kiowas, unable to mount any serious attack without the Cheyennes' support, feinted an attack on the agency stock and then withdrew from the region, moving to the Llano Estacado in Texas. On July 20, as the warriors retreated from the vicinity of Supply, they seized seven horses belonging to civilians from a pasture just outside the post.[31] Another band made a similar effort at Cimarron Redoubt but failed.

Cheyennes were accounted for in camps south of Supply on the Canadian River, but Davidson wondered how it could be that the "Kiowas can so multiply themselves as to appear at so many different points," unless they were aided by other tribes.[32] Little Robe denied Davidson's implied accusation and informed the colonel that the Kiowas had been joined by hostile Osages. That alliance proved ineffective, however, for when a small white settlement on Medicine Lodge Creek in Kansas was at-

[30] Post Adjutant, Camp Supply, to William Harper, July 4, 1872, in *ibid*. Patrols were made on June 3, 9, 21, July 4, 8, 17, 25, 31, and August 2, 10, 27, 1872.

[31] Davidson to AAG, Dept. of Mo., June 23, 1872, in *ibid*.

[32] Davidson to AAG, Dept. of Mo., Aug. 2, 1872, in *ibid*.

tacked in early August the Indians got the worst of it, losing one Osage and two Kiowas.[33]

By the end of August seventy-five Arapaho lodges had been moved to within a mile and a half of Camp Supply, and fifty lodges of Cheyennes under Stone Calf had moved to within twenty-five miles of the post. The main Cheyenne winter camps were located on the Canadian, west of Antelope Hills.

In early September a small party of Arapahoes slipped away from one of the bands camped near Supply for another attempt on the Utes. The expedition was generally unsuccessful, and the Arapahoes turned to raids on white settlers, on September 15 stealing twenty horses from settlers at Cimarron Pass, seventy-five miles south of Fort Lyon. When the theft was reported to Colonel Davidson, he immediately wrote John D. Miles (who had replaced Brinton Darlington as Indian agent on June 1, 1872, upon the latter's death), seeking recovery of the animals. When that effort failed, Davidson made a personal appeal to the chiefs, for by then most of the Arapahoes had returned and were camped near the post. Thirteen horses were returned in October.[34]

Just about the time the stolen horses were recovered, Davidson learned of another incidence of violence. According to the Indians, some peaceful Northern Cheyennes were returning home after a visit to the Southern Cheyennes when they were fired upon by a group of buffalo hunters on Walnut Creek. One Indian was killed. Being too few in numbers to fight, the Indians slipped away and later encountered a Richard Jordan and his wife in the vicinity. The Northern Cheyennes killed Jordan and took his wife captive, being careful to leave the Jordan horses in camp to show that they were not on a maraud-

---

[33] Davidson to AAG, Dept. of Mo., Aug. 10, 1872, in *ibid.*

[34] John R. Brooke to AAG, Dept. of Mo., Sept. 20, 1872 (copy), Camp Supply, Letters Received, Box 2; Davidson to AAG, Dept. of Mo., Oct. 7, 21, 1872, in *ibid.*

ing expedition but had committed the act in revenge.[35] Davidson alerted authorities, but the northbound party was out of his
jurisdiction.

Indian violence did not frighten off the Kansas whisky traders.
Smuggled liquor flowed freely in Arapaho and Cheyenne villages. In November, 1872, in a drunken shooting spree Walk-a-
Bit, an Arapaho, was killed, and Ben Clark's Cheyenne wife was
seriously wounded.[36] A week later two whisky ranches were
established on the Dodge–Supply road inside Kansas, one at
Bluff Creek, the other on the Cimarron.

Lacking the authority to take action against civilians outside
Indian country, Colonel Davidson was limited to strengthening
Cimarron Redoubt and ordering all approaching wagon trains
from Kansas to be searched. Agent Miles for his part urged that
the full power of the Bureau of Indian Affairs be brought to
bear to halt the illegal traffic. He charged that certain Indians,
among them John F. Brown, a Seminole, and Black Beaver,
a Delaware, brought liquor into Indian country as agents of
white traders.[37]

In the second week of January, 1873, Agent Miles reported
that forty gallons of whisky had arrived at a Cheyenne camp
and that within two hours twelve hundred Indians were drunk.
The Indians insisted that they had taken the liquor from a deserted buffalo hunter's camp, but a reliable witness denied the
story. Arapaho camps continued to welcome Dodge City merchants who would trade a bottle of liquor for a buffalo robe or
a pony. Miles appealed to the tribesmen to return to the reserva-

[35] Davidson to AAG, Dept. of Mo., Oct. 20, Nov. 2, 1872, Fort Supply, Letters
Sent, Vol. 28.

[36] Miles to Hoag, Dec. 12, 1872, Jan. 1, 1873, Central Superintendency, FOF,
Letters Received.

[37] Davidson to AAG, Dept. of Mo., Dec. 8, 1872, Post Adjutant, Camp Supply
to Alfred Von Wilke, Feb. 22, 1873, Fort Supply, Letters Sent, Vol. 28; Miles to
Hoag, Dec. 12, 20, 1872, Jan. 12, 1873, in *ibid.*

tion and do business with the legitimate, licensed traders. They ignored him, and he resolved to deal with the trouble at its source.

Using information gathered from distraught Indian women, Miles formed a plan. Evidence pointed to five whisky ranches on the Dodge–Supply road: one at the Cimarron, two at Bear Creek, and two on Bluff Creek. In his capacity as Indian agent, Miles asked Colonel Davidson for a military escort to protect his charges from the liquor traffic. J. J. Hoag, an agency employee, would accompany Camp Supply troops as Miles's legal representative, pointing out individuals and property dangerous to the general welfare of Indians.

Such maneuvers were of questionable legality, Miles readily admitted, but they were logically defensible. The Medicine Lodge Treaty of 1867 with the Cheyennes and Arapahoes allowed the Indians the right to hunt buffalo in Kansas, south of the Arkansas River, as long as they found animals in sufficient numbers to warrant doing so. It therefore followed, Miles maintained, that, since it was lawful for the Indians to hunt south of the Arkansas, the same law must protect the hunters and that the Indian intercourse laws were applicable south of the Arkansas, within Kansas, even as they were applicable in the Indian country. Such an interpretation was also important, Miles continued, so that prisoners would be brought to the district court in Kansas rather than in Fort Smith. Miles concluded, "If we are to go to Arkansas for trial we had just as well liberate them and go home and say free whiskey and free trade."[38]

On January 24, 1873, Lieutenant R. B. Pratt and twenty men of the Tenth Cavalry departed Camp Supply to support Miles's efforts to control the liquor traffic. Three caches discovered on the road just north of the post were destroyed, and several In-

[38] Miles to Hoag, Jan. 16, 28, 1873, Central Superintendency, FOF, Letters Received.

dian ponies and robes were recovered. The two ranches at Bluff Creek had been warned of the approaching force, and Lieutenant Pratt returned to post. The expedition had been a successful one. Troops had arrested fourteen offenders, dumped more than four hundred gallons of liquor, and chased about thirty traders from the Indian camps. Eight of the prisoners were sent to Topeka for trial, and two other men, "Slippery Jack" Gallagher and one "Frenchy," escaped by giving three privates a forty-dollar bribe en route to Kansas.[39]

Correctly assuming that the Kansans would resume operations, on February 5, Lieutenant Joseph M. Kelley and fourteen men of the Tenth Cavalry accompanied Miles to the whisky ranches northeast of Bear Creek. The surprised traders decided to fight it out and barricaded themselves inside the log houses. For three days the traders withstood the siege, but when Captain James J. Gageby and a company of the Third Infantry arrived with a small cannon, they broke from hiding. All escaped in spite of determined efforts to capture them.[40]

The excitement of January and February, 1873, was not concerned only with whisky traders. About January 15 a party of seventeen young Cheyennes slipped from their winter camps on foot to seek the Utes once again. Twelve of the party returned on March 10 to tell a gruesome tale of ambush. Following a tributary of the Canadian in New Mexico, the Indian youths passed several settlements where they were treated kindly. But

[39] Miles to Hoag, Sept. 1, 1873, *Annual Report of the Commissioner of Indian Affairs For the Year 1873*, 220; Post Returns, Camp Supply, Jan., 1873. An unfortunate incident of the raid was that on the return to Camp Supply the temperature suddenly dipped below zero, causing one of the prisoners to develop pneumonia. Not being allowed out of the damp cellar where he was confined, the man died, and later developments and testimony showed him to have been entirely innocent of the charge of whisky selling. Medical History of Fort Supply, Vol. 166, 20.

[40] Medical History of Fort Supply, Vol. 166, 20; Post Returns, Camp Supply, Feb., 1873.

on the night of February 26, while camped about eighty miles east of Fort Bascom, they were surprised and fired upon by soldiers and citizens. Two dead were left where they fell, and three wounded were hidden and left behind.[41]

Little Robe immediately sent three young men to aid the wounded. He then went to Camp Supply, where he protested to Agent Miles, who was sympathetic but reminded the chief that his braves had been more than one hundred miles from the reservation when they were attacked and that the Indians had often been warned of the consequences of leaving the reservation.

Feeling was high in the Cheyenne camps, and braves were reported to be drinking heavily.[42] Looking for someone on whom to vent their rage, the Cheyennes chose sixteen railroad survey crews camped nearby. One party of workers was driven from the Cimarron River, and on March 18 a band of forty to fifty Cheyennes entered another camp twenty miles east of Camp Supply, beat the cook with clubs and an ax, shot at him with arrows and revolvers. and then carried off, burned, or destroyed everything in the camp. The next day E. N. Deming and his three assistants were killed near the Cimarron, just below the Kansas line. Other survey crews were stalked by Indians until they found refuge in settlements.[43]

[41] Miles to Hoag, Mar. 15, 1873, General Order No. 5, Headquarters, Dept. of Mo., Mar. 17, 1873 (copy), Central Superintendency, FOF, Letters Received; *House Exec. Doc. No. 1*, 43 Cong., 1 sess., 46; Brooke to AAG, Dept. of Mo., Mar. 15, 1873, Fort Supply, Letters Sent, Vol. 28.

[42] Miles to Hoag, Mar. 15, 1873, Williams to Hoag, Mar. 31, 1873 (copy), Hoag to H. R. Vlum, Apr. 1, 1873, Williams to Hoag, Mar. 22, 1873 (copy), Central Superintendency, Letters Received.

[43] Theodore H. Barrett to Pope, Apr. 8, 1873 (copy), Camp Supply, Letters Received, Box 2; Barrett to Secretary of the Interior, Apr. 4, 1873 (copy), Central Superintendency, Letters Received; Hoag to E. P. Smith, Apr. 15, 1873, Central Superintendency, FOF, Letters Sent; Miles to Hoag, Mar. 29, 1873, Central Superintendency, FOF, Letters Received. The dead surveyors' bodies were not found until May 14, 1873, and then only after Indians told a party of hunters where to look.

Theodore H. Barrett, chief surveyor, indignantly demanded military escorts for his crews. In reply General Pope admitted that the region was dangerous but asked why the crews had not sought protection before instead of after the attacks. Detachments from Fort Dodge and Camp Supply were sent to the points indicated by Barrett, with the reminder from Pope that escorts would always be furnished the surveyors if they made their locations known to commanders at Fort Larned, Fort Dodge, or Camp Supply.[44]

Military authorities assessed the attack on the surveyors as retaliation for the ambush of the Cheyenne party near Fort Bascom. What was even more serious was the state to which liquor had reduced the Cheyennes. Bull Bear, a Cheyenne chief, later told Special Agent John F. Williams that the Cheyennes were on a huge drunk, and the fact that the dead surveyors' bodies were found buried in sand indicated their state of intoxication, for Cheyennes customarily left their victims exposed.[45]

Lieutenant Colonel John R. Brooke, who replaced Colonel Davidson as commanding officer of Camp Supply in February, 1873, believed that the Cheyennes would send a large party of young warriors to the Fort Bascom vicinity to complete the revenge. Brooke's fears seemed well founded when several warriors departed the Cheyennes' camp on April 8. Fortunately, the band returned to camp upon word from Grey Bear that the three wounded men had arrived safely from New Mexico Territory.[46]

Military protection allowed Barrett to concentrate his crews into three or four parties and continue the survey. General Pope,

[44] Pope to Townsend, Apr. 8, 1873, Dept. of Mo., Letters Sent, Vol. 84, Records of the War Dept., National Archives, Washington, D.C.

[45] Hoag to Smith, Apr. 11, 15, 1873, Central Superintendency, FOF, Letters Sent; Miles to Hoag, Apr. 25, 1873, A. E. Reynolds to Miles, Central Superintendency, FOF, Letters Received.

[46] Brooke to AAG, Dept. of Mo., Apr. 4, 8, 1873, Fort Supply, Letters Sent, Vol. 28.

as commander of the Department of the Missouri, was not bound to extend the escort into Indian Territory, since that country, except for Camp Supply, had been placed under the jurisdiction of the Department of Texas in December, 1871. Nevertheless, he assumed responsibility for the region. Two companies of the Sixth Cavalry were stationed on the Arkansas River southwest of Wichita, Kansas, to scout from the southern line of Kansas to the Cimarron River. Three companies of the same regiment at Fort Dodge would scout south and east from that post, and troops from Camp Supply were directed to patrol north and east to the point where the Cimarron meets the southern border of Kansas.

This elaborate system of patrols had a dual purpose: to protect the surveyors and at the same time control the Indians. Up to that time the policy of the Department of the Missouri had been merely to take efficient precautionary measures. Now, instead of keeping the troops at the posts and sending them out only upon report of trouble, the commanders kept large portions of the cavalry force in the field. "In this manner," explained General Pope, "the necessity of watching has been thrown upon the Indians and not, as hitherto, upon the troops shut up in posts for a large part of the season."[47]

Besides taking an active part in this comprehensive network of patrols, Camp Supply was ordered to escort and protect all properly authorized parties of surveyors whose work lay within its jurisdiction—ordinarily any part of the Indian Territory between the southern border of Kansas and the North Fork of the Canadian.

Through April and May, Captain Adna R. Chaffee and Lieutenant William Harper alternated in commanding the Sixth Cavalry escort detail assigned to the surveyors. In June, Cap-

---

[47] Barrett to Pope, Apr. 8, 1873 (copy), Pope to Brooke, Apr. 14, 1873, Camp Supply, Letters Received, Box 2; *House Exec. Doc. No. 1*, 43 Cong., 1 sess., 43.

tain Ezra P. Ewers with a company of Fifth Infantry carried on until relieved in mid-June by details from Fort Sill. During the three months only one minor incident occurred. On June 3 several young Cheyennes entered a surveyors' camp and demanded rations. Sergeant Hamlin and his troops ordered them out, whereupon the Indians strung their bows and appeared to be about to attack. They left, however, after firing a few harmless shots into the air.[48]

During this period, though incidents involving the Indians all but ceased, horse thieves and highwaymen were busily taking over the whisky business or practicing their own specialized trades. Slippery Jack Gallagher and Frenchy, who had escaped their guards on the way to trial for selling whisky, formed a gang in Indian country with Bob Hollis and several deserters from Camp Supply. Using Baker's Ranch on the Cimarron as headquarters, Gallagher and his band systematically robbed teamsters, travelers, and messengers of their mounts. In one bold masquerade in April, 1873, Gallagher and Hollis impersonated Fort Sill scouts and spread an alarm—false, of course—of an Indian uprising, in an effort to frighten survey crews away from their stock and equipment.[49]

Troops from Camp Supply made futile efforts to capture Gallagher. On April 28 he held up a stage, then ran off some horses, and eluded pursuit by scout Amos Chapman and ten others. General Pope wrote to General E. P. Townsend, of the Division of the Missouri:

It is foolish and unjustifiably reckless to have a small party go

[48] Adna R. Chaffee to Post Adjutant, Camp Supply, Apr. 29, 1873, Fort Supply, Letters Received, Box 2; Post Adjutant, Camp Supply, to Ezra P. Ewers, June 14, 1873, Fort Supply, Letters Sent, Vol. 28; Miles to Hoag, June 13, 1873, Central Superintendency, FOF, Letters Received.

[49] Miles to Hoag, April 14, 17, 1873, Central Superintendency, FOF, Letters Received; Brooke to AAG, Dept. of Mo., Apr. 20, 1873, Fort Supply, Letters Sent, Vol. 28.

into that country. The danger is not as great from the Indians as from the gangs of white horse-thieves, buffalo hunters, and whiskey sellers, who would not hesitate a moment to kill a small party in so remote a country.[50]

Gallagher and Hollis were cornered in May, 1873, after stealing some livestock. Hollis was slightly wounded in the ensuing chase, and the stolen stock was recovered, but the two men managed to reach their hiding place. Gallagher vowed to sell his horse for a railroad ticket away from his past, and Hollis told William M. Lee, "The country is getting too warm, I think I'll emigrate." When thefts resumed in the Camp Supply area a few weeks later, it was assumed that Gallagher had returned—or had never left. Colonel Brooke enlisted the aid of Cheyenne scouts, but they too were mystified by Slippery Jack's escapes.[51]

During the late spring and summer details from Camp Supply and Fort Dodge closely patrolled the areas assigned to them. The Indians remained quiet, but whisky traders and desperadoes were only temporarily checked. Far-ranging scouts by the Sixth Cavalry at Fort Dodge between June and October, 1873, and the authorization of United States marshals to patrol the Indian country finally put an end to most of the Kansas whisky traffic.[52] New Mexican traders, however, were quick to take their places in the Indian camps.

In early June, 1873, the Cheyennes camped on the Washita, southeast of Antelope Hills, to make medicine. The peaceful Arapahoes camped along the North Fork of the Canadian, be-

[50] Pope to Townsend, April 8, 1873, Dept. of Mo., Letters Sent, Vol. 84; Miles to Hoag, Apr. 28, 1873, Central Superintendency, FOF, Letters Received.

[51] W. M. Lee to Miles, May 10, 1873, Central Superintendency, FOF, Letters Received; Brooke to R. I. Dodge, May 21, 1873, Fort Supply, Letters Sent, Vol. 28.

[52] Reports and Journals of Scouts and Marches, Fort Dodge, Kansas, 1873 to 1879, 1–29, typescript copy in Walter S. Campbell Collection, University of Oklahoma Library. (Hereinafter this series of reports will be cited as Reports of Fort Dodge, 1873–79, with appropriate pages.)

tween Sheridan's Roost and the agency. New Mexican traders, frightened from the Kiowa and Comanche camps by patrols from Fort Bascom, sought customers among the Cheyennes. Moving up the Canadian, touching the headwaters of the creeks flowing north and south into the Canadian and Red rivers, the traders camped on Elk Creek. From there they sent scouts to find the Cheyenne camps.[53]

On July 12 forty New Mexicans packed two hundred kegs of whisky into the Cheyenne camps, were paid, and left the next day. Scouts Ben Clark and Ed Guerrier reported the transaction to Agent Miles. The traders frequently carried off thirty to sixty ponies in return for whisky, giving rise to fears that the Indians would raid Texas herds to replace their losses. Miles decided to try to bring the Cheyennes to the agency, but Little Robe beat him to camp with a wagonload of liquor, and the agent found the Indians incapacitated when he arrived on August 10.[54]

Colonel Brooke made earnest attempts to capture the traders, but they operated from a point south and west of Camp Supply filled with ample natural cover. Furthermore, the Indians shielded the culprits, and the agency itself was so far from the lines of travel that seldom could it pass along any intelligence to the commanding officer at Camp Supply. Finally Colonel Brooke sought aid from officers in New Mexico Territory.

Colonel J. Irwin Gregg, of the District of New Mexico, replied that the illegal trade was conducted by the boldest and most unscrupulous members of the frontier population and that these men seemed to have the sympathy of the settlers and the topography of the country in their favor. Still, he added, the fact that New Mexicans were involved did not necessarily mean that the

[53] Brooke to AAG, Dept. of Mo., June 2, 19, 30, 1873, Fort Supply, Letters Sent, Vol. 28.

[54] Brooke to AAG, Dept. of Mo., July 16, Aug. 16, 1873, Fort Supply, Letters Sent, Vol. 29; Clark to Miles, July 22, 1873 (copy), Miles to Hoag, July 28, Aug. 11, 1873, Central Superintendency, FOF, Letters Received.

trade was carried on from New Mexico. The commander was certain that the trade did not reach the Indian camps by any route between Fort Bascom and Fort Sumner. His suggestion was a series of scouts about one hundred miles west of Camp Supply that would cut off all the traders' trails both north and south of the Canadian. That was preferable, he said, to extending the Fort Bascom patrols to over three hundred miles. Gregg gave assurances that every possible effort would be made to accomplish the desired end. "However," he commented, "I do not anticipate success."[55]

In addition to efforts to capture, or at least halt the activities of, horse thieves and whisky peddlers, the garrison at Camp Supply continued to patrol the Cimarron River in co-ordinated regular scouts with Fort Dodge. Alternate detachments from the two posts moved up and down the river watching for trade irregularities, offering escort to travelers, locating stray Osage hunters, and warning white buffalo hunters out of Indian country.[56]

In September, Agent Miles persuaded a party of Cheyennes and Arapahoes to visit Washington, D.C., and in their absence the Indian lodges moved closer to Camp Supply. As had been the case when the chiefs visited Washington in April, 1871, a party of Cheyennes bolted toward Raton Pass, ostensibly to attack the Utes but more likely to replace horses traded for whisky. At almost the same time a large party of Kiowas who had been camped on the Washita moved rapidly onto the North Fork of the Red River, beating a retreat from recent depreda-

[55] J. I. Gregg to AAG, Dept. of Mo., Aug. 29, 1873 (copy), Camp Supply, Letters Received, Box 2.

[56] Report of Joseph Kerin, Sept. 27, 1873, Reports of Fort Dodge, 1873–79, 18–22; Dodge to AAG, Dept. of Mo., Oct. 27, 1873, Dept. of Mo., Letters Received, Records of the War Dept., in Donald J. Berthrong Collection, University of Oklahoma Library.

tions in Texas. Hoping to forestall Cheyenne participation in a Kiowa war, Brooke wisely ordered the Cheyennes closer to the post.

When Colonel Brooke received word from Agent Miles—and later read in the *St. Louis Democrat* of October 9, 1873—that troops from Fort Lyon were in pursuit of raiding Cheyennes, he became alarmed. Should a clash occur in Colorado Territory, he felt sure that the Cheyennes would join the Kiowas and Comanches in a war. Returning bands of Cheyennes were questioned on October 17, and they acknowledged having been followed by a small party of civilians but claimed that there was no fight. Brooke was relieved.[57]

Of the reported 200 Cheyennes who had left camp, it appeared that 160 had gone to Colorado and returned safely. Another party of about 30 under White Eagle had gone up the Canadian to visit the graves of the 2 Indians who had been killed near Bascom in February, 1873. One group of about 10 had gone on a raid into Texas. They had been attacked by civilians and troops from Fort Union, New Mexico Territory, and had scattered, leaving behind all their stolen stock. One of these Indians had fallen on a courier from a survey party and killed him in retribution.[58]

On November 21, Big Bow and a band of Kiowa warriors visiting the Camp Supply area contributed to the unrest by murdering Jacob Dilsey as he was en route to Camp Supply with a wagonload of wild turkeys. His charred, scalped body was found by Lieutenant Frank West near Osage Springs on the Supply–agency road. Brooke sought permission to "mete out

[57] Brooke to AAG, Dept. of Mo., Sept. 5, 8, 11, Oct. 13, 17, 1873, Fort Supply, Letters Sent, Vol. 29; Pope to James Biddle, Nov. 3, 1873, Dept. of Mo., Letters Sent, Vol. 85.

[58] Brooke to AAG, Dept. of Mo., Oct. 27, 1873, Fort Supply, Letters Sent, Vol. 29.

just punishment" to Satanta and Big Bow, who were camped on the Canadian, but was refused for fear such an expedition would lead to a general outbreak.[59]

Once again snows forced the soldiers back to camp, where rumors abounded. As winter moved into 1874, the word in Camp Supply was that preparations on a grand scale were being made for an immediate campaign against the Indians and that troops were gathering at Fort Sill and Fort Bascom and Camp Supply.[60]

[59] Brooke to AAG, Dept. of Mo., Dec. 3, 1873, Statements of Frank West, Ben Clark, Amos Chapman, Feb. 10, 1874, Statement of James Richmond, Apr. 4, 1875, in *ibid.*

[60] Lee and Reynolds Co. to Miles, Dec. 18, 1873 (copy), Central Superintendency, FOF, Letters Received.

Chapter IV

Camp Supply in
the Indian Territory Expedition
1874–75

Eᴀʀʟʏ ɪɴ December, 1873, United States deputy marshals gathered on the Kansas border to halt civilian trespass of the Indian Territory. Leaving Caldwell on January 16, 1874, Marshals Benjamin Williams and William Talley moved south under orders to halt illegal trade with Indians and to arrest trespassing buffalo hunters. On the first sixty miles of their trip they found great numbers of skinned buffaloes—at one point twenty-six carcasses within a half-mile radius—mute evidence of persistent invasion.

Realizing that they were powerless to eject hunters even if they found them, Williams and Talley proceeded to Camp Supply to seek military assistance. Colonel Brooke approved their request, and Lieutenant Henry P. Kingsbury and seven men of the Sixth Cavalry joined the marshals on January 29. The following day, as the escort plodded through a snowstorm on the Cimarron, six hunters, temporarily sheltered in a dugout on the riverbank, were found and arrested. The next morning Lieutenant Kingsbury and three men followed Williams south on the Cimarron, while the remaining four troopers accompanied Talley northeast to the Harker Trail and then south. When the troops returned to the agency in February, they had raided four camps and taken twelve prisoners.[1]

Wholesale slaughter of buffaloes by the renegade hunters had

---

[1] B. Williams to Miles, Feb. 6, 1874, Central Superintendency, Letters Received.

the immediate effect of causing the Indians to demand higher prices for the consequently smaller numbers of robes. The Arapahoes' price of fifteen dollars a robe appeared steep, and licensed traders moved on. Agent Miles was faced with a dilemma. The few sales made it necessary for the Indians to return to the agency to draw upon winter subsistence stores, while normally they would have been able to sustain themselves for some months with profits of the winter chase. Because his storehouses were not prepared for such an emergency, Miles forecast that he would run out of rations in early spring, several months before the arrival of the next year's supplies.[2]

About the same time word filtered through the Cheyenne camps that the Kiowas had been attacked by troopers in Texas and that three warriors, including Lone Wolf's son, had been killed. Kiowa and Comanche chiefs appealed to the Cheyennes to join them in a war of vengeance. Whisky runners, slipping past the marshals and patrols, left well-liquored camps to deliberate the proposal. Large shipments of spirits, promoted by Gallagher and Frenchy disguised as Cheyennes, changed hands within ten miles of Camp Supply. With the Cheyennes uneasy about the supplies of food and whisky more plentiful than good water, the prospects for peace in the spring appeared dim.[3]

In mid-March, 1874, a new band of horse thieves, led by Hurricane Bill Martin, entered into competition with Gallagher, Hollis, and Frenchy for the spoils of the Indian country. The Cheyenne camps of Little Robe and Bull Bear on the Cimarron near the Salt Plains lost forty-three horses to Martin on March 11. A few days later a band of one hundred visiting Northern Arapahoes lost nearly fifty horses to two white men on Crooked Creek. When the Indians arrived at Camp Supply on March 26

[2] Miles to Hoag, Jan. 13, 1874, Central Superintendency, FOF, Letters Received.

[3] Miles to Hoag, Jan. 24, 1874, Reynolds to Lee, Mar. 3, 1874 (copy), in *ibid.*; Brooke to AAG, Dept. of Mo., Mar. 1, 18, 1874, Fort Supply, Letters Sent, Vol. 29.

en route to the Cheyenne and Arapaho Agency, they were so destitute that the officers took up a collection to buy them provisions.[4]

Little Robe refused to break his treaty word and go north of the Kansas line in pursuit of thieves, but his son and four others, urged on by Frenchy, sought out Bill Martin near Sun City, Kansas. Failing to find their own spotted ponies, the Indians stole about twenty horses and fifty head of cattle from local citizens. Five Kansans tracked the band over exceedingly rough country until Captain Tullius C. Tupper and a troop of the Sixth Cavalry joined them on the morning of April 11. That afternoon, on Bull Bear Creek, the Indians were overtaken and the stock recovered. Little Robe's son and another brave were so closely pursued that they abandoned their ponies and opened fire from behind rocks in a gulch, each sustaining dangerous wounds before they managed to escape.[5]

By the end of April, Gallagher's and Martin's gangs were infesting the trails between the Cheyenne and Arapaho Agency and Caldwell, stealing Indian animals or dealing out whisky. Three United States deputy marshals and a patrol from Camp Supply were not enough to drive these desperadoes from their rendezvous on Turkey Creek, near the Cimarron, but in early May troopers from Fort Sill succeeded in chasing Gallagher and five men into Texas, possibly wounding Slippery Jack.[6]

[4] Miles to Hoag, Mar. 28, 1874, Central Superintendency, FOF, Letters Received; Hoag to Smith, Apr. 23, 1874, Central Superintendency, FOF, Letters Sent; H. L. Chipman to AAG, Dept. of Mo., Mar. 26, 1874, Fort Supply, Letters Sent, Vol. 29.

[5] Tullius C. Tupper to Post Adjutant, Fort Dodge, Apr. 21, 1874, Reports of Fort Dodge, 1873–79, 34–36; Miles to Hoag, May 1, 1874, Central Superintendency, FOF, Letters Received.

[6] Miles to Brooke, Apr. 25, 1874, Miles to Hoag, May 1, 9, 12, 16, 1874, Central Superintendency, FOF, Letters Received; Hoag to Smith, May 18, 1874, Central Superintendency, FOF, Letters Sent. "Frenchy" was arrested in Wichita, Kansas, selling stolen horses about mid-July, 1874, and Martin was arrested on July 22, also in Wichita.

Fear of Indian trouble ran high when Little Robe's wounded son presided at the Cheyenne medicine on the Washita in late May. In a short time Colonel Brooke received word that two small parties of Cheyennes had left camp "for the purpose of stealing stock and taking scalps, if possible." One of the bands reportedly struck a party in Texas, but were driven off. The other band approached a surveyor crew, who fired on them, wounding one Cheyenne. Finally, when John F. Holloway was murdered on May 21 at the agency and the Cheyennes moved near the camps of the Kiowas and Comanches on Red River, it was assumed that hostilities were imminent.[7]

The long-anticipated Indian war gained momentum in June, 1874. On June 9 a Kiowa party under Stone Wolf attacked and killed two buffalo hunters named Dudley and Wallace fifteen miles southeast of Adobe Walls in the Texas Panhandle, scalping and mutilating their bodies. Two nights later a combined camp of retreating surveyors and Deputy Marshals E. C. Lefebvre and William Talley was raided, and the marshals lost their mounts.[8]

More and more the unpledged Cheyennes were tending toward open warfare. A party of Cheyennes ran off Miles's agency stock and refused to give it up. The Indians moved their camps far off the reservation to the Sweetwater River in Texas. The problems of low rations, whisky merchants, buffalo hunters, and horse thieves—now reportedly scalping victims to make the murders appear to be the work of Indians—made the Cheyennes even angrier.

---

[7] Brooke to AAG, Dept. of Mo., May 18, 29, 1874, Fort Supply, Letters Sent, Vol. 29; Miles to Hoag, May 16, 1874, Central Superintendency, FOF, Letters Received; Miles to Smith, Sept. 30, 1874, *Annual Report of the Commissioner of Indian Affairs for the Year 1874*, 233.

[8] E. C. Lefebvre to Miles, June 14, 1874, Central Superintendency, FOF, Letters Received; Brooke to AAG, Dept. of Mo., June 15, 1874, Statement of Richmond, Apr. 4, 1875, Fort Supply, Letters Sent, Vol. 29.

Kiowa and Comanche forces, as an example to the Cheyennes, divided into small parties and moved north to pillage along the Dodge–Supply road. On June 19 the Camp Supply mail party on the way to Dodge was attacked by Indians north of Buffalo Creek. Two days later Major Charles E. Compton and an escort of the Sixth Cavalry received the same treatment en route to Camp Supply, south of Buffalo Creek. In that attack one citizen and one enlisted man were wounded. On the return to Fort Dodge on June 24, Major Compton was again fired upon, but this time at defensible Bear Creek Station, and four Indians were killed and several more wounded.[9]

Several Cheyenne leaders, including Grey Beard and Medicine Water, eventually joined the hostiles. A combined Cheyenne, Comanche, and Kiowa force numbering nearly three hundred attacked Adobe Walls on the Canadian River on June 27. Twenty-eight buffalo hunters and one woman were trapped in the Adobe Walls station for a full day although miraculously they repulsed each wave of attackers. At day's end the Cheyennes had lost six men; the Comanches and inhabitants of Adobe Walls, three each.

Hostile Cheyennes, Comanches, and Kiowas hovered about the Cheyenne and Arapaho Agency, killed herders, and so harassed the compound that Agent Miles abandoned the post on July 2, taking his employees to the safety of Caldwell. Along the route Miles found the scalped body of William Watkins, the charred remains of Patrick Hennessey and his three companions, and several burned-out ranches.[10]

In late June and early July Camp Supply was in as great a

[9] Brooke to AAG, Dept. of Mo., June 22, 1874, Fort Supply, Letters Sent, Vol. 29; Post Returns, Camp Supply, June, 1874; *Record of Engagements*, 39–40.

[10] Berthrong, *Southern Cheyennes*, 385–86; Miles to Smith, July 7, 1874, Upper Arkansas Agency, Letters Received; Miles to Hoag, July 10, 1874, Central Superintendency, FOF, Letters Received.

state of turmoil as were the Indian camps. Colonel Brooke and three companies of the Third Infantry were preparing for transfer to the Department of the Gulf, and at the same time Lieutenant Colonel William H. Lewis and his command of two companies of the Nineteenth Infantry were taking station at Camp Supply. On July 4, 1874, Colonel Lewis accepted command of the post, and Colonel Brooke and the Third Infantry moved out the following day. It was not until July 10 that the post learned of the events at Adobe Walls and subsequent depredations.[11]

There was a division of opinion about what to do with the hostile Indians. Superintendent Enoch Hoag, Agent Miles, and Agent Lawrie Tatum advocated military chastisement of warring tribes. The Executive Committee of the Society of Friends disagreed, asking for understanding, not troops. Among the military, General Pope sympathized with the Indians, outlining the evils of whisky traders, buffalo hunters, and horse thieves. General Sheridan, on the other hand, blamed the Indian unrest on the immunity the tribes had come to expect from three years of raiding in Texas and in the Indian country.[12]

Until this policy conflict was resolved, Camp Supply, with two companies each of the Nineteenth Infantry and the Sixth Cavalry, was under orders to watch the Indians closely, prevent depredations, scout continually to the east and northeast, and aid Fort Dodge in keeping open the Dodge–Supply road. Additional frontier preparations included the summoning of three companies of the Fifth Infantry to hold positions along the southern line of Kansas and patrol the Chisholm Trail from Caldwell to the agency. Major Compton at Fort Dodge had general charge of the country along Medicine Lodge Creek, both east and west of that stream, and four companies of his cavalry

[11] Post Returns, Camp Supply, July, 1874; W. H. Lewis to AAG, Dept. of Mo., July 10, 1874, Fort Supply, Letters Sent, Vol. 29.

[12] Berthrong, *Southern Cheyennes*, 388.

scouted south and southeast of the post, while five companies of infantry lined the Arkansas River and guarded the Atchison, Topeka, and Santa Fe lines. Troopers from Fort Lyon, Colorado Territory, patrolled the valley of the Arkansas and moved east to close the gap to Fort Dodge.[13]

General Sheridan insisted on an immediate attack. Ten companies of the Sixth Cavalry were gathered from various points on the frontier and ordered to move to Fort Sill on a sweep of the Indian reservations. Pope replied to this demand on July 16, acknowledging the need of some measure, but suggesting that a large movement of cavalry at the present time was not the best solution. For the time being, he felt, it would be better to devote the cavalry to the protection of frontier settlements. Then, when cold weather moved in, a campaign much like 1868 would be instituted. It was feared that if the cavalry moved against the hostiles immediately nearly all the Indians would return to the agencies, only to sally forth again once the troops had left.[14]

Before Sheridan could review the opinion of General Pope, the Bureau of Indian Affairs and the Interior Department made their decision, recommending that the military use all available force to check the warring bands. On July 20 officials of the Department of the Missouri ordered troops at Camp Supply to "attack any hostile Indians whom you may meet in or out of the Indian country." The next day further authority was received from the Department of the Interior, through the War Department, to punish the hostiles wherever they might be found, even to following them onto the reservations.[15] General Pope of the Department of the Missouri and General C. C.

13 AAG, Dept. of Mo., to Lewis, June 30, 1874, Camp Supply, Letters Received, Box 2; AAG, Dept. of Mo., to Thomas Osborn, July 8, 1874, Pope to Sheridan, July 10, 1874, Dept. of Mo., Letters Sent, Vol. 87.

14 Pope to Sheridan, July 16, 1874, Dept. of Mo., Letters Sent, Vol. 87.

15 AAG, Dept. of Mo., to Lewis, July 20, 1874, Camp Supply, Letters Received, Box 2; Lewis to AAG, Dept. of Mo., Aug. 25, 1874, Fort Supply, Letters Sent, Vol. 29.

Augur of the Department of Texas went about the task of organizing the attack.

Plans for the campaign were completed by late July. The Department of the Missouri arranged a three-pronged attack. Colonel Nelson A. Miles commanded eight companies of the Sixth Cavalry and four companies of the Fifth Infantry in a move south against the hostiles on the reservations. Major William Price would move with four troops of the Eighth Cavalry east of Fort Union, New Mexico Territory, along the Canadian to Antelope Hills, where he would join Colonel Miles. At the same time Lieutenant Colonel Thomas H. Neill would join one company of the Sixth Cavalry and four companies of the Fifth Infantry at the Cheyenne Agency, where he could either receive surrendered Indians or strike those remaining at war.[16]

General Augur of the Department of Texas likewise employed three columns. Colonel Ranald S. Mackenzie with eight troops of the Fourth Cavalry, four companies of the Tenth Infantry, and one of the Eleventh Infantry marched north from Fort Concho, Texas, searching the headwaters of Red River. Lieutenant Colonel John Davidson operated west of Fort Sill with six troops of the Tenth Cavalry and three companies of the Eleventh Infantry, while Lieutenant Colonel George P. Buell scoured the territory between Mackenzie and Davidson, commanding four troops of the Ninth Cavalry, two troops of the Tenth Cavalry, and two companies of the Eleventh Infantry.

Colonel Miles received orders to organize his part of the campaign, called the Indian Territory Expedition, on July 27, 1874. The better part of the next two weeks was spent collecting his command at Fort Dodge and placing his 744 soldiers under responsible officers. Majors Charles E. Compton and James Biddle each commanded four troops of cavalry, Captain H. B. Bristol

[16] Pope to AAG, Military Div. of Mo., Sept. 7, 1874, *Annual Report of the Secretary of War for the Year 1875*, 30.

commanded four companies of infantry, and Lieutenant Frank D. Baldwin was placed in charge of 39 guides and trailers.[17]

In general, Miles's force would operate in the Indian Territory between Camp Supply and Fort Sill in much the manner proposed by Pope to Sheridan in mid-July. Camp Supply served as the supply depot for the Department of the Missouri in this campaign, as it had in 1868, holding clothing, ammunition, subsistence, forage, and other necessary items. Besides equipping Miles, the post was ordered to provision Major Price and his command whenever requested. At all times Supply was ordered to have on hand not less than fifty days' subsistance for one thousand men and twelve hundred animals.[18]

Major Compton and his cavalry battalion, one company of infantry, and selected guides left Fort Dodge August 11, scouting to the southwest. The remainder of the command, under Miles, departed on August 14, moving directly south on the Dodge–Supply road. After crossing the Beaver, Lieutenant Baldwin and his scouts left the main body to reconnoiter west to Adobe Walls. Late on August 18, Miles and the Indian Territory Expedition arrived at Camp Supply.[19]

After taking on fifteen days' supplies, Miles resumed his march on August 20, moving toward the Dry Fork of the Washita. At this junction intelligence was received of Lieutenant Baldwin's engagement with hostile Indians thirty miles east of Adobe Walls, and Miles quickly directed his command south-

[17] Nelson A. Miles to Pope, Mar. 4, 1875, *ibid.*, 78; Nelson A. Miles, *Personal Recollections of General Nelson A. Miles*, 164; Special Orders 114, Headquarters, Dept. of Mo., July 27, 1874, in Joe E. Taylor (ed.), "The Indian Campaign on the Staked Plains, 1874–75," *Panhandle-Plains Historical Review*, Vol. XXXIV (1961), 14–16.

[18] Pope to Miles, July 29, 1874, Pope to William Price, Aug. 12, 1874, Dept. of Mo., Letters Sent, Vol. 87; Pope to Lewis, Sept. 2, 1874, Camp Supply, Letters Received, Box 2.

[19] Miles to Pope, Mar. 4, 1875, *Report of the Secretary of War, 1875*, 78–79; Post Returns, Fort Dodge, Aug., 1874; Post Returns, Camp Supply, Aug., 1874; Miles, *Personal Recollections*, 164.

west to the Canadian. Lieutenant Baldwin reported in on August 24, having observed Indian signs nearly the entire distance from Adobe Walls.

To trap the Cheyennes, Kiowas, and Comanches now retreating southwestward before his main body, Miles made forced marches for about one hundred miles to a spot near the headwaters of the Washita River. There the Indians were engaged on August 30. After a two-day running fight of twenty-six miles, the Indians were routed, at a cost of one soldier and one Delaware scout wounded.[20]

It was now the final day of August, and Miles found himself rapidly exhausting provisions. Far removed from his source of supply, and as yet unable to link with Major Price, he set up camp, and thirty-six wagons under Captain Wyllys Lyman were detached to meet a supply train from Camp Supply at Oasis Creek on the Canadian.[21]

Camp Supply was ill-equipped with transportation facilities to handle the requisition chores for Miles's command. Lieutenant Cornelius Gardner and thirty men of the Nineteenth Infantry from Camp Supply had accompanied the expedition on August 20 as escort to a train of five wagons. When the wagons were returned to camp nine days later in need of repair, Colonel Lewis was presented with a serious problem. He had requests from Miles for 290,000 pounds of rations, forage, ammunition, quartermaster equipment, and ordnance stores, to be delivered to an advance party at the Canadian on September 10. Yet Lewis found himself with only enough fresh mule teams and wagons to deliver 25,000 pounds of the order.

[20] Miles to Pope, Aug. 25, 1874 (copy), Central Superintendency, Letters Received; Miles to AAG, Dept. of Mo., Sept. 1, 1874, in Taylor (ed.), "Indian Campaign on the Staked Plains," *loc. cit.*, 21–24.

[21] Miles to Pope, Sept. 14, 1874, in Taylor (ed.), "Indian Campaign on the Staked Plains," *loc. cit.*, 34–35. Oasis Creek was named by Miles, and lay approximately ten miles west of Antelope Hills, on the north side of the Canadian.

General Pope, in an effort to ease Lewis' concern, reported that Colonel Miles had been informed before he marched that the Department of the Missouri did not have the facilities to supply him in the field and that he must send his own teams with proper escort to Camp Supply. Lewis was advised to remind Miles of this understanding and then do his best to support him with whatever he could.

Official justification of his position was not the real question, and Lewis was eager to give Miles as much aid as possible. Without proper authorization he ordered the post quartermaster to employ a civilian ox train of fourteen wagons to assist the government transportation. With this help a total of 92,000 pounds of supplies was moved. Under the direction of Captain Charles W. Holsenfrillen a guard of 29 men of the Nineteenth Infantry and 110 men of the Sixth Cavalry left the post on September 4 bound for the Canadian rendezvous.[22]

In the meantime, Captain Lyman had traveled 120 miles to Oasis Creek, arriving five days early on September 5. Urgently needing the supplies, he ordered Lieutenant Frank West and an escort to set out in the direction of Camp Supply. West located the train and returned it to Commission Creek, where the exchange of goods was made on September 7. The transfer was made quickly and without incident, except for the slaying of a turkey-hunting teamster barely one mile from camp. Captain Holsenfrillen, his men, and the empty wagons retraced their route 48 miles to Camp Supply, arriving on September 10. Lyman moved west to rejoin Miles.[23]

While encamped waiting for Lyman, Miles selected Lieuten-

22 Post Returns, Camp Supply, Aug., Sept., 1874; Lewis to AAG, Dept. of Mo., Aug. 31, Sept. 3, 1874, Lewis to Miles, Sept. 3, 7, 1874, Fort Supply, Letters Sent, Vol. 29; Pope to Lewis, Sept. 2, 1874, Camp Supply, Letters Received, Box 2.

23 Medical History of Fort Supply, Vol. 166, 29; Wyllys Lyman to G. W. Baird, Sept. 25, 1874, in Ernest R. Archambeau (ed.), "The Battle of Lyman's Wagon Train," *Panhandle-Plains Historical Review*, Vol. XXXVI (1963), 93.

ant Frank D. Baldwin and three men to carry dispatches to General Pope at Fort Leavenworth by way of Camp Supply and Fort Dodge. Leaving the main camp on September 6 at 8:30 P.M., the messengers spent the entire first night in the saddle. When forty miles out from the command, at 4:40 A.M. on the seventh, the party halted for a meal. No sooner had a cup of coffee been heated than the lookout on a knob spread the alarm: "They are coming!"

Gathering their rifles, the four men took positions. In fifteen minutes twenty-six Indians came dashing over the hill within fifty yards of the men. The four fired in a volley, instantly killing three warriors. In a moment the Indians had circled the bluffs, and brisk firing continued for an hour. In desperation the lieutenant ordered his men to saddle up, draw pistols, and charge the Indians.

Somehow managing to break through the Indians' line, the messengers alternately trotted their horses and dismounted to fire whenever the Indians gained on them. Somehow another band of fifteen Indians maneuvered in front of the messengers, and again, yelling, the four men charged through the line, killing two or three Indians. The chase continued for eight miles until the soldiers came upon a ravine from which they could hold the last seven raiders at bay.

Rain began to fall, and the Indians did not pursue the attack. Baldwin and his men started out once more. At dusk, a safe distance away, they made camp. On the morning of September 8, as they neared the banks of the Washita, they ran directly into a camp of about one hundred Comanches. Covered with blankets to protect themselves from the cold, Baldwin and his men had stumbled past the camp picket before they realized their predicament. In almost unbelievable style the tired riders once again galloped directly through the Indians, stopping only long enough to capture a stray lookout and his two horses. "We had grown desperate," Baldwin later wrote, "and not having any thought of being able to get through, we were bound to put on a bold front and sell out for all we were worth after gaining timber, before doing which we had to swim the Washita River three times."

Careful never to leave the woods, and crossing the Canadian only after dark, the party stumbled upon Captain Lyman's train near Oasis Creek. There they obtained fresh horses, and two more scouts joined Baldwin. Lyman moved out on the morning of September 9, but Baldwin rested during the day, traveling the final seventy-five miles to Camp Supply after dark. When the lieutenant and his crew reached the post, they had ridden from 8:30 P.M., September 6, to 10:00 A.M., September 10, with only fourteen hours' rest.[24]

In the meantime, after leaving camp on September 9, Captain Lyman moved steadily along. As the train approached a ridge between the Washita and Canadian rivers a party of Kiowas and Comanches launched an attack on both flanks of the convoy. Proceeding very slowly under these extremely hazardous circumstances, Lyman corralled the train at a point two miles from the Washita. One man was already dead, Wagoner McCoy lay mortally wounded, and Lieutenant Granville Lewis was severely crippled with a bullet in the knee. In addition, enough mules had been disabled to retard progress, Lieutenant West counted only twelve mounted men, and communication with Colonel Miles was cut off. Word was sent to Camp Supply for relief.[25]

[24] *Ibid.*; Frank D. Baldwin to Alice B. Baldwin, Sept. 17, 1874, reprinted in *Winners of the West*, Vol. IX (Aug., 1932), 3–4; Alice Blackwood Baldwin (ed.), *Memoirs of the Late Frank D. Baldwin*, 78.

[25] Lyman to Commanding Officer, Camp Supply, Sept. 10, 1874, *Report of the Secretary of War, 1875*, 86; Lyman to Baird, Sept. 25, 1874, in Archambeau (ed.), "Lyman's Wagon Train," *loc. cit.*, 93–100; J. W. McKinley, "J. W. McKinley's Narrative," *Panhandle-Plains Historical Review*, Vol. XXXVI (1963), 68.

Shortly after dark on September 10 scout William F. Schmalse dashed out of the besieged camp on horseback, crashing the Indian line. Hotly pursued, the scout spurred his mount into a large buffalo herd, causing it to bolt and thereby enabling him to escape in the turmoil and darkness. Schmalse rode his horse to death but arrived at Camp Supply at 8:30 A.M. on September 12.

Restricted by the number of available horses and mules at Camp Supply, Colonel Lewis mounted only fifty-eight cavalry and scouts and loaded five wagons. The rescue party, under the command of Lieutenant Henry Kingsbury, left the post at noon and reached the crippled train, eighty-eight miles southwest, at 2:00 A.M. on September 14. The Indians, however, had moved on, and, escorted by Lieutenant Kingsbury, Captain Lyman was able to rejoin Miles, who by that time had begun to move east in search of his train.[26]

The Kiowas and Comanches who left Lyman's train on the morning of September 12 had traveled only a few miles when they spied a party of six messengers. Scouts Billy Dixon and Amos Chapman, Sergeant Zachariah T. Woodall, and Privates Peter Rath, John Harrington, and George W. Smith, all of the Sixth Cavalry, had left Miles's camp on McClellan Creek late on September 10 to take dispatches to Camp Supply. At 6:00 A.M. on the twelfth the band of 125 hostiles came upon them.

Dismounting, the couriers lay against a hillside preparing for an attack. Private Smith, holding the horses, was critically wounded in the first volley. With the Indians surrounding all positions, the men decided to make a dash for a mesquite flat several hundred yards away, but abandoned the idea when Chapman received a bullet in the leg and Harrington and Woodall were also wounded. Choosing a second-best defense,

---

[26] Miles, *Personal Recollections*, 172; Post Returns, Camp Supply, Sept., 1874; Lewis to AAG, Dept. of Mo., Sept. 12, 1874, Fort Supply, Letters Sent, Vol. 29.

the men crawled into a ten-foot-diameter buffalo wallow. Smith was left for dead on the field. As each man reached the wallow, he drew his knife and commenced piling dirt around the sides.

The fight continued throughout the day, the wounded men concealing their crippled condition by sitting upright. Wave after wave of Indians was turned back. About 3:00 P.M. a rainstorm, followed by a norther, engulfed the battlefield, forming two-inch-deep pools of blood and water in the little wallow. When the Indians moved out of range for better shelter from the cold and rain, Private Rath returned to Smith's side for his cartridge belt and pistol, only to find him still alive. The men carried Smith back to the wallow, but he died during the cold night.[27]

At nightfall Dixon and Rath gathered tumbleweed beds for the four wounded, and all huddled together without food or warm clothing. Rath went for help shortly after dark but returned in two hours, unable to find the Camp Supply road in the dark. At the first hint of daylight Dixon started toward Camp Supply and had gone only about a mile when he met Major Price's command. Price allowed his surgeon to examine the men but offered no other aid, except for a few pieces of hardtack. It was not until midnight on September 13 that support from Miles arrived.[28]

The wounded were placed on wagons and a few days later joined with Lieutenant Kingsbury's escort for Captain Lyman's

---

[27] Miles, *Personal Recollections*, 173–74; Olive Dixon, *The Life of Billy Dixon*, 199–202; Charles E. Campbell, "Down among the Red Men," *Collections of the Kansas State Historical Society*, Vol. XVII (1926–28), 654–55.

[28] Dixon, *Billy Dixon*, 210–13; W. R. Price to AAG, Dept. of Mo., Sept. 24, 1874, in Taylor (ed.), "Indian Campaign on the Staked Plains," *loc. cit.*, 51–52. Frederick Remington painted a picture called "Caught in the Circle," inspired by the story of the buffalo wallow fight. Remington probably heard the tale from officers of the Sixth Cavalry during the Sioux campaign of 1890–91, and in the telling of the story details became confused, for the painting shows only three troopers and one scout, instead of four troopers and two scouts.

new train seeking subsistence at Camp Supply. The couriers and the wounded of Lyman's command were given medical treatment upon their arrival at Camp Supply on September 18.[29]

The problems which Lyman had encountered in bringing supplies, plus the events of the Baldwin and Chapman scouting parties, indicated to Miles that he was too far into the field to freight in his own supplies. Miles and General Pope had distrusted each other since Civil War days, and the colonel was reminded of this when he wrote his wife that the Department of the Missouri was not adequately supporting him. Custer, he complained, was furnished four hundred wagons but went no farther from Camp Supply than the Indian Territory Expedition, which had only sixty. Moreover, he wrote, on September 14 he received

> one of those cold blooded letters from Department Headquarters saying to the commanding officer of Camp Supply that I must get my supplies with my own wagons and that he was not to furnish me more. It was another case of one man [Pope] thinking he knows more five hundred miles away than one who is on the ground. I felt enraged and sent my dispatch accordingly.[30]

Colonel Lewis was still having a very difficult time meeting all the demands of the Indian Territory Expedition. Camp Supply was well stocked with provisions; the problem was to transport them to the men in the field. The garrison fluctuated with Miles's demands for officers and men, but through most of the late summer and early fall Supply operated with about two hundred officers and men, who made patrols of the surrounding

[29] Amos Chapman suffered the most serious wound, and his left leg was amputated above the knee. *Medical History of Fort Supply*, Vol. 166, 29. All six messengers were awarded the Medal of Honor, but in 1916, because they were not military personnel, Chapman's and Dixon's names were stricken from the list.

[30] Quoted from Virginia W. Johnson, *The Unregimented General: A Biography of Nelson A. Miles*, 55.

country, performed the labor of the post, and furnished guard details to hay contractors, two redoubts, and the mail escort. Any emergency, such as the assistance sent to Lyman's train, cut the operational garrison nearly in half.

Colonel Miles, unaware of Lewis' predicament, informed General Pope of the need for a permanent supply camp on the Canadian, just off Oasis Creek. Pope, eager to contribute to the success of the expedition, yet aware that Colonel Lewis had earlier warned him that he could not accommodate large requisitions from the field, compromised by charging Lewis with the establishment and protection of Miles's suggested supply base but ordering all contractors' trains to proceed directly through Camp Supply nonstop to the depot.[31]

Such a compromise was not at all acceptable to Colonel Lewis. It was obvious that his garrison would soon be responsible for guarding the trains from Camp Supply to the Canadian, and he could not spare enough men to hold a depot with stores for one thousand men and fifteen hundred animals. In fact, reported Lewis on September 15, because of the Lyman detail, his present command consisted of only seventy-nine infantrymen and no cavalry. Certainly he was in no position to establish new camps, for necessary duties had already spread his men dangerously thin.

At last Colonel Lewis' plight was understood, and Camp Supply was relieved of any responsibility for establishing Miles's depot. As an alternative Pope ordered Major Price to turn over his supplies to Miles and then take post on the Canadian, near Antelope Hills, keeping the trail open between Miles and Camp Supply. Miles was warned that if he moved farther west his own troops must keep the lines to Price open. Camp Supply would

31 Lewis to AAG, Dept. of Mo., Sept. 12, 1874, Fort Supply, Letters Sent, Vol. 29; Pope to Lewis, Sept. 5, 1874, Camp Supply, Letters Received, Box 2.

continue escort duties, but only between the camp and Fort Dodge.[32]

Thousands of pounds of clothing, ammunition, rations, and forage were directed to Miles and Price through the fall of 1874. Infrequently even cattle were herded to the expedition. On October 1, 1874, more than 450,000 pounds of subsistence, grain, and equipment for Miles was in motion between Fort Dodge and Camp Supply. Although not required to furnish escorts below Camp Supply, for that was Price's duty, Lewis was reinforced by Major James Biddle and half the Sixth Cavalry regiment after September 26 and was then able to offer protection to government and contractors' trains all the way from Fort Dodge to Price's camp on the Canadian.[33] Miles and Mackenzie's activities in the Texas Panhandle were gradually forcing the Indians toward Camp Supply and the Cheyenne Agency, and one officer and seventy-five to one hundred enlisted men usually guarded the teams. In most instances a supply train ran about a dozen wagons, but sometimes as many as fifty vehicles went south in convoy.[34]

Early in November, 1874, Miles moved near Adobe Walls. Lewis, ever ready to support the troops in the field, voluntarily assumed responsibility for the supply of two new locations, one a depot near Miles, the other a new camp on the Washita. Com-

[32] Lewis to AAG, Dept. of Mo., Sept. 15, 1874, Fort Supply, Letters Sent, Vol. 29; Pope to Lewis, Sept. 17, 18, 1874, Camp Supply, Letters Received, Box 2; Pope to Sheridan, Sept. 18, 1874, Pope to Miles, Sept. 13, 18, 1874, Dept. of Mo., Vol. 87.

[33] Miles detached Biddle's battalion in order to reduce his command to a more maneuverable number, and also to seal off the Cheyenne northern escape route. Miles to Pope, Mar. 4, 1875, *Report of the Secretary of War, 1875*, 79; Miles to AAG, Dept. of Mo., Oct. 12, 1874, in Taylor (ed.), "Indian Campaign on the Staked Plains," *loc. cit.*, 62.

[34] In October, 1874, some 53,000 rations and 218,000 pounds of grain were delivered to the Indian Territory Expedition through Camp Supply. Lewis to AAG, Dept. of Mo., Sept. 22, 24, Oct. 1, 4, 7, 8, 10, 20, 25, Nov. 4, 8, 1874, Fort Supply, Letters Sent, Vol. 29.

modities at Camp Supply seemed inexhaustible. Every week thousands of pounds of material left the post. By the end of November nearly 300,000 rations of bacon, beans, peas, coffee, and sugar were being kept in readiness for any of the three depots. In addition, warehouses at the post held almost 100,000 pounds of grain and more than 107,000 pounds of ordnance stores, medical supplies, and clothing.[35]

In December it was decided that a permanent supply post would be established at Miles's station near Adobe Walls, on the Sweetwater in the Texas Panhandle. Camp Supply was charged with provisioning that outpost. Plans were announced for 1,000,000 pounds of grain, 650,000 pounds of contractors' goods, and 106 mule teams and wagons to haul stores to the cantonment.[36]

The first shipments began late that month. Trains of mixed cargo, with subsistence sufficient for 500 men and the same number of animals, carried loads of up to 600,000 pounds of grain and 60,000 rations, presumably enough supplies to last the post until May, 1875. December was indeed a busy month, for, in addition to the accumulation of supplies for the camp on Sweetwater, Colonel Lewis sent 500,000 pounds of grain and 7,000 rations to the Washita camp of the expedition.[37]

The best-laid plans, however, often went awry when confronted with the unpredictable weather of the plains. The first ox train left Camp Supply on December 16, but was stalled less than forty miles west of the post when a snowstorm struck with paralyzing fury. A large number of animals froze to death, and only a few wagons were able to continue. Wintry blasts held all other trains at Camp Supply until January 16, when a combined

35 Lewis to AAG, Dept. of Mo., Nov. 10, 25, 1874, Lewis to Miles, Nov. 8, 1874, Fort Supply, Letters Sent, Vol. 29.

36 Pope to Lewis, Dec. 10, 1874, Camp Supply, Letters Received, Box 2.

37 Pope to Lewis, Dec. 14, 17, 29, 1874, in *ibid.*; Lewis to AAG, Dept. of Mo., Dec. 24, 25, 26, 30, 1874, Fort Supply, Letters Sent, Vol. 29.

government and contractor's train ventured out. In order to pick up the excess supplies left by the frozen ox train, the Lee and Reynolds Company of Camp Supply was commissioned to join a government convoy on January 23. By month's end Major James Biddle, commander of the new Sweetwater cantonment, had most of his supplies.[38]

The tactics of Miles, Mackenzie, Davidson, and Buell in the fall and winter months of 1874 continued to move the hostiles eastward. Kiowas and Cheyennes surrendered at the Darlington Agency as early as October 3. Step by step the Cheyennes were being driven past Camp Supply and toward the agency. At only one point did troops operating out of Camp Supply engage the Indians. On November 3, Lieutenant Henry J. Farnsworth and a company of the Eighth Cavalry scouted west of the post. On November 6, about thirty miles out, they were surprised by a large force of retreating Cheyennes. The detachment of twenty-eight men fought the entire afternoon, killing at least four Indians and wounding several more. Victory did not come easy; Farnsworth lost one trooper killed and four wounded.[39]

With surrenders increasing daily, in January, 1875, Colonel Miles made one final southwestward campaign around the eastern edge of the Staked Plains. Moving into Fort Sill, he turned directly north and passed through Camp Supply in February. When he reached Fort Dodge several days later, the Indian Territory Expedition disbanded.

Only the most hardy Cheyennes remained unaccounted for when the campaign closed, and it was well known that the winter had been hard on them and that they could not hold out for long.

---

[38] Lewis to John A. Runker, Jan. 4, 1875, Lewis to AAG, Dept. of Mo., Jan. 7, 15, 20, 23, 31, 1875, Fort Supply, Letters Sent, Vol. 29; AAG, Dept. of Mo., to James Biddle, Jan. 16, 1875, Dept. of Mo., Letters Sent, Vol. 88.

[39] H. J. Farnsworth to Field Adjutant, Wingate Battalion, Eighth Cavalry, Nov. 7, 1874 (copy), Central Superintendency, Letters Received; William H. Leckie, *The Buffalo Soldiers*, 132.

At last, on March 6, more than eight hundred Cheyennes under Stone Calf surrendered to Colonel Neill at the Cheyenne and Arapaho Agency.[40]

The close of the long campaign against the Cheyennes, Kiowas, and Comanches was no less exhausting for the men at Camp Supply. As early as February patrols were pushing the Indians toward the agency by scouring the Canadian River trails. In addition, fresh supplies had to be freighted to the agency to feed both the increased numbers of Indians who had surrendered and the soldiers stationed at the new post near by. The first load of 20,000 pounds of subsistence, carried in twenty-five mule-drawn wagons, left Camp Supply the second week of March, and such deliveries continued through the spring.[41]

Then, when at last it seemed that warfare had subsided, the Cheyennes broke loose again. Colonel Neill, under orders to send the ringleaders of the past war to prison at St. Augustine, Florida, gathered his captives on April 6. Taunts from Indian women caused Black Horse to resist and break toward the lodges. Guards' bullets brought the fugitive to the ground, but stray rounds hit the Indian camp, causing pandemonium. Half the Cheyennes fled to nearby hills, where they dug up hidden arms and ammunition. Three charges mounted by troops under Colonel Neill could not dislodge them. When the sporadic firing broke off at dusk, Neill had lost nineteen wounded men, one of whom later died.[42]

40 Medical History of Fort Supply, Vol. 166, 30; Miles to Pope, Mar. 4, 1875, *Report of the Secretary of War, 1875*, 82; Thomas H. Neil to Pope, Feb. 23, 1875 (copy), Camp Supply, Letters Received, Box 1.

41 Pope to Lewis, Mar. 8, 1875, Camp Supply, Letters Received, Box 1; Neil to AAG, Dept. of Mo., Mar. 16, 1875, Cheyenne and Arapaho Agency, Letters Received, Records of the Office of Indian Affairs, National Archives, Washington, D. C.

42 Neil to AAG, Dept. of Mo., Apr. 7, 1875, *House Exec. Doc. No. 1*, 44 Cong., 1 sess., 87; Peter M. Wright, "Fort Reno, Indian Territory, 1874–85" (Unpublished M.A. thesis, University of Oklahoma, 1965), 4–7.

During the night the Cheyennes slipped away, leaving behind seven dead. Two companies of the Tenth Cavalry were immediately ordered up the North Canadian in pursuit. Two-thirds of the warriors were found ninety miles northwest of the agency near the Cimarron, but the others continued their flight.

Fort Dodge and Camp Supply were not alerted to the outbreak until April 10. Moving into action, troops from Fort Dodge scouted the Dodge–Supply road and Medicine Lodge Creek, while on April 13, Colonel Lewis, uninformed about the direction taken by the escapees, ordered Captain Adna R. Chaffee and sixty men of the Sixth Cavalry and Nineteenth Infantry to seek Indian signs south and east of the post.[43]

Captain Chaffee returned to post on April 23 without having sighted any Indians. Three other companies led by Captain William A. Rafferty, provided with stores from Camp Supply, pursued the main group of Indians on the Cimarron and eventually brought that group, and another near the Antelope Hills, to the agency.

The sixty-six Cheyennes who refused to surrender crossed the Arkansas west of Fort Dodge, heading north. At daylight on April 23 they were intercepted by Lieutenant Austin Henley and forty men of the Sixth Cavalry out of Fort Wallace. In the desperate fight that ensued, Henley killed nineteen warriors and eight women and children, ending all resistance. At last the eight-month war was over.[44]

[43] Pope to Compton, Apr. 10, 1875 (copy), Pope to Lewis, Apr. 10, 1875, Camp Supply, Letters Received, Box 1; Lewis to Biddle, Apr. 13, 1875, Lewis to AAG, Dept. of Mo., Apr. 14, 1875, Fort Supply, Letters Sent, Vol. 29.

[44] Berthrong, *Southern Cheyennes*, 402–404; Lewis to W. A. Rafferty, Apr. 17, 1875, Fort Supply, Letters Sent, Vol. 29; *Record of Engagements*, 46–47.

Chapter V

Indians, Whites, and Thievery
1875–79

WITH THE Cheyennes subdued, the Department of the Missouri reassessed its line of frontier posts. Camp Supply was still looked upon as only a supply depot, and physical permanency notwithstanding, the settlement on Wolf Creek remained a camp, not a fort. The appraisal did result in the expansion of two new cantonments, however. The so-called Post at Cheyenne Agency, established by Lieutenant Colonel Thomas H. Neill in July, 1874, and the Cantonment on the Sweetwater, Texas, organized by Major James Biddle in January, 1875, were stabilized. Throughout the spring and summer of 1875, Camp Supply served as a maintenance base and sent several outfitting expeditions to both locations, reducing its own garrison to fewer than 150 officers and men to staff the new outposts.[1]

Although the recent Indian raids had been dealt with successfully, other problems did not end. Horse thieves, whisky peddlers, and buffalo hunters quickly returned to Indian Territory. Because the defeated Indians had fewer horses, military herds became more inviting to the thieves, who stole twelve mules at Cimarron Redoubt on March 12 and struck the post again a few weeks later.[2]

During this resurgence of lawlessness a small Cheyenne hunting party who entered the Camp Supply area was mercilessly

[1] Post Returns, Camp Supply, Mar.–Sept., 1875; Lewis to AAG, Dept. of Mo., Apr. 13, 1875, Lewis to Biddle, May 17, 1875, Fort Supply, Letters Sent, Vol. 29.
[2] Lewis to AAG, Dept. of Mo., Mar. 21, 1875, Fort Supply, Letters Sent, Vol. 29.

harassed by thieves. Deputy Marshal Benjamin Williams joined these Cheyennes and with an escort from the Cheyenne Agency arrested ten men on June 23.[3] Captain Philip H. Remington, temporary commander at Camp Supply, informed General Pope: "The country between this [post] and Dodge is so thoroughly infested with horsethieves as to make it very unsafe for Government trains, especially to travel over the route without the utmost precaution." Moreover, whisky ranches were being rebuilt on the Dodge–Supply road, and scouts observed a concentration of buffalo hunters operating south and east of Antelope Hills, unmistakably within Indian Territory.[4]

When in August, 1875, two companies of Sixth Cavalry were transferred from Camp Supply, the post retained only two companies of the Nineteenth Infantry and one troop of the Fifth Cavalry, a total of seventy-eight men and five officers. The garrison was much too small to control the peddlers, vagrants, and hunters who prowled the Indian country. The additional troops needed to combat illegal trespass and watch the Indians were not forthcoming, and this duty gradually passed to the garrison at the Cheyenne Agency.

The shift in responsibility was sometimes awkward, as in the case of a party of seventeen Arapahoes who headed northward from their agency on August 14, taking with them a number of ponies belonging to other Indians. A detachment of the Fourth Cavalry under Lieutenant James Thompson pursued from the agency, but because of the breakdown of communications with Camp Supply a patrol under Lieutenant Edward L. Keyes from that post scouted in the opposite direction, allowing the Arapa-

[3] Benjamin Williams to Miles, July 5, 1875 (copy), Central Superintendency, FOF, Letters Received. In July the prisoners were taken to Wichita, Kansas, for trial—four men for horse theft and six for buffalo hunting in Indian country. Miles to Smith, July 22, 1875 (copy), Central Superintendency, FOF, Letters Received.

[4] Philip H. Remington to AAG, Dept. of Mo., June 23, 1875, Fort Supply, Letters Sent, Vol. 29.

hoes to disappear across the Kansas line. Patrols of this nature, some lasting twenty days, continued to aid the agency garrison during the transitional period, especially during the Cheyenne and Arapaho annual hunt. Other patrols sought hunters' camps within the Indian reservation.[5]

Several thieves and at least one murderer were rounded up near Camp Supply by these patrols, but the Cheyenne and Arapaho camps, even those within twenty-five miles of the post, were still not safe. Deputy Marshal Ben Williams rightfully predicted trouble from white hunters out of the Texas Panhandle. On October 18 a squad of hunters fired on four Indians about fifty miles above their camps on Wolf Creek, killing one mule. Then, in what might be called poetic justice, the hunters, fearing that more Indians would come to the rescue, quickly departed the scene, leaving behind five worn horses. The Indians retrieved them, and the owner of the dead mule was compensated with two of the horses.

Anticipating difficulty, E. C. Lefebvre, the deputy marshal assigned to the Arapahoes, telegraphed General Pope for a special military detail to accompany his charges, who were about to separate from the Cheyennes' winter camp and go up Wolf Creek. Within a few days Lieutenant Horace S. Bishop and fifteen enlisted men from Camp Supply joined the Arapahoes, allowing the escort from the agency garrison to follow the Cheyennes up the Beaver.[6]

Disturbing news of an engagement between a patrol from Fort Wallace and a band of Arapahoes near Buffalo Station, Kansas, brought reinforcements to the Arapaho escort. Apparently those Arapahoes who had made good their escape from the

---

[5] Post Returns, Camp Supply, Aug., 1875; Covington to Smith, Aug. 16, 1875 (copy), Central Superintendency, FOF, Letters Received; J. H. Bradford to AAG, Dept. of Mo., Aug. 22, 26, 1875, in *ibid*.

[6] Williams to Miles, Oct. 22, 1875 (copy), Central Superintendency, FOF, Letters Received.

agency on August 14 had reached the Red Cloud Agency. About October 1 a party of thirty Arapaho men and five women, three of whom had just arrived from the south, left the camp near Red Cloud Agency in a reverse journey to join the Southern Arapahoes. According to the Indians, soon after crossing the Republican River and the Kansas Pacific Railroad, on October 26, they sighted troops but were not themselves discovered. The following day the Arapahoes went into camp on a tributary of the Republican River, and two of the party took the travel pass from their agent and backtracked in search of lost ponies. While the men were absent, a detachment of the Fifth Cavalry entered the camp. A woman told them that the group had obtained a pass but that the two men had it. It was decided to send one Arapaho with Captain John M. Hamilton in search of the trackers while the troopers remained at the camp. The officer and the young Arapaho had proceeded about half a mile from the camp when Hamilton demanded that the youth surrender his revolver. When the Indian refused, he was shot at three times but managed to escape. The shots were heard in camp, where general fighting broke out. Two Arapahoes were killed before the group managed to escape from the soldiers.[7]

Assuming that the escaping Arapahoes could join the winter camps as easily as the agency, Captain James H. Bradford, now commanding Camp Supply, reinforced the escort with the Arapahoes by sending Lieutenant Edward M. Hayes and thirty-one men of the Fifth Cavalry. As expected, the fugitives entered the camps in bands of eight or nine, beginning on November 5. They were immediately taken prisoner by the escorts and transferred, under guard, to the Cheyenne and Arapaho Agency.[8]

As the winter hunt continued into February, 1876, buffaloes

[7] Miles to Smith, Nov. 5, 1875 (copy), in *ibid.*; *Record of Engagements*, 48.

[8] Pope to Commanding Officer, Camp Supply, Oct. 28, 1875, Camp Supply, Letters Received, Box 1; Bradford to AAG, Dept. of Mo., Oct. 30, Nov. 4, 6, 1875, Fort Supply, Letters Sent, Vol. 29.

became so scarce that Agent Miles recalled the Indians. Beginning on March 1, parties began returning to Darlington. Lieutenant Hayes remained with the Arapahoes until they entered the agency, and by April 1 nearly all the hunting parties of both tribes had returned.[9]

At Camp Supply the spring and summer months of 1876 were spent in ordinary post duty. After February 21 the Cheyenne and Arapaho Agency garrison and the cantonment on the Sweetwater, in Texas, were named, respectively, Fort Reno, Indian Territory, and Fort Elliott, Texas. A change in title did not alter procedure, and for the most part Fort Reno continued to offer protection to Cheyenne and Arapaho hunting parties, while the 150-man garrison at Camp Supply provided the field patrols with rations and forage. Such was the case for the Cheyenne and Arapaho hunts in June and July.[10]

After the Fifth Cavalry transferred to the Department of the Platte in June, only sixty to seventy men, in two companies of the Nineteenth Infantry, remained at Camp Supply. When the Cheyenne and Arapaho winter hunt moved into the vicinity during October, the camp's garrison was too small even to perform its supply function for the escorts out of Fort Reno.[11]

In the absence of cavalry at Camp Supply horse thieves plundered at will. Two mounts were stolen from the Fourth Cavalry escort with the Cheyennes, and a few days later, on February 3, 1877, outlaws made away with seventeen Cheyenne horses and mules from Kiowa Medicine Lodge Creek. Altogether the Indian losses to horse thieves during the 1876–77 winter

[9] Miles to Hoag, Aug. 31, 1876, *Annual Report of the Commissioner of Indian Affairs for the Year 1876*, 46–47; Edward M. Hayes to Post Adjutant, Camp Supply, Mar. 1, 1876, Camp Supply, Letters Received, Box 1.

[10] Miles to William Nicholson, June 19, July 5, 1876, Central Superintendency, FOF, Letters Received.

[11] Bradford to AAG, Dept. of Mo., Oct. 20, 1876, Fort Supply, Letters Sent, Vol. 29; Post Returns, Camp Supply, Oct.–Dec., 1876.

hunt amounted to about 150 animals.[12] Colonel Lewis was powerless to stop these outrages. Not only did he suffer from an undermanned garrison but also he had only five horses capable of making a chase. And even when the outlaws were put on the run, they inevitably lost themselves in the trackless No Man's Land squeezed between Texas and Kansas east of New Mexico Territory. In Colonel Lewis' opinion, a series of scouts west of Indian Territory as far as Palo Duro Creek and beyond, if necessary, was the only solution to the raids.[13]

William Nicholson, acting superintendent of Indian affairs, sought aid from General Pope in curbing the thefts. He concluded: "As you are aware, it is just such deeds as this extensive horse stealing that incite these Indians to acts of retaliation and depredation, and they should be stopped."[14]

When at last Deputy Marshal William Malaley was authorized military support, he captured a thief, Joseph Harriman, on March 8, northwest of Camp Supply. It was an important arrest because Harriman made a full confession of organized thievery in the region. Apparently bands of outlaws were gathering large numbers of stolen animals in Ellsworth and Russell counties, Kansas, and then selling them. Agent Miles understood that there was "a stolen pony in almost every stable from the Cimarron to the Platte."[15] General Pope would eventually recognize the serious conditions in Indian Territory and advise full garrisons for Forts Reno and Elliott and Camp Supply, but for the

[12] William Malaley rescued about forty-four head, reducing the sale value loss to the Indians to approximately $3,000. Miles to Nicholson, Aug. 31, 1877, *Annual Report of the Commissioner of Indian Affairs for the Year 1877*, 82.

[13] Lewis to AAG, Dept. of Mo., Feb. 10, 1877, Fort Supply, Letters Sent, Vol. 29; Miles to Nicholson, Jan. 1, 1877, Central Superintendency, FOF, Letters Received.

[14] Nicholson to Pope, Mar. 2, 1877, Central Superintendency, FOF, Letters Sent.

[15] Miles to Nicholson, Mar. 28, 1877, Central Superintendency, FOF, Letters Received; Nicholson to Pope, Apr. 9, 1877, in *ibid*.

Camp Supply, Indian Territory, as shown in *Harper's Weekly Magazine* (February 27, 1869).

Issue of rations to Indians at Camp Supply in the spring of 1870, photographed by William S. Soulé.

This teamster's cabin, erected about 1869, is on the grounds of what is now Western State Hospital, Fort Supply, Oklahoma.

Ground plan of Camp Supply, December, 1870:

1	Infantry Barracks	12	Post Bakery
2	Cavalry Barracks	13	Butcher Shop
3	Company Mess Houses	14	Post Hospital
4	Laundress' Quarters	15	Quartermaster Corral
5	Ordnance Storehouse	16	Carpenter and Saddle Shops
6	Commissary Storehouse	17	Blacksmith Shop
7	Quartermaster Storehouse	18	Meetinghouse
8	Commissary Office	19	Cavalry Stables
9	Infantry Guardhouse	20	Cavalry Guardhouse
10	Adjutant's Office	21	Post Trader
11	Officers' Quarters		

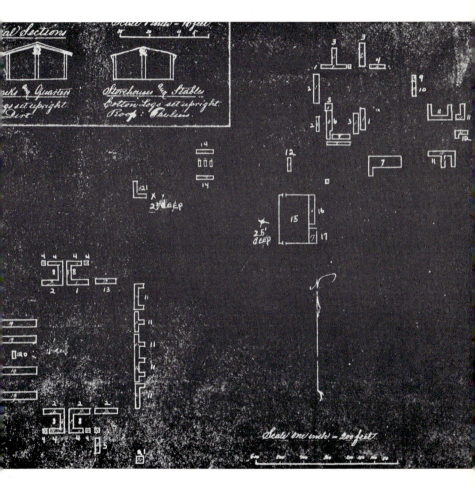

The original guardhouse, or jail, at Fort Supply.

The hospital building at Fort Supply.

Woodward County Collection
University of Oklahoma Library

Major General Philip H. Sheridan, commander of the Department of the Missouri. Camp Supply was established to supply Sheridan's troops in 1868.

This building, sometimes referred to as the Opera House, erected in 1874, was also the headquarters building and library of Fort Supply. The recreation building in the rear was added in 1880.

The Lee and Reynolds shop building was removed from old Fort Supply and reconstructed where the Western Cattle Trail crosses Otter Creek.

Barracks on the north side of Fort Supply.

Ground plan of Fort Supply, 1886:

1	Commanding Officer	41	Post Quartermaster Office
2–9 and 46	Officers' Quarters	42	Commissary Sergeant
10–16	Company Barracks	43–44	Subsistence Officer
17	Commanding Officer's House	45	Quartermaster's House
18 and 22	Ordnance Stores	46	Regular Noncommissioned Service Officers
19–20	Hospital	48	Armory
21	Bakery	49	Carpenter Shop
22	Old Ordnance Store	51–54	Civilian Employees' Quarters
23–26	Icehouses	55–57	Quartermaster Stables
27–29	Married Men's Quarters	58	Butcher Shop
30	Old Picket Building	59–62	Married Men's Quarters
31	Guardhouse	63–64	Schoolhouse and Reading Room
32	Magazine	65–71	Bathhouses
33–34 and 50	Blacksmith		
35–38	Cavalry Stables		
39–40 and 47	Quartermaster Stores		

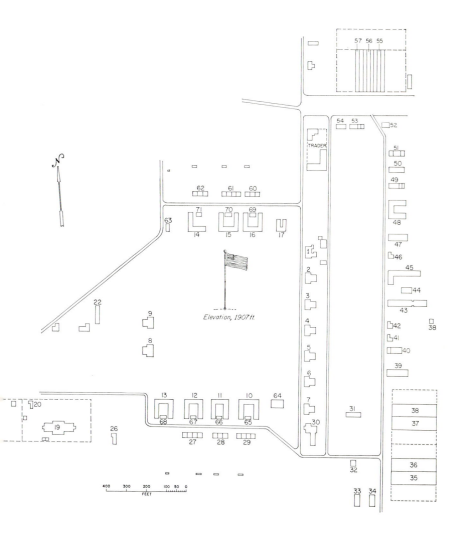

Elevation, 1907 ft.

400 300 200   100 50 0
FEET

Cavalry inspection at Fort Supply, about 1890.

time being the Cheyennes and Arapahoes could only finish their winter hunts and return to the agency in March, 1877.

In July new arrivals entered Indian Territory, bound for the Cheyenne and Arapaho Agency. The Northern Cheyennes, distinct from the Southern Cheyennes since the early nineteenth century, were being joined with their brothers as part of the peace settlement following the Sioux War on the Northern Plains. Escorted by Lieutenant Gerry W. Lawton and 15 troopers of the Fourth Cavalry out of Fort Robinson, Nebraska, about 950 Northern Cheyennes traveled for seventy days before reaching Darlington Agency on August 5.[16] The warriors had serious doubts about Indian Territory, and, after taking stock of the agency location and climate, they decided that they wanted to return to the High Plains. Agent Miles feared that only force would bring them under control.

One reason the Northern Cheyennes were reluctant to establish in Indian Territory was the prevalence of horse thieves. There was no denying that the thieves were bold and unscrupulous. The outlaws showed their hand at Camp Supply early in October, 1877, when they removed three saddle horses from nearby stables. A short time later reports from the Texas Panhandle alerted stockmen to the activities of the notorious Chummy Jones.

When riders with a Fort Elliott wagon train observed that they were being followed on an early October trip to Fort Sill, word was returned to the post. Captain Wirt Davis and ten troopers of the Fourth Cavalry were ordered after the suspects. Some distance southeast of the post five horse thieves, including Chummy Jones and Charley Morrow, were captured with 139 head of stock, and all were delivered to Fort Sill. For some reason the commanding officer at Fort Sill refused to take custody of Jones and Morrow, and Captain Davis decided to take

16 *Sen. Rep. No. 708*, 48 Cong., 2 sess., v; *Dodge City Times* (July 14, 1877).

them to Fort Elliott. In a few hours Davis returned to Fort Sill and told the authorities that the prisoners had escaped but that he "didn't believe they would ever steal any more horses." The next scouting party out of Fort Sill found Jones and Morrow hanging from a tree, "both dead as mackerels."

More trouble was in store for Captain Davis thirty miles from Fort Elliott. An ambulance, whose driver was accompanied by a sergeant, was traveling in advance of the rest of the men. The vehicle passed a tent, and just as Captain Davis was about opposite it a white man burst out of the tent and commenced firing. The first shot grazed Davis, and the next killed his horse. Soldiers riddled the man with bullets, but not before another man had stepped from the brush and killed the ambulance driver. Captain Davis and his men began firing into the brush, and the bushwhacker fell dead in the trail. The man who had fired from the tent was identified as Johnny Jefferson, an alleged horse thief.[17]

Stealing continued, with Arapaho horse herds the target. On October 23 they lost forty-two horses. By good luck a party of Indians recovered thirty-eight of the horses three days later when they chanced on three of the thieves near the Salt Fork of the Arkansas.[18]

Another band of outlaws was discovered later that month about fifty-five miles southwest of Camp Supply. A Mr. Ivey, employed by Lee and Reynolds to recover stolen horses, stumbled onto the thieves' rendezvous. Ivey dropped his gun and threw his hands into the air, the signal for a parley. The result of the interview was an agreement that Ivey could have the ponies if he could take them, but seven heads peering from behind the barricade were sufficient discouragement. Upon hearing of this incident, the commanding officer at Camp Supply

[17] *Dodge City Times* (Oct. 6, 27, 1877).

[18] Miles to E. A. Hayt, Nov. 17, 1877 (copy), Central Superintendency, FOF, Letters Received.

sent out Lieutenant William Leeper and a squad of the Fourth Cavalry, but the prairie pirates relocated before their arrival.[19]

About November 15 the Darlington Agency tribes began moving west on their annual hunt. Buffalo herds in Indian Territory were rapidly being depleted, and the remaining animals were gradually moving from the reservation to the northern Texas Panhandle. In the winter of 1876–77 the Indians killed only about seven thousand buffaloes, while commercial hunters collected more than double that amount.[20]

The scarcity of buffaloes in central Indian Territory forced other tribes to the western limits, near Camp Supply, for their winter chase. Under the escort of Subagent Charles McCarlow and eight men of the Fourth Cavalry, about eight hundred Pawnees left their agency on November 1 in search of herds. After several weeks without success they moved west to Camp Supply, demanding rations. Under General Orders of December, 1874, Major Henry A. Hambright, the new commander, could not issue rations to these Indians, and the request was denied. The escort was allowed to draw regular supplies, however.

The Pawnees were desperate. Their subsistence stores were used up, they had found no buffalo meat, and their small annuity payments had been turned over to the post trader. Before they left Camp Supply, in order to buy food they disposed of their shirts, pants, coats, vests, hats, boots, shoes, and all other salable possessions to the soldiers at the post for prices ranging from twenty-five cents to three dollars.

As the Pawnees moved west of the post on November 27, an advance party of Cheyennes made its appearance at Camp

[19] Post Returns, Camp Supply, Oct., Nov., 1877; *Dodge City Times* (Oct. 27, Nov. 3, 1877).

[20] Miles to Nicholson, Aug. 31, 1877, *Report of the Commissioner of Indian Affairs, 1877*, 82.

Supply.[21] Observers at the camp knew that there was bad blood between the Cheyennes and the Pawnees. According to one source, the Pawnees, passing near the Cheyenne camps on their way west, had driven off ponies, used them until the horses' backs were sore, and then cut them loose. The Cheyennes were already angry about the abuse of their ponies. The invasion of their hunting preserve could lead to war.[22]

Captain Sebastian Gunther and Company H, Fourth Cavalry, brought the main party of Cheyennes and Arapahoes to Camp Supply on December 3. One cavalry officer etimated the total number of Northern Cheyennes, Southern Cheyennes, Arapahoes, and Pawnees camped near the post at two thousand. To settle differences among the Indians a council was held, the result of which allowed the Cheyennes hunting privileges south of the post, the Pawnees west, and the Arapahoes northwest. The Cheyennes left Camp Supply on December 15.[23]

Prospects for both a successful and a peaceful hunt dimmed with each day on the plains. The Pawnees, who had reached the range three weeks early, were accused of overworking the herds, leaving nothing for the Cheyennes and Arapahoes. After only a week of effort a band of three hundred Cheyennes, under Little Raven, Black Crow, and Dull Knife, returned to Camp Supply seeking rations. Amos Chapman reported Indians so hungry that they readily ate dead horseflesh. Pawnees and Cheyennes expressed their discontent not only to each other but to soldiers as well. Pawnee hunters encountered Sergeant Storr of Camp Supply while he was hunting, stole his game, and then fried skunk meat in his frying pan. A week later the Indians shot a civilian, having mistaken him, they said, for a big turkey.[24]

[21] H. A. Hambright to AAG, Dept. of Mo., Nov. 27, 1877, Fort Supply, Letters Sent, Vol. 29½; Medical History of Fort Supply, Vol. 168, 145.

[22] *Dodge City Times* (Dec. 8, 1877).

[23] *Ibid.* (Dec. 15, 1877); Medical History of Fort Supply, Vol. 168, 149.

[24] Post Adjutant, Camp Supply, to Lee and Reynolds Co., Dec. 19, 1877, Ham-

More audacity was reported from Kansas. One D. Sheedy alerted Dodge City to "another sneaking, treacherous outrage perpetrated by the noble red man" in late December. He reported that five Northern Cheyennes burst into his cattle camp in Comanche County, "in their accustomed insolent manner," brandishing guns. They killed a cow and stole four horses while the unarmed men in camp watched.[25]

Old Cactus, a *Dodge City Times* correspondent at Camp Supply, fueled the creeping hysteria by informing his readers that Stone Calf of the Cheyennes could scarcely contain his warriors, who were bent on committing depredations, that Dull Knife and Standing Elk of the Northern Cheyennes were aching for an outbreak, and that even Powder Face and Big Mouth of the Arapahoes were hostile. If the Cheyennes and Pawnees confronted each other and the Fourth Cavalry escorts intervened, he wrote, the "whole posse of red devils would no doubt turn on them, causing general war."[26]

The 1877 winter hunt furnished only 219 robes to the Cheyennes after they had made repairs to their lodges.[27] Starving Pawnees, Cheyennes, and Arapahoes gave final proof that the dwindling buffalo herds could no longer support the Indians.

On January 2, 1878, the escorts for the Pawnees, Cheyennes, and Arapahoes were directed to return their charges to the agencies by way of Camp Supply, where they would be given rations. By that time about seven hundred Northern and Southern Cheyennes had surrounded Camp Supply, able to survive only by killing their horses and dogs and a few wolves. On January 2 these Indians were given a partial ration. Another seven hundred

bright to Commanding Officer, Fort Reno, Dec. 21, 1877, Fort Supply, Letters Sent, Vol. 29½; *Dodge City Times* (Dec. 15, 1877).

[25] *Dodge City Times* (Dec. 22, 1877); Miles to Hayt, Dec. 20, 1877, Central Superintendency, FOF, Letters Received.

[26] *Dodge City Times* (Jan. 19, 1878).

[27] Miles to Nicholson, Aug. 31, 1878, *Annual Report of the Commissioner of Indian Affairs for the Year 1878*, 55.

Cheyennes and Arapahoes were expected at the post in time for the January 5 issue. The Pawnees were eighty-five miles from the post, suffering severely from exposure.

In small bands the Cheyennes and Arapahoes entered Camp Supply. Over one thousand rations of flour and beef were issued. All the Arapahoes except for five lodges and all the Cheyennes but for two bands under Little Robe and Whirlwind, numbering fifty lodges in all, departed for the agency on January 7. Some of the remaining Cheyennes moved directly into the agency from the Washita, and others were reported near Adobe Walls.

The Pawnees, being farthest away and in the worst condition, were not present for the January 5 ration. They struggled into the post shortly thereafter, the main body finally arriving on January 24. Flour and bacon were issued, bringing the total number of rations issued by Camp Supply that month to 657 for men and 1,137 for women and children.[28] In a few days the Pawnees moved on toward their own agency.

Horse thieves had no qualms about striking the destitute Indians. Cavalry mounts were also fair game. While they were looking for stolen horses, two Fourth Cavalry guards for the Pawnees were surprised by five white men and robbed of their mounts. On January 20 eight lodges of Cheyennes arrived at Camp Supply on foot, having been robbed of twenty-six horses, and Lieutenant Otho W. Budd, who led a company in pursuit of the thieves, was turned back by a heavy snowstorm, which caused his own horses to stampede.[29]

It was an open secret that Dodge City afforded a no-questions-asked market for stray horses. Certain civilians, ranchers, and traders surrounding the Indian Territory, either from fear or from motives of personal interest, furnished supplies to the

[28] Hambright to S. Gunther, Jan. 2, 4, 1878, Hambright to AAG, Dept. of Mo., Jan. 2, 6, 23, Feb. 3, 1878, Fort Supply, Letters Sent, Vol. 29½.

[29] Hambright to AAG, Dept. of Mo., Jan. 23, Feb. 17, 1878, in *ibid.*; *Ford County Globe* (Feb. 5, 19, 1878).

desperadoes and marketed the stolen property. Instead of aiding the military, some Kansans and Texans seemed more disposed to throw the authorities off the track or conceal the stolen stock. Under such circumstances it was nearly impossible for troops to arrest the outlaws or curb the lawlessness.

As spring broke over the prairies, rumors of an outbreak by Northern Cheyennes flooded the Southern Plains. Amos Chapman learned that at the mid-April councils at Fort Reno the Indians threatened that unless they received better provisions they would leave the reservation. The warnings issued by Dull Knife and Standing Elk at Camp Supply the previous December and January could not be disregarded either. These Cheyennes had vowed to die on the field of battle rather than see their women and children starve. Major Hambright believed the threats and asked for an additional cavalry troop. With maximum cavalry strength at Camp Supply, the roads north and south of the Canadian, as well as the trails leading along the Cimarron, could be patrolled for signs of pending trouble.[30]

Tension increased during the summer months of 1878. On June 16, Little Raven, Left Hand, and Yellow Bear stampeded a herd of cattle passing near their camp, making off with forty-three head. Rations ran low, and the Interior Department failed to recognize the need for twelve months' subsistence now that the winter chase was in the past. In August, Spotted Horse, a Pawnee chief, prowled the plains near Camp Supply and killed ten or twelve buffaloes. Major Hambright was forced to arrest him and inform the Pawnee agent that there were only a few buffaloes near Camp Supply and that the Pawnees should not be allowed to spread the word that the buffaloes were running.[31]

The Northern Cheyennes were particularly vociferous in their

[30] Hambright to AAG, Dept. of Mo., Apr. 14, 21, 1878, Fort Supply, Letters Sent, Vol. 29½.

[31] Hambright to AAG, Dept. of Mo., July 13, 1878, Hambright to Agent Ely, Pawnee Agency, Aug. 20, 1878, in *ibid.*

contempt for agency life. Their plans to leave were widely broadcast within the agency, but no one knew exactly when they would go until friendly Southern Cheyennes informed Miles that the date would be September 5. Major John K. Mizner, commanding Fort Reno, acted on the advice of the agent and ordered two troops of the Fourth Cavalry under Captain Joseph Rendlebrock to follow the fugitives and return them to the agency. At the same time a messenger was sent with a warning to Camp Supply. He arrived at the post at 6:00 P.M. on September 7.[32] Upon receipt of the communication Major Hambright immediately directed Captain William C. Hemphill to move north on the Dodge–Supply road, follow the Indian trail, and overtake the Indians with all due speed. Company I, Fourth Cavalry, assisted by Amos Chapman, left the post at 8:30 P.M. the same evening.[33]

Rendlebrock, in the meantime, found that the Northern Cheyennes had not left the reservation but had only shifted their village a few miles farther from the agency. The command sent word to Major Mizner and camped about two miles from the Indians. A courier was then dispatched to Camp Supply canceling the prior order. Recall was received at Camp Supply at 4:30 P.M. on September 8, about twenty hours after Captain Hemphill had left the post. After an exhausting ride a scout reached Hemphill with orders to return, which he did on September 10.[34]

On September 9 a band of 92 Northern Cheyenne warriors and 268 women and children led by Dull Knife and Little Wolf slipped away from their lodges at the agency, making a break

[32] Wright, "Fort Reno," *loc. cit.*, 41–42; W. C. McFarland to Joseph Rendlebrock, Sept. 6, 1878, *Report of the Secretary of War, 1878*, 46.

[33] Hambright to AAG, Dept. of Mo., Sept. 8, 1878, Fort Supply, Letters Sent, Vol. 29½.

[34] Mizner to Rendlebrock, Sept. 8, 1878, *Report of the Secretary of War, 1878*, 46; Campbell, "Down among the Red Men," *loc. cit.*, 676; Hambright to Commanding Officer, Fort Reno, Sept. 9, 1878, Fort Supply, Letters Sent, Vol. 29½.

for the Northern Plains. American Horse and an agency police-
man notified John Miles in the early-morning hours, and he in
turn alerted Mizner. Only then did messengers return to Rendlebrock's command.[35] After consultation Major Mizner authorized
Captain Rendlebrock to lead Troops G and H, Fourth Cavalry,
after the fleeing Indians and force them to return immediately.

Rendlebrock's battalion of four officers and eighty-one enlisted men struck the Cheyennes' trail about noon and proceeded
sixty miles before making camp at 10:00 P.M. When they were
about forty miles out of Fort Reno, Rendlebrock sent couriers
to Camp Supply asking Major Hambright to patrol the Bear
Creek area, where it was most likely that the Cheyennes would
cross the Dodge–Supply road. The message was received at
Camp Supply at 8:00 A.M. on September 12, and two and a half
hours later Captain Hemphill and Company I, Fourth Cavalry,
were on the Dodge–Supply road headed for Bear Creek,
Kansas.[36]

Hemphill stopped only for supper at Snake Creek and arrived
at Bear Creek, approximately fifty-four miles from Camp Supply, near midnight. The next day pickets were sent to find signs
of either the Indians or Captain Rendlebrock. The road was
patrolled from Bear Creek to Bluff Creek, and when no one had
been found by 4:00 P.M., the troops proceeded toward Fort
Dodge, where they arrived about noon on September 14.[37]

By that time the Department of the Missouri had mobilized

---

[35] Wright, "Fort Reno," *loc. cit.*, 44; Dennis Collins, *The Indians' Last Stand
or the Dull Knife Raid*, 240–41.

[36] *Army and Navy Journal*, Vol. XVI (Oct. 12, 1878), 150; *Report of the
Secretary of War, 1878*, 45; Hambright to AAG, Dept. of Mo., Sept. 12, 1878,
Fort Supply, Letters Sent, Vol. 29½.

[37] William C. Hemphill to J. P. Hatch, Nov. [?], 1878, Dept. of Mo., Letters
Received, typescript in the Walter S. Campbell Collection, University of Oklahoma Library. (Hereinafter this report will be cited as Hemphill, Report, OU.)
Hambright to Commanding Officer, Fort Reno, Sept. 15, 1878, Fort Supply, Letters Sent, Vol. 29½.

great numbers of troops to head off the Indians. Captain Philip H. Remington marched with Company F, Nineteenth Infantry, from Fort Dodge west to Pierceville, Kansas, hoping to intercept the Dull Knife band, and on September 13, Colonel John Davidson at Fort Sill sent Troop C, Fourth Cavalry, to Fort Reno to control the remaining Cheyennes. Mounted infantry troops left Fort Wallace by special train to cut off trails and crossings east and west of the post. Two infantry companies from Fort Hays were posted at crossings on the Kansas Pacific Railroad between Hays and Wallace, and Fort Lyon was ordered to scout the country east and west of its post.[38]

Captain Rendlebrock continued to search for Indian trails. The Northern Cheyennes, however, were not intimidated and attacked cattlemen and ranch property in their path. On September 12 two young nephews of Charles Colcord were killed near Salt Fork, and their horses and one mule were seized. On the same day John Evans, a herder for the D. Sheedy camp, was slain, and the Indians made off with more than sixteen hundred dollars' worth of equipment. The next afternoon a drover named Dow was killed, and one man and two children were wounded at the E. W. Payne ranch.[39]

Willing to swap danger for distance, the Northern Cheyenne warriors sent their women and children ahead on September 13 and retraced their own trail to meet the slowly gaining troopers. Rendlebrock's command was surprised to find the Indians drawn up for battle when the two forces finally met forty miles northeast of Camp Supply. Through the help of an Arapaho scout

[38] Post Returns, Fort Dodge, Sept., 1878; Pope to Sheridan, Sept. 11, 12, 1878, Div. of Mo., Letters Received, Walter S. Campbell Collection, University of Oklahoma Library.

[39] Report of Captain William C. Wedemeyer in James van Voast to AAG, Dept. of Mo., Oct. 29, 1878, Dept. of Mo., Letters Received, Walter S. Campbell Collection, University of Oklahoma Library. (Hereinafter this report will be cited as Wedemeyer, Report, OU.)

named Chalk, a parley was held, and the Indians were informed that they must return to the agency. Little Wolf preferred to dispute the passage through the range of bluffs near Turkey Springs and refused the order.

At that moment, about 250 yards from the cavalry line Chalk spied several ponies that had been stolen from him. Seizing a revolver from one soldier and mounting another's horse, he made a wild charge against the seven Cheyennes holding the animals. Firing his revolver at close range, Chalk hit four of the seven Indians, receiving wounds in both thighs and the bowels in return.[40]

Fighting immediately broke out. Some of the Indians charged the soldiers, attempting to encircle them, while others fired from the bluffs surrounding the conference site. The cavalry, momentarily thrown into confusion, retreated to a draw, where they took up positions against the withering fire. Hemmed in on all sides, the troopers kept up constant but ineffective fire until dark. About 8:00 P.M. seven men broke for fresh water but were repulsed. In return the Cheyennes set fire to the prairie, but at no cost to the troopers. On the morning of September 14, after nearly thirty hours of attacks and counterattacks, the detachment made a final determined effort to break the Indians' position. Advance and flanking columns forced the Indians' lines to buckle, enabling the troops to reach the springs, after which they turned and in a final skirmish put the Indians to flight.

A courier from the besieged command reached Camp Supply at 9:00 A.M. on September 16. Major Hambright ordered a medical officer and an ambulance into the field to meet Rendlebrock and bring in the wounded. Several hours later the command

---

[40] Mari Sandoz, *Cheyenne Autumn*, 38–39; George B. Grinnell, *The Fighting Cheyennes*, 404–405; Campbell, "Down Among the Red Men," *loc. cit.*, 678; *Dodge City Times* (Sept. 28, 1878).

staggered into Camp Supply, bearing three killed and three wounded. The unofficial count of Indian casualties was thought to be fifteen killed and about thirty wounded. Twenty-odd Indian ponies were estimated killed.[41]

Captain Hemphill had meanwhile provisioned his command at Fort Dodge on September 14 and then, after gaining permission from Colonel Lewis, had returned fifty miles south to his Bluff Creek bivouac to continue sentry duty on the Dodge–Supply road. A courier arrived there at 2:00 A.M. on September 16 and reported that Kollar's Ranch, twenty-four miles southeast, had been raided the night before. At daylight the command started for the ranch, where they arrived that afternoon. While circling for a trail, they spotted six Indians and gave chase, but the Indians disappeared into the hills. Hemphill's troops remained close by throughout the night.[42]

Camp Supply also received news of the attack on Kollar's Ranch. Harry Coons, one of Hemphill's scouts, brought the news on the morning of September 17 and was followed a few hours later by a stagecoach that had passed so near the point of conflict that the driver and passengers had heard heavy firing. Coons reported Captain Hemphill to be but a few miles north of the Cimarron, checking the ranches in that area. In an effort to bolster Hemphill's command, should he contact the Indians, Major Hambright took command of Rendlebrock's forces and ordered three junior officers and forty men of Companies G and H, Fourth Cavalry, to reinforce and assist the Cimarron reconnaissance. They departed at 10:00 A.M., September 17, and

[41] *Army and Navy Journal*, Vol. XVI (Oct. 12, 1878), 150; Grinnell, *Fighting Cheyennes*, 404–405; *Dodge City Times* (Sept. 28, 1878); Hambright to Commanding Officer, Fort Elliott, Sept. 16, 18, 1878, Fort Supply, Letters Sent., Vol. 29½.

[42] Hemphill, Report, OU. Henry Kollar's camp on Bluff Creek was raided on September 15. Warren Richardson was killed; two others were wounded. Mr. Kollar lost property valued at $1,800. Wedemeyer, Report, OU.

were expected to intercept Hemphill at the Cimarron crossing about 5:00 P.M.[43]

Captain Joseph Rendlebrock and Sebastian Gunther remained at Camp Supply with twenty-eight men of the Fourth Cavalry until September 19, when they were directed to join their detachments and make all efforts to communicate with Hemphill. With the scene of action shifting northward, reserve Companies B and F, Fourth Cavalry, from Fort Elliott were transferred to Fort Dodge. Lieutenant Clarence Mauck and his command reached Camp Supply at 4:00 P.M. on September 22 and left for Dodge twelve hours later.[44]

On September 17, Hemphill continued to search the country bordering Bluff Creek and the Cimarron crossing. While in pursuit of a small band of Indians, he stumbled upon two herders from the Driskill Ranch seeking help after a sunrise attack.[45] Hemphill and his men did not cover the twelve miles to the ranch before dark, and it was morning before they found the Indians' trail. A few hours later Hemphill drew up before what appeared to be a large force of Indians concealed in the breaks of Sand Creek. Each fourth man was holding four horses or mules, and the effective command of thirty or so men attempted to drive the Indians into the open. The skirmish lasted about an hour, and no one was wounded, but Hemphill was forced to retire to Bluff Creek. He remained there until dark and then marched for Fort Dodge, arriving at 3:00 A.M. on September 19.[46]

At Dodge, Hemphill was joined with a company of the Sixteenth Infantry who had arrived by rail from Fort Riley only

[43] *Dodge City Times* (Sept. 28, 1878); Hambright to Commanding Officer, Fort Elliott, Sept. 18, 1878, Fort Supply, Letters Sent, Vol. 29½.

[44] Medical History of Fort Supply, Vol. 168, 186; Pope to Sheridan, Sept. 20, 1878, Div. of Mo., Letters Received, Walter S. Campbell Collection, University of Oklahoma Library.

[45] J. W. Driskill lost fifty-five head of horses and an unknown number of cattle. Wedemeyer, Report, OU.

[46] Hemphill, Report, OU; Post Returns, Fort Dodge, Sept., 1878.

the day before his appearance. Captain Charles E. Morse assumed command of the combined force, including a group of about thirty-five cowboys from Dodge City. The troop train of the Santa Fe line departed at 9:00 A.M. on September 19, for Pierceville, Kansas, some forty miles west of Fort Dodge.[47]

Twenty miles out, at Cimarron Station, Captain Morse alighted from the train to find a group of armed civilians reporting a hostile band of Indians. Unable to verify the story, Morse continued on to Pierceville, where Colonel C. H. Smith and Company D, Nineteenth Infantry, had been stationed since September 17. Convinced that the Indians had not yet crossed the Arkansas, the entire command marched about forty miles south to Crooked Creek, where they spent the night of September 20.

On the twenty-first, shortly after daybreak, word reached Morse that the fugitive Indians had recently camped at Sand Creek. While he was en route, he received further information from Fort Dodge that Captain Rendlebrock and Companies G and H, Fourth Cavalry, were about to join him. The two commands met about noon, and Captain Rendlebrock assumed full command as the senior officer. The march then resumed, and a halt was not called until 4:30 P.M., when Sand Creek was reached.

The troopers began making camp, but the Dodge City cowboys decided to look around. Less than half an hour later rapid firing was heard in camp, and the alarm was given. Lieutenant Abram E. Wood and Company G, Fourth Cavalry, were the first to reach the scene of battle, quickly followed by Captain Hemphill and Company I. Captain Gunther's Company H and Captain Morse's infantry remained in camp. A force of about one hundred Indians met Wood and put up heavy resistance. As

---

[47] *Ibid.*; C. E. Morse to Post Adjutant, Fort Dodge, Sept. 27, 1878, Dept. of Mo., Letters Received, Walter S. Campbell Collection, University of Oklahoma Library. (Hereinafter this report will be cited as Morse, Report, OU.)

night set in, Wood and Hemphill were forced to retreat three miles back to Sand Creek, leaving the Indians in their stronghold.

In the morning Rendlebrock learned that the Indians had departed, moving west. After more than two hours' rapid march they finally caught up with the Cheyennes. The infantry was ordered forward in an advance column, and after they had gone about two hundred yards, skirmishing began. Both sides took up positions and maintained heavy, if not too accurate, fire until 4:30 P.M., at which time Rendlebrock ordered his men to withdraw. The troops made camp about one and a half miles from the site of the engagement, and during the night of September 22, the Northern Cheyennes once again escaped unchecked. Rendlebrock returned to the campsite set up two days earlier, where, the following night, supply trains from Fort Dodge arrived with rations and ammunition.

The next two days were spent in indecision, Rendlebrock moving about the Sand Creek area and then north to the Arkansas River, finally crossing it about four miles west of Cimarron Station. On September 25, Colonel William H. Lewis joined the main command, bringing Captain Mauck's detachment of Fourth Cavalry, plus Captain James H. Bradford and another company of the Nineteenth Infantry. Colonel Lewis assumed command and sent Captain Morse and his company of the Sixteenth Infantry to Fort Dodge.[48]

The following morning, after locating the Indian trail where it crossed the Arkansas, the troops renewed the chase. The next day, near Punished Woman's Fork of the central Kansas Smoky Hill River, the Indians reversed their direction and set up an ambush. In a sharp encounter the Dull Knife band fired on the troopers while they were struggling to take five wagons across a difficult stretch of trail. Lewis ordered the cavalry near him to

[48] *Ibid.*

drive the Indians from the nearest ridge, and when that was accomplished, the command fell back under cover. Indians occupied three sides of the ravine, but Colonel Lewis and Captain Mauck remained mounted, directing their forces. In the wild shooting Colonel Lewis was fatally injured by a bullet that struck him in the thigh, cutting the femoral artery. The troops lost three other men wounded. One Indian was killed.[49]

On the morning of the twenty-eighth, Captain Mauck, now senior officer, picked up the trail of the Northern Cheyennes and sent an ambulance to Dodge with the wounded. Mauck retained his command until he reached Fort Sidney, Nebraska, on October 19. Hemphill remained at Fort Sidney only long enough to organize the escort of another band of Northern Cheyennes, who had taken no part in the outbreak, back to the Cheyenne and Arapaho Agency in Indian Territory.[50]

For the most part, after Captain Hemphill carried the colors of Camp Supply against the Northern Cheyennes on September 12, the post could do no more. The camp was too far south to provide supplies and much too undermanned to send troops. After the death of Colonel Lewis, the commanding officer at Fort Dodge, Major Hambright, assumed command of that post on October 22, and Captain William J. Lyster succeeded him at Camp Supply.[51]

Matters concerning the agency's wards continued to be an

[49] C. C. Gardner to AAG, Dept. of Mo., Oct. 10, 1878, Dept. of Mo., Letters Received, Walter S. Campbell Collection, University of Oklahoma Library; *Dodge City Times* (Oct. 5, 1878); Hemphill, Report, OU; *Army and Navy Journal*, Vol. XVI (Oct. 19, 1878), 166; *Harper's Weekly Magazine*, Vol. XXII (Oct. 19, 1878), 827.

[50] *Sen. Rep. No. 708*, 48 Cong., 2 sess., 130; Hemphill, Report, OU. Captains Rendlebrock and Gunther were court-martialed at Fort Reno in February, 1879, for their conduct in the pursuit of the Dull Knife band. This information can be found in Wright, "Fort Reno," *loc. cit.*, 60–61. The remainder of the Dull Knife story on the Northern Plains can be found in *Record of Engagements*, 80–85.

[51] Post Returns, Fort Dodge, Oct., 1878; Post Returns, Camp Supply, Oct., 1878.

important responsibility of the post. On November 16, Captain Lyster received confidential information that Little Robe and about three hundred Cheyennes had left their reservation without permission ten days earlier and were somewhere between Antelope Hills and the Staked Plains. Apparently the Cheyennes had asked permission to be absent a month or two for a hunt, but the agent had told them that they must wait until the cavalry escorting the Northern Cheyennes from Fort Sidney returned. The Indians replied that by then it would be too late and started out alone.[52]

Captain Mauck and the Fourth Cavalry, including Captain Hemphill, escorted a band of Northern Cheyennes to Camp Supply on November 27. During the September outbreak these Indians had been at Fort Sidney under the care of Ben Clark. The three companies of the Fourth Cavalry under Mauck reached Reno on November 29, and after a conference it was decided that Little Robe in the Texas Panhandle would be looked after by another unit of cavalry from Fort Elliott.[53]

Just as the Outbreak of 1874 had encouraged the establishment of Forts Reno and Elliott, the Dull Knife raid awarded permanent status to Camp Supply. In December, 1878, the camp on Beaver River was officially named Fort Supply.[54] In addition, it was decided by the Department of the Missouri that a new military station should be established midway between Fort Supply and Fort Reno for the future protection of Kansas against runaway Indians. With rare foresight the Secretary of War suggested in his 1879 report that, whatever the attitude of

---

[52] W. J. Lyster to Mizner, Nov. 16, 1878, Lyster to AAG, Dept. of Mo., Nov. 18, 1878, Fort Supply, Letters Sent, Vol. 29½; *Dodge City Times* (Nov. 30, Dec. 7, 1878).

[53] Medical History of Fort Supply, Vol. 168, 197; *Dodge City Times* (Nov. 16, 23, Dec. 14, 1878).

[54] General Orders No. 9, Headquarters, Div. of Mo., Dec. 30, 1878, Fort Supply, Letters Received, Box 3.

the Indians might be then, the future value of such a post would be to "maintain them in possession of their lands and to protect them against broils and difficulties with the whites, both respectable persons and outlaws."[55]

To strengthen the defenses of Fort Supply and at the same time staff the new cantonment, Regimental Headquarters of the Twenty-third Infantry was transferred to Indian Territory. The field staff, band, and Companies E, F, and H, under the command of Colonel Jefferson C. Davis, left Fort Leavenworth on January 27, 1879, on the Atchison, Topeka and Santa Fe Railroad. Company B joined the command at Topeka on the same day, and the entire force arrived in Dodge City at midnight on January 28, after a rail trip of 369 miles. After remaining in Dodge City a few days, the command took the Dodge–Supply road on February 3 and marched 93 miles to Fort Supply in six days.[56]

General Sheridan originally proposed Sheridan's Roost on the North Canadian as the best location for the new camp, but he later settled on a spot known as Barrel Springs. Lieutenant Colonel Richard I. Dodge, commanding the detachment of the Twenty-third Infantry attached to the new cantonment, preferred a point on the south bank of the North Canadian about 3 miles directly south of Barrel Springs. The troops spent their first night at this spot on March 6. The Cantonment, as it was called, was 70 miles by road from Fort Supply and 60 miles from Fort Reno. Wichita, Kansas, 150 miles north, was the nearest railroad and telegraph station and the point from which stores were shipped.[57]

[55] *Annual Report of the Secretary of War for the Year 1879*, 74.

[56] Post Returns, Fort Supply, Jan., 1879; Henry C. Keeling, "My Experiences with the Cheyenne Indians," *Collections of the Kansas State Historical Society*, Vol. XI (1909–10), 305.

[57] *Ibid.*; *Dodge City Times* (Jan. 18, 1879); Dodge to AAG, Dept. of Mo., [March, 1879], Cantonment, I.T., Letters Sent, Vol. 17, Records of the War Dept., National Archives, Washington, D. C.

The subsequent return of Little Chief and the captured Northern Cheyennes from Dull Knife's band created new tensions in Indian Territory. In April, 1879, in an effort to remove some of the discontent, Little Chief was given permission to visit Washington.[58] Yet the unrest continued. Southern Cheyennes and Arapahoes complained that the northern tribesmen were already stealing horses and making preparations for the next flight.

On March 26, 1879, mindful of the mistakes of September, 1878, the Department of the Missouri ordered a cavalry force from Fort Elliott to aid Fort Supply in keeping watch on the Northern Cheyennes. On April 2, Amos Chapman informed Major Alexander J. Dallas, commanding Fort Supply, that on a recent visit to Fort Reno the Northern Cheyennes had told him that they would not take Dull Knife's route when they left the reservation. Rather, they would pass south of Fort Supply, move to a point at or near the mouth of the Palo Duro Creek, a tributary of the Beaver, and cross the Santa Fe tracks east of Fort Lyon.[59]

Lieutenant Abiel L. Smith and Company B, Fourth Cavalry, an aggregate of forty-six men, arrived at Fort Supply from Fort Elliott on April 6 to begin temporary service. The next morning, in an effort to foil the Northern Cheyennes' plans, Smith took the field to establish a camp on the Cimarron and from there scout the Dodge–Supply road for any attempt by Indians to escape northward. Contact with cattlemen in the area was recommended as one way to obtain the latest information about the Indians.

Shortly afterward, on April 14, a small body of Indians set up camp near Fort Supply, and Amos Chapman set out to learn their intentions. Lieutenant Smith was directed to station him-

[58] Hayt to Miles, Apr. 4, 1879, Central Superintendency, Letters Sent.

[59] A. J. Dallas to AAG, Dept. of Mo., Apr. 2, 4, 1879, Fort Supply, Letters Sent, Vol. 29½.

self about thirty miles south and east of the Cimarron to cover any break past Chapman. Neither Chapman nor Smith actually caught sight of the Indians, but Chapman was able to track them forty miles before concluding that the group was made up of ten Cheyennes who had been looking for stock but were returning to the agency empty-handed. Lieutenant Smith returned to his station, this time camping on Snake Creek, Kansas. Cattlemen were alerted to possible trouble, and several drove their herds nearer Fort Supply.[60]

When the break of the Northern Cheyennes had not materialized by May 9, Lieutenant Smith was reassigned. Still the rumors of Northern Cheyenne discontent persisted. Mysteriously, Southern Cheyennes and Arapahoes lost one or two of their best horses from each herd during May. Most of the Indians complained to Colonel Dodge at Cantonment and Major Dallas at Fort Supply, casting suspicion on the Northern Cheyennes.[61]

Acting on a strong complaint by Stone Calf, Major Dallas dispatched Lieutenant William Leeper and a squad of cavalry to recover a dozen missing ponies, authorizing the force to proceed as far as the Kansas line. Lieutenant Leeper picked up a warm trail but halted just inside Indian Territory, where he allowed William Wells, a post employee, to continue into Kiowa, Kansas. There, with the aid of some civilians, the suspected thief, William Parker, was arrested and placed in the custody of the United States marshal. Seven of the lost ponies were subsequently recovered.[62]

Unknown to Leeper, a party of Southern Cheyennes and

[60] Dallas to Abiel L. Smith, Apr. 6, 1879, Dallas to AAG, Dept. of Mo., Apr. 7, 16, 1879, in *ibid.*; *Dodge City Times* (Apr. 12, 1879); *Ford County Globe* (Apr. 15, 1879).

[61] Dallas to AAG, Dept. of Mo., May 4, 1879, Fort Supply, Letters Sent, Vol. 29½; Dodge to AAG, Dept. of Mo., May 16, 1879, Cantonment, I.T., Letters Sent, Vol. 17.

[62] Dallas to AAG, Dept. of Mo., May 10, 1879, Dallas to Miles, May 10, 1879, Fort Supply, Letters Sent, Vol. 29½.

Arapahoes, still believing the Northern Cheyennes to be the thieves, were searching the canyons between the North Fork of the Canadian and the Cimarron for their stolen animals. What their actions were on that trip are not fully known, but on his return from Kansas, Wells found the Sheedy Ranch ransacked and abandoned and plentiful Indian signs in the vicinity. Wells refused to name the Indians as the depredators but warned that it would be unwise for red men to stray above the North Canadian since the cowboys were in a touchy mood.[63]

The Northern Cheyennes never made their advertised break north, although fears that they would do so persisted until June. Possibly Little Chief was favorably disposed toward peace after his return from Washington, or the extensive military preparations of the Department of the Missouri may have prevented the exodus. Six companies of infantry were stationed at Cantonment, and four more were on duty at Fort Supply. In addition, Forts Reno, Elliott, and Dodge held cavalry units on guard under momentary orders to take the field. Dull Knife's raid had been a success in part because of the faulty communication among the posts below the Arkansas. Beginning in June, 1879, that situation was corrected, when details from Cantonment, Reno, Elliott, and Supply worked through the summer linking their respective posts with telegraph lines.

In the meantime, Fort Supply was given a new assignment under orders of the Department of the Missouri. On May 5 the command was authorized to employ all necessary force to expel parties of boomers attempting to make settlements south of the Kansas line.[64] The boomer movement called for white settlement of the unoccupied lands of the Indian Territory, and for some months in the spring of 1879 it generated a great deal of

---

[63] Dallas to AAG, Dept. of Mo., May 17, 27, 1879, in *ibid.* Because of the sudden departure of mounted men from his post, Major Dallas asked officers at the Cantonment to check out the Sheedy Ranch.

[64] Dallas to AAG, Dept. of Mo., May 5, 1879, in *ibid.*

excitement. Two days after being placed on stand-by, Fort Supply was ordered into action by telegram.

On May 9 a message was sent to Lieutenant Smith's camp at Snake Creek ordering his troops to proceed as rapidly as possible to Arkansas City, Kansas, where they were to help eject intruders from Indian Territory. On the same day Captain William C. Hemphill and another company of the Fourth Cavalry were detached from the Fort Supply garrison and ordered to Coffeyville, Kansas, for a like purpose. Cantonment troops were similarly drawn out, taking post at the nearest point where the Kansas line crossed the Reno–Wichita road.[65]

Hemphill's detail immediately headed northeast, carrying the colors of Fort Supply to this new challenge to the Indian Territory. Moving across the country without regard for established road or trails, they proceeded by way of the Pawnee Agency to Coffeyville, a distance of 280 miles, arriving on May 21. The company remained there for ten days, performing the duties assigned to it. On May 24 two scouting parties, each made up of one corporal and six privates, penetrated the Indian Territory, one moving southwest and the other southeast. After covering forty miles and failing to find any unauthorized persons in the territory, they returned to camp. On May 31, when the emergency was apparently over, a telegram from the Department of the Missouri ordered the detached company to return to Fort Supply by way of Fort Reno.

The command left Coffeyville on June 3 and traveled the 226 miles to Fort Reno in nine uneventful days, arriving on June 11. The troops stayed at Fort Reno until June 24, when they were ordered to resume their march to Fort Supply. The troops covered the remaining 130 miles, reaching the post at midnight on June 30. The expedition had totaled 636 miles.

[65] Dallas to Smith, May 9, 1879, Dallas to AAG, Dept. of Mo., May 9, 15, 1879, Dallas to Commanding Officer, Cantonment, I.T., May 14, 1879, in *ibid.*

Lieutenant Smith and the company of the Fourth Cavalry detached from Fort Elliott returned to Fort Supply from their post at Arkansas City on July 3. Two days later Smith left for the camp on Snake Creek set up before the assignment to the Kansas line. But by that time there was no longer a real danger of a Northern Cheyenne break, and the detail was relieved on July 20 and left for Fort Elliott the next day.[66]

Only one event of note interrupted the quiet at Fort Supply during Captain Hemphill's absence. On the morning of June 9 a band of ninety Pawnees, escorted by twenty-six men of the Nineteenth Infantry, arrived at the post. These Indians had been stealing ranch stock near their agency, Major Dallas was informed, and it was feared that the cattlemen would retaliate. In the hope of preventing trouble, the commanding officer at Fort Gibson arranged to send the Pawnees to hunt buffaloes some distance from the agency—and from the cowboys. After clearing the situation with the department commander, Fort Supply allowed the Indians to hunt buffalo for a few days within forty-five miles of the post. The hunt was a surprising success: 150 buffaloes were brought down with bows and arrows. The hunt ended on June 30, and the Indians peacefully headed back to their agency on July 2.[67]

As the fall of 1879 turned toward the decade of the 1880's, Fort Supply closed a chapter on Indian matters. For more than ten years the post had guarded white men from the Indians, Indians from the white men, and Indians from each other. In those years the "temporary camp" for the expedition of 1868 had experienced three Indian wars, controlled illegal trespass by whites, and become senior post among the military guardians of the Indian country. The end of Indian resistance to the white

---

[66] Post Returns, Fort Supply, May–July, 1879.

[67] Dallas to AAG, Dept. of Mo., June 8, July 1, 1879, Dallas to A. C. Williams, July 1, 1879, Fort Supply, Letters Sent, Vol. 29½.

man did not, however, mean that Fort Supply could diminish its interest in the red man. In 1879 the Great Plains were in the midst of a great cattle boom and ranchers, like boomers, were unwilling to respect Indian boundaries. The decade of the 1880's would call for new responsibilities for the Fort Supply garrison.

Chapter VI

Soldier and Citizen at Fort Supply

Life at Fort Supply, deep within Indian Territory, was a true pioneer experience. In just ten years an energetic garrison had transformed the post from a temporary supply depot to an established guardian of the frontier. Transportation links with surrounding settlements attracted a civilian population, and in a short time social life flourished. The post had many attributes of a frontier settlement.

In 1872, Fort Supply consisted of a complex of officers' quarters, barracks, stables, offices, and hospital. Private H. Harbers, stationed at Camp Supply in September, 1872, remembered construction at the post as "a continuous duty every day. There was no lay-off."[1]

Stability, however, was not to be confused with luxury. Mrs. Frances M. Roe, who accompanied her husband to Camp Supply in May, 1872, wrote that "this place is quite as dreadful as it had been represented to us." Quarters, she found, were nothing more than huts built of logs, with canvas to partition the rooms. Sand and dirt floors encouraged the growth of little white toadstools, and the cottonwood logs "have the bark on, and the army of bugs that hide underneath the bark during the day and march upon us at night is to be dreaded about as much as a whole tribe of Indians!"

To Mrs. Roe, danger lurked almost everywhere at Fort Sup-

---

[1] H. Harber's "Service Account" in Percy M. Ashburn, *A History of the Medical Department of the United States Army*, 98.

ply: she feared that a sudden downpour of rain might wash away her house; she considered the Negro troops of the Tenth Cavalry good soldiers but better thieves; and she was certain that hostile Indians surrounded the post.

> The [Indians] have a disagreeable way of coming to the windows and staring in. Sometimes before you have heard a sound you will be conscious of an uncomfortable feeling, and looking around you will discover five or six Indians, large and small, peering at you against the windows, each ugly nose pressed flat against the glass! It is enough to drive one mad. You never know when they are about, their tread is so stealthy with their moccasined feet.[2]

Fort Supply continued to expand until progress was interrupted by the Outbreak of 1874. The reduced garrison could not easily keep such a large post in repair, and the military cutback after the Indian wars resulted in further deterioration. A fire at the post on July 1, 1877, destroyed three sets of officers' quarters and very nearly spread to the rotted logs of several other buildings. Disaster was averted only through the efforts of the entire command. Two days later, recognizing the perilous condition of the fort, Captain William J. Lyster, the new commanding officer (who had lost all his personal possessions in the fire) began a rebuilding program.[3] This program continued through 1877 and into the following year. Stockade or picket-wall structures were replaced with rows of frame buildings. When cost prohibited a complete replacement of the extensive sets of barracks, about six hundred cedar logs were cut to replace every fourth cottonwood log.[4]

[2] Roe, *Army Letters*, 54, 57–59, 64–65, 77.

[3] Consolidated Quartermaster Correspondence, Envelope 3182, Records of the War Dept., National Archives, Washington, D.C.; Lewis to AAG, Dept. of Mo., July 2, 1877, Fort Supply, Letters Sent, Vol. 29; *Dodge City Times* (July 7, 1877).

[4] *Dodge City Times* (Sept. 1, 1877); Hambright to AAG, Dept. of Mo., Feb. 17, 1878, Fort Supply, Letters Sent, Vol. 29½.

Water, ice, and fresh vegetables at Fort Supply were both necessities and luxuries. None were easy to come by, but ingenuity and persistence made them available by one means or another.

In the beginning water (of insufficient quantity and poor quality) was hauled from Wolf Creek. It was carted by wagons to barrels behind the officers' quarters, the laundry, and the barracks. Mrs. Roe commented that the water was "so full of alkali that we are obliged to boil every drop before it is used for drinking or cooking, and even then it is so distasteful that we flavor it with sugar or lemons so we can drink it at all."[5] One or two wells within the post were pressed into duty during dry periods, but it was not until a windmill and clay pipes were installed in late 1879 that the post was assured adequate water.[6]

Usable ice was a rare commodity at Fort Supply. Each winter great blocks of ice were cut from Wolf Creek and stored for later distribution. Before 1875 ice was temporarily deposited in a sand hill covered with manure, but it usually melted before mid-June. In 1872 an unsuccessful attempt was made to cart ice from Fort Dodge, but it succumbed to the summer heat and melted in thirty-six hours. Construction of special icehouses in 1875 allowed storage in quantities, depending upon the severity of the winter. In 1877, for example, about 450 tons of ice were stored, but the mild winter of 1878 provided only 55 tons.[7]

Improper nourishment was common at frontier posts. Scurvy often affected entire garrisons, and to forestall the disease military authorities encouraged the cultivation of vegetable gardens near the post. An attempt was made at Fort Supply to grow vegetables in 1871, but heat, drought, and grasshoppers killed the crop. The following year was one of "discouraging success";

[5] *Army Letters*, 70–71.

[6] Granville O. Haller to Chief Quartermaster, Dept. of Mo., June 9, 1880, Fort Supply, Letters Sent, Vol. 29½; *Ford County Globe* (Sept. 28, 1879).

[7] Medical History of Fort Supply, Vol. 166, 16, 19, Vol. 168, 113, 153.

the garrison managed to grow some watermelons and cucumbers, but they were destroyed in an Indian raid. In 1873 a new garden was staked out about three miles from the post, and about twenty acres were cultivated, but with no results. The next year the post medical officer observed, "Although there is nominally a Post garden here, it scarcely deserves the name and is not worth the timber that fences it."[8]

Not until 1877, a year of abundant rains, did the garden furnish a good supply of vegetables. Years of failure had taught the gardeners much. Drainpipes were installed to prevent flooding—on one occasion water had covered the garden to a depth of three feet—and crops were selected carefully. In later years the post gardener and the medical officer co-operated to make Fort Supply one of the healthiest posts on the plains. In 1879 crops suffered disaster from drought, but after 1880 the new post windmill provided enough water for irrigation.[9]

Military life at Fort Supply in the 1870's was rigorous. Until the garden began producing vegetables, the main diet consisted of salt pork, hard bread, and coffee in winter and dried beef, fresh game, and fruits in summer. The barracks were not styled for comfort. Pay for a private was only thirteen dollars a month, and his duty was hazardous. A soldier from Fort Supply made some interesting comments to the editor of the *Ford County Globe* on November 1, 1878:

> Thirty seven men is at present the maximum number allowed a company of infantry and to my certain knowledge there never is that number in a company. I have known 37 men borne on the rolls of a company, but after deducting the extra duty and daily duty men, which comprises about 40% of the number reported,

[8] *Ibid.*, Vol. 166, 16, 19, 24; Brooke to AAG, Dept. of Mo., Dec. 8, 1873, Fort Supply, Letters Sent, Vol. 29.

[9] Medical History of Fort Supply, Vol. 168, 109–28; *Dodge City Times* (July 7, 1877, Mar. 30, Apr. 20, 1878); *Ford County Globe* (Feb. 19, 1878, Sept. 28, 1879).

besides orderlies, sick "dog robbers," etc. which at times will average more than 10% of the total number—there was seldom 15 men remaining on for actual duty. And then deduct 5 Sergts., 4 Corporals, 2 musicians, and we have a company as follows: Three commissioned officers, (who are not counted in the aggregate of enlisted men), 9 non-commissioned officers, two musicians, and in the name of all that is absurd, 6 privates. Yes, 6 privates soldiering in a company of infantry available for duty.

Since the visit of the band to this post the military ceremonies have been imposing: reviews, dress parades, and guard mounts ad lib. We all like to see fine military turnouts, but when 2 commissioned officers, 3 sergeants, 2 or 3 corporals, and 5 or 6 dilapidated privates constitute the entire strength of a company marching on parade to martial strains of 20 brass horns and a big drum major covered with gold lace leading them, the situation becomes rather ridiculous.[10]

The weather in northwest Indian Territory did not make life more pleasant—or less exciting. In July and August temperatures regularly ranged around the one-hundred-degree mark, and from November to March a sudden blue norther could bring a rapid drop in temperature. Surgeon Peter J. A. Cleary testified in 1875 that "the thermometer during the latter part of March [went] from 40 to 92 in twenty-four hours and down to 20 in the succeeding forty-eight."[11] Winds were constant—from the south in summer, from the north in winter. In good years twenty-five inches of rain fell, but in bad years, fewer than ten. Sometimes rain came too quickly, and the post, located on low ground between two streams, was flooded. Wolf Creek overflowed its banks in December, 1877, and swift water undermined the Lee and Reynolds bunkhouse, which collapsed, killing one employee. Electrical storms were equally dangerous. On one occasion lightning struck a tent, injuring the five occupants.[12]

[10] *Ford County Globe* (Nov. 12, 1878).
[11] Medical History of Fort Supply, Vol. 166, 36.
[12] *Dodge City Times* (Dec. 29, 1877); *Ford County Globe* (Aug. 6, 1878).

Congressional failure to renew special pay allowances for Civil War soldiers automatically reduced the postwar privates' pay from sixteen to thirteen dollars a month. As Rickey commented, "The desertion of about one-third the total number of enlisted men in the Regular Army in 1872 in part reflects their reaction to the pay cut."[13] Fort Supply was no exception; its desertion rate equaled the national average. Colonel Nelson lost large numbers of men in March, 1872. Patrols were sent out day and night to capture deserters, but to no avail. Nelson reported:

> Still the men went. Many were caught and when put in confinement tools were handed in nightly thru the prison gratings for them to escape with. I was in the heart of Indian country and must use stringent measures to stop all this. When as a matter of prison discipline and to mark escaped deserters I had the hair cut short of all deserters in the guard house, I believe it effectively stopped the combination to aid the escape of prisoners.[14]

Desertions were reduced by the passage of a new pay bill on May 15, 1872, but there were always some runaways from Supply, as from every post. A spate of desertions in 1878 caused a standard reward of twenty-five dollars to be posted for the capture of the men.[15]

Most troopers were good soldiers, however, and Fort Supply had its share of them as well. Private Harbers recalled one night in 1872 when he was on guard duty after several Indian attempts had been made on the Fort Supply herds:

> At night the sentries had importuned the Commanding Officer to allow the three men of each [guard] post to be together, so as to have protection in case of a surprise attack as sentries had been shot at post and it would not be found out until the hour call would be made. One night on No. 2 Post (I was on that Post) and

[13] Don Rickey, Jr., *Forty Miles a Day on Beans and Hay*, 127.
[14] Nelson to AAG, Dept. of Mo., Mar. 10, 1872, Fort Supply, Letters Sent, Vol. 28.

Humpy Brown was on No. 3 Post (the hay stack). At 8:20 I went to the farthest end of my beat to exchange the situation before going back to meet the other sentry and told him that Humpy Brown did not report and I was going to call for the Corporal of the Guard. When the grand round came, the officer in charge asked me what was the matter. They hunted in the hay stack and found Brown with two arrows in his neck. They asked him why he did not call out, and he said, "Oh! I was waiting for the man to show himself before seeing me—and I was going to get him." They took him to the hospital and extracted the arrows. He recovered.[16]

Soldiers at Fort Supply regularly sounded off through the two Dodge City newspapers. The *Dodge City Times* received comments from Old Cactus and Young Cactus, while the *Ford County Globe* printed letters from Jerry, Reville, and Domingo. Perhaps the most perceptive critic and satirist was Jerry. In a communication of December 20, 1878, he combined the usual complaints of being overworked and underfed with a comment on the recent desertions:

At break of day the soldier is called from the land of dreams in order that it may be ascertained if during the night he evacuated the ranch. Answering to his name he is allowed 20 minutes to wash and arrange his toilet for breakfast, which consists of stale bread, muddy, weak coffee and the time-immemorable hash, which latter is compounded from refuse bits of bread, meat, etc. accumulated from the day previous.

Then ten minutes are allowed before fatigue call, when he goes forth to labor. Some as mechanics, others to saw wood, dig sewers, build roads, blast rock, burn lime, mound brick, drive teams, police the garrison, and other care for public property and animals, and other things.

---

[15] *Dodge City Times* (June 1, 1878, Jan. 18, 1879); *Ford County Globe* (July 22, 1879).

[16] Harber, "Service Account," *Medical Department*, 100.

At 11:45 there is recall from fatigue and all hands repair to their quarters where another feast is spread, comprising beef, thin bean soup or water and stale bread.

At 1 pm each one resumes his work which lasts until fifteen minutes to sundown. The recall is again sounded and supper is announced. Supper is the most transparent meal in the army. A slice or two of bread with a pint or two of the inevitable weak coffee fills the bill of fare for supper.

At sundown all are assembled for retreat or parade, and here the scene changes, for instead of the laborer of a few minutes ago the man is now transformed into a soldier and is put through the maneauvers [*sic*] of drill. Darkness comes on and this servant of Uncle Sam is dismissed, but not for the night. Oh no! for at 8:30 he is again called out to satisfy his superiors that he is still present in propria persona. This being satisfactorily settled he is allowed to retire to dream, perhaps of the reign of terror or the dark days of the inquisition.[17]

Communication links were vital for a frontier post. As the first outpost in western Indian Territory, Camp Supply was originally joined to Fort Dodge and later to Fort Sill by roads established in the troop movements of the Campaign of 1868. Since Fort Sill was 196 miles south and Fort Dodge 93 miles north, Supply concentrated on maintaining contact with the latter post. The outbreak of 1874 brought two new posts to the region, Fort Reno and Fort Elliott. Fort Reno was linked to Wichita on the north and Fort Sill to the south, but Fort Supply and Fort Elliott, in the Texas Panhandle, had a close bond. In 1879, Cantonment was established midway between Forts Supply and Reno. This post merged with the eastern Sill–Reno–Wichita network of roads, while Forts Supply, Elliott, and Dodge formed a western transportation system.

Until 1872, Fort Supply received its supplies by wagon 166 miles from Fort Hays by way of Fort Dodge. After the Santa

[17] *Ford County Globe* (Jan. 1, 1879).

Fe Railroad reached Fort Dodge in 1872, the distance was cut to the Dodge–Supply road. Freighting between the posts was carried out by private contractors, but the threat of Indian attacks forced the military to furnish escorts. Both freighters and troopers suffered on winter details. More than once men had to be thawed from leather saddles, lost limbs to frostbite, and died in blizzards.

By 1877 the Dodge–Supply road was a familiar trail to most travelers in western Kansas and the Indian Territory. Thirteen miles from the Arkansas River Bridge at Dodge City was Mulberry Creek, where water could be found in even the driest seasons, and the Pat Ryan farm was located nearby. Fourteen miles farther, over a rolling prairie, was the first stopping point, Bluff Creek. Banks as high as two hundred feet walled in the creek, and the Silas Maley ranch offered accommodations, or there was a camping spot on a little plateau not far away.

From Bluff Creek the road continued fourteen miles on a level prairie into Bear Creek valley. The decaying station established in February, 1872, remained at this onetime Cheyenne hunting camp as a relic of days past. Bear Creek, too, afforded water for stock the year round. The second day on the trail ordinarily ended at Red Clarke's Boss Ranch, near the old Cimarron Redoubt.[18] Sandy beds and low banks characterized the Cimarron at that point, fifty-five miles from Dodge City.

The thirty-eight miles from the Cimarron to Camp Supply was the most difficult part of the trip. For eight miles south the road crossed and recrossed deep gulches, wound like coils by Snake Creek. It was another five miles to Buffalo Creek and a splendid camping ground for the third night. The final day of the four-day trip began with a ten-mile trek to Gypsum Creek, one of the more interesting streams on the road. After three more

18 After 1875, Upper Bear Creek Station and Cimarron Redoubt were abandoned, and in time they were replaced by ranches.

miles the traveler reached Sand Creek with its high banks, followed in four miles by Devil's Gap, where General Sully met the Indians in September, 1868. Before much farther Camp Supply could be seen from the top of the divide overlooking Beaver River.[19]

As a railroad center, Dodge City supplied both Fort Supply and Fort Elliott. There was a Dodge–Elliott road—in fact, there were three alternate routes of one road—but it was not as practical as the route to Elliott by way of Camp Supply.[20] The Supply–Elliott road was an easy-to-travel, well-marked road, used more by hunters than by freighters. The abundance of good campsites did not call for a rigid four-day schedule, as the Dodge–Supply road did.

Eighteen miles southwest of Fort Supply the traveler crossed Wolf Creek, which offered the first of several camping spots. It was at that point that hunters usually unlimbered their gear in preparation for hunting the buffaloes that ranged immediately south. It was only ten miles more to Willow Springs and another well-watered camp. Rock Springs, eight miles away, and Commission Creek, eight miles farther, were also camping points. The Polly Hotel at Commission Creek served the less adventurous. Commission Creek was crossed twice in three miles, and three miles past the south ford the traveler crossed the one hundredth meridian, the boundary between Indian Territory and Texas.

---

[19] *Dodge City Times* (June 1, July 7, 21, Aug. 25, 1877); *Ford County Globe* (Feb. 5, 1878).

[20] One trail from Dodge City to Fort Elliott proceeded down Crooked Creek to Mulberry Creek and due south, a distance of 170 miles; another left the Dodge-Supply road at the Cimarron crossing, moved past Bear Creek to Kiowa Medicine Lodge Creek and south to Wolf Creek crossing, thence to the Supply-Elliott road crossing of the Canadian, a route of 160 miles; and probably the best trail for water and wood was the patch 160 miles due south through no man's land, often called the Jones-Plummer Cattle Trail. *Dodge City Times* (Sept. 29, 1877).

Twelve miles into the Texas Panhandle the Boggy River offered good water, wood, and buffalo grass. Three miles more and the traveler could purchase refreshment at the A. G. Springer ranch on the Canadian River. The next twelve miles took the traveler past Cottonwood Springs and onto the Washita River. There also was a well-stocked ranch. Gageby Creek and the settlement of the same name were reached nine miles out, and an equal distance brought the traveler to Fort Elliott and Sweetwater City.[21]

Mail call was an exciting event at Fort Supply. Government mail contractors early made the post a weekly stop, and in 1871 twice-weekly mail was delivered on an irregular schedule. Numerous complaints were made about the indifferent service, but Fort Supply was not able to improve it. The Department of the Missouri could not justify better delivery because it estimated that the mail from Dodge to Supply cost nearly three thousand dollars a year.[22]

After the establishment of Fort Elliott in 1876, Fort Supply carried from eight hundred to one thousand pounds of mail and express twice each week to that post. The *Dodge City Times* calculated the cost of this service to the military at about $6,000 a year.[23] Panhandle residents joined with personnel at Fort Supply in protests about the service, and in 1878 Lee and Reynolds Company received a subcontractorship of $4,400 a year to deliver the mail from Dodge to Elliott. The mail from Dodge City to Fort Supply was thereafter regularly delivered twice each week, and Reynolds then carried the mail to Fort Elliott. This

21 *Ibid.* (June 1, Sept. 1, 1877).

22 Jacobs, "Military Reminiscences," *loc. cit.*, 29; AAG, Dept. of Mo., to Commanding Officer, Camp Supply, Feb. 8, 1871, Camp Supply, Letters Received, Box 1; Brooke to AAG, Dept. of Mo., Dec. 23, 1873, Fort Supply, Letters Sent, Vol. 29.

23 (Sept. 29, 1877).

service was only token improvement for Fort Supply, and in June, 1878, more than two hundred persons signed a petition for mail delivery from Dodge City three times a week. In response to the demands, a Tuesday-Thursday-Saturday schedule was granted in November, 1878.[24] In January, 1879, Supply residents requested six mails a week from Dodge, but were refused. By June, 1879, the Reynolds stage line was carrying mail, express, and passengers 185 miles from Dodge City to Fort Elliott, by way of Fort Supply, in 40 hours. A round-trip ticket cost $35.[25]

Military men and civilians at Fort Supply met on an equal footing at the post trader's store. As early as the spring of 1869, Fort Supply had a self-appointed merchant, and later John F. Tappan officially served as sutler for a few months. The isolation of the post caused Colonel A. D. Nelson to recommend the appointment of a single person to barter with the Indians and the military, and the secretary of war responded on November 17, 1870, by appointing Albert E. Reynolds official post trader.[26]

Reynolds, in partnership with W. M. D. Lee, held a monopoly at the post store, subcontracted with Fort Supply for hay and wood, dealt with the Indians for buffalo robes, and eventually developed the first stage route to Fort Elliott. In 1872, when General William B. Hazen drew the attention of his friend Representative James A. Garfield to the machinations of post trader J. S. Evans at Fort Sill, Reynolds was said to possess material information regarding Evans' relationship to Secretary of War William Belknap. It was also stated that Lee and Reynolds paid ten thousand dollars outright for their extensive privileges at

[24] *Dodge City Times* (Mar. 9, Apr. 6, June 8, 1878) ; *Ford County Globe* (Mar. 19, Nov. 5, 1878).

[25] *Ford County Globe* (June 24, Sept. 16, 1879).

[26] Nelson to AAG, Dept. of Mo., July 2, 1869, Fort Supply, Letters Sent, Vol. 25; Nelson to AAG, Dept. of Mo., Dec. 30, 1870, Fort Supply, Letters Sent, Vol. 26.

Fort Supply,[27] but there was no investigation at the post and the firm retained the tradership. In later years Lee and Reynolds established a tradership at Fort Elliott, had some business enterprises at the Cheyenne and Arapaho Agency, and owned several ranches near the Texas–New Mexico line.[28] Through hard work and public service Lee and Reynolds became highly respected in Indian Territory.

By the close of the 1870's there were other businessmen at Fort Supply, and many stores had opened on Washington Avenue. Tailors advertised "genuine Parisian style," and bootmakers, barbers, and dry-goods merchants offered good wares and services at reasonable prices.

Fort Supply had its share of fights among the men, some quite brutal. Eye gouging, thumb pulling, and nose biting were common injuries at Fort Supply in the typical style of frontier brawling. Each fracas was investigated by the officer of the day, in the absence of civil authorities. Intoxication lay at the bottom of most of the fights, and the week following payday was the most critical time of the month.

Post records show few incidents of murder, and only one real troublemaker appears to have located at the post. Bill Gibbs, a twenty-four-year-old Negro wagon boss for Lee and Reynolds, went to Fort Supply in 1877. On August 3, while Gibbs was leading a wagon train to Fort Elliott, an argument erupted between him and the train's Mexican cook, Joe Campo, resulting in the latter's dismissal. Campo left for Fort Supply to pick up his pay, but after a few moments Gibbs followed him and ordered him

27 R. H. Pratt to Hazen, Nov. 25, 1871, quoted in Kroeker, "William B. Hazen," *loc. cit.*, 189.

28 "Catalogue of Ranches of the Texas Pan-Handle," in the Laura V. Hamner Collection, Panhandle-Plains Historical Society, Canyon, Texas. References to the LS ranch, owned partially by W. M. D. Lee, and the LF ranch, owned by Lee and Albert Reynolds, are in the *Dodge City Times* (May 1, 1880, Jan. 29 and Feb. 24, 1881, and Dec. 7, 1882).

back to work. The Mexican refused, and when Gibbs reached for his revolver, Campo also drew. Both men fired at the same time. The wagonmaster's bullet creased Campo's scalp, but Gibbs took a ball through the lungs. Campo turned himself in to Fort Supply authorities, and Gibbs was taken to the fort hospital, where, though seriously wounded, he recovered.[29]

Gibbs learned nothing from his shooting scrape and continued to create disturbances at the post. He took particular delight in making uncomplimentary remarks about George Thomas' wife. On March 23, 1878, Thomas approached Gibbs, who was seated on a wheelbarrow in front of the post butcher shop, and asked him whether he had a pistol. Gibbs immediately drew a revolver from his hip pocket, just as Thomas leveled a navy six-shooter at him. Thomas fired and hit his mark. The wounded Gibbs ran inside the butcher shop, but Thomas kept firing until Gibbs sagged to the floor, dead. The post sympathized with Thomas, but he was culpable for firing in the crowded market, although luckily none of the bystanders were wounded. Thomas was bound over to the marshal at Fort Reno.[30]

In November, 1878, the people of Fort Supply were observers of an unusual shooting incident on the Supply–Elliott road. The incident resulted in the death of A. G. Springer and his barkeeper, Tom Ledbetter, in a row with four soldiers at the Springer whisky ranch.

A. G. Springer was a salty cowman who lived in the Texas Panhandle about fifty miles southwest of Fort Supply on the road to Fort Elliott. Because his ranch was only twelve miles

[29] *Dodge City Times* (Aug. 11, 18, 1877). Upon recommendation of the Commanding Officer at Camp Supply charges were dropped against Campo. Post Adjutant, Camp Supply, to U.S. Marshal, West District of Ark., Sept. 2, 1877, Fort Supply, Letters Sent, Vol. 29; *Dodge City Times* (Sept. 1, 1877).

[30] *Dodge City Times* (Mar. 30, 1878); *Ford County Globe* (Apr. 2, 1878); Hambright to U. S. Marshal, West District of Ark., Apr. 7, 1878, Hambright to AAG, Dept. of Mo., Mar. 24, 1878, Fort Supply, Letters Sent, Vol. 29½.

down the Canadian from Indian Territory, Springer knew that his spread would probably be struck at the outset of any Indian uprising. To protect his property he built "Fort Sitting Bull," two small log buildings about one hundred feet from either side of the ranch, accessible only through an underground passage from the house.[31] In February, 1877, a Cheyenne hunter ventured too close to the buildings, and Springer shot him down, defending his action on the grounds that the Indian was off the reservation.[32]

On the night of November 16, 1878, the army paymaster, Major A. J. Broadhead, was en route to Fort Elliott, escorted by thirteen soldiers of the Nineteenth Infantry out of Fort Dodge. As was customary, the escort pitched camp about fifty yards from Springer's ranch. After nightfall some soldiers visited the bar of the ranch, where liquor was being served. Sergeant Patrick Kerrigan joined Springer in a game of cards. Apparently Kerrigan believed that he was being cheated. When he protested, Springer drew a revolver and beat him over the head. Then Springer fired some shots to force the soldiers back to their camp.

Soon afterward the soldiers were fired upon in their tents, and two privates were wounded. At this point of the story the facts are unclear. Some of the soldiers said that they observed four men approaching, presumably highwaymen. Other versions reported that the shots came from the ranch. The major ordered his escort to attack, and a deadly fire was poured into the night. A volley hit the ranch, and Springer was struck in the neck, and the ball passed through his body and into Ledbetter, who was standing behind him. Both were killed.[33]

---

[31] *Dodge City Times* (June 1, 1878).

[32] Lewis to AAG, Dept. of Mo., Feb. 8, 1877, Fort Supply, Letters Sent, Vol. 29.

[33] *Dodge City Times* (Nov. 23, 1878); *Ford County Globe* (Nov. 26, 1878); Post Returns, Camp Supply, Nov., 1878. A different account is offered in Laura V. Hamner, *Short Grass and Longhorns*, 39–40.

A coroner's inquest made up of Panhandle citizens returned the verdict that Springer had fired the first two shots and that Ledbetter was trying to prevent him from shooting again when the men were killed. The soldiers were exonerated from blame, since they had acted in self-defense. Lieutenant Thomas M. Wenie of Fort Elliott took possession of the ranch property, valued at about fifty thousand dollars, until Springer's brother could arrive from Delaware.[34]

Hunting was the most popular recreation at Fort Supply among both military personnel and civilians. Game was an important item of food at the fort. Within ten to fifteen miles of the post buffaloes, elk, antelopes, turkeys, rabbits, quail, and grouse could be found in abundance. Organized parties of hunters beat the creatures toward the post, where the best shots bagged them. In winter detachments of ten men and an officer moved near the Cimarron, killed what game they could in ten days, and brought the meat back to the garrison for the troops.

For a time in 1877 and 1878 baseball was a popular pastime. The cavalry and infantry regiments played on company levels, and the best squads of each league met in a short series, which the cavalry usually won. In the spring of 1878 a new game, croquet, swept the post. A *Globe* reporter wrote: "Croquet seems to be the great outdoor amusement at this place. No less than three grounds are occupied on fair days, and it has entirely taken the place of baseball."[35] Among those less athletically inclined, rides and picnics were popular.

Evening amusements included strolling shows, magicians, road companies, and band concerts. In spite of the fort's relative

[34] *Dodge City Times* (Nov. 30, 1878, Apr. 3, 1880). In April, 1880, three enlisted men from the escort detachment were arrested for the Springer death under warrant issued by the Wheeler County, Texas, Grand Jury. The results of the trial are not known.

[35] *Ibid.* (May 18, 1878) ; *Ford County Globe* (Apr. 30, 1878).

[36] *Dodge City Times* (May 18, 25, 1878) ; *Ford County Globe* (May 21, 1878).

isolation the men were regularly exposed to cultural events. Professor Petrie was acknowledged a conjurer with "scarcely an equal in this country," and the Texas Star Troupe presented performances of high quality. On another occasion, however, five strolling players inflicted "horrid punishment" on the Fort Supply patrons of the arts and were labeled "humbugs." One attendant lamented, "The Indians have not taken us yet, but this strolling show has."[36]

The arrival of the regimental band on its tour of the posts offered the best entertainment. Usually spending two to three weeks at each post where units of the regiment were stationed, the band performed at concerts and dances. The Nineteenth Infantry band visited Fort Supply in 1878, and in 1879 and 1880 the bands of the Twenty-third and Twenty-fourth infantries were stationed at the post.

Holidays were observed at Fort Supply. While Christmas time, when Lee and Reynolds "set 'em up" for the boys, was pleasant, the Fourth of July was the event of the year. In 1878 a baseball game opened the festivities and was followed by foot, sack, and wheelbarrow races. In the last contest of the day entrants tried to catch a greased pig, the prize being the pig. Music and dancing out-of-doors closed the program.

In 1879 the Fourth of July celebration was even more elaborate. A federal salute with full band was held at daylight, after which shooting matches for small money prizes were held. Races were then run, but the most exciting event was the greased-pole climb for a prize of a twenty-day furlough. After retreat, dances were held for the men and officers.[37]

Clubs and societies were another outlet for the men at Fort Supply. Two of the less important clubs were the Gutter Snipes and the Knights of the Big Canteen. There was constant talk of forming a literary society at the post, but it was never organized.

[37] *Ford County Globe* (July 22, 1879).

Old Cactus tried to promote it, giving as his reason the "education, natural intelligence and stamina" of the officers and tactfully noting that the enlisted men were also a noble lot:

> Among the three small companies here we find . . . two ex-Congressmen (Rebel), five ex-state M.C. [members of Congress], two ex-clergymen, one ex-lawyer, two ex-judges, four squires, four ex-school teachers, two professors, four agitators, 13 of the brotherhood, one Polish count, six strikers, three professional dog-robbers and ten ex-commercial drummers.[38]

For the "gentry" there was the exclusive Camp Supply Social Club. Grand balls ("hops" in the military term), were held for the officers, their ladies, and certain privileged civilians, such as Lee and Reynolds. Dancing began about 8:00 P.M., and before long individual or community singing of German, Irish, and southern songs delighted the gathering. After 11:00 P.M. the sideboard in the adjoining room was spread with ice cream, cake, pie, sandwiches, ham, cold beef, roast antelope, venison, canned fruits, tea, coffee, and milk. About 3:00 A.M. the festivities drew to a close.

On Christmas Eve, New Year's Eve, and St. Patrick's Day the Officers' Club joined the Camp Supply Social Club in presenting spectacular balls. The uninvited called the social elite the "wash tub aristocracy," but the Yuletide dances and the Seventeenth of Ireland Ball became traditional events. Old Cactus skillfully recorded the ejection of an uninvited guest from one such occasion:

> He went to considerable expense to secure a proper outfit that is, white gloves, etc. for the purpose of adorning his handsome person to an irresistible and fascinating status, thereby securing in his own imagination the exclusive attention of the ladies to his fascinating form. But alas! when he entered the ball room one of the committee waited upon him for the purpose of getting a sight

[38] *Dodge City Times* (Sept. 1, 1877).

at his "credentials"—his ticket. Unluckily he did not possess this. He was then politely informed that his presence was not required. After a furtive attempt to bulldoze another one of the committee as to the absolute necessity of his presence in order to give the ball social standing he made for the door in this manner:

"Is this a dagger which I see before me."
(And gave a tremendous roll on the r-r-r in dagger.)
"The handle towards me hand—
Come let me clutch thee,"
(Long strides, three stamps and a tragical snort.)
"I have thee not
(Gives sixteen jumps, interspersed with several of his most bewitching snorts.)
"And yet I see thee still"
(Makes devious punches in the air, three high-falutin snorts and a blur-r)
"Art thou but
a dagger of the mind, a false creation,
proceeding from the heat-oppressed brain.
(This is somewhat difficult for it presupposes a brain. But the close is grand, and so appropriate.)
"There is no such thing;
It is the position which informs thee to mine eyes."[39]

The men at Fort Supply had indeed developed an active social schedule. They had demonstrated that life among buffalo hunters and Indians could not dull aesthetic tastes.

[39] *Ibid.*

Chapter VII

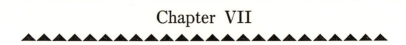

Cattle, Reservations, and Trails
1880–89

THE DECADE of the 1880's opened with serious doubts regarding the continuance of Fort Supply. It had accomplished its main purpose—pacification of the Plains Indians. Colonel Granville O. Haller of the Twenty-third Infantry submitted his semiannual report in September, 1880, commenting that it might be best to close the station. Colonel Haller listed a number of drawbacks to the post. First of all, he explained, its location made its service to the frontier almost negligible. Moreover, the site of the post buildings, in an indefensible low point, make the stockade vulnerable to punishing gunfire from attackers on the higher sand hills if times of stress should return. Haller agreed with Colonel John Davidson, who in May, 1872, had suggested a better site a short distance away. In addition, the post covered too large an area, comprising more than 165 acres. Haller compared the post buildings to "a line of peaked-roofs running through Pennsylvania Avenue, from the U.S. Capitol to the President's Mansion, in Washington, if the shingled roofs were placed in a row."[1]

The post was in such poor repair that it would hardly justify rehabilitation costs. The cottonwood logs had been partly replaced by the Twenty-third Infantry in 1879, but more than twenty thousand logs needed to be replaced. Floors remained a

---

[1] Haller to Inspector General, Dept. of Mo., Sept. 5, 1880, Office of the Inspector General, Letters Received, Records of the War Dept., National Archives, Washington, D.C.

luxury at the post, and "the Officers Quarters seem to harbor snakes."

Still another drawback was the fact that the post had no military reservation. Haller considered a reservation not only proper but necessary. Fort Supply lay within the Cherokee Outlet, and agents of the Cherokee Nation were beginning to lease certain sections of land to cattlemen. Finally, the fort had lost its importance, according to Haller, because the legal state of affairs in Indian Territory did not allow the military to prevent depredations of civilians or Indians on private or government property.[2]

The inspection report of Captain George M. Randall, Twenty-fourth Infantry, in September, 1881, substantiated Haller's remarks.[3] Request for abandonment of Fort Supply was forwarded through the Department of the Missouri, but when it reached the desk of General of the Army Philip Sheridan, the refusal was quick and emphatic. Sheridan, on November 30, 1881, wrote that Fort Supply

> was built under my direction of logs, originally, and has been improved, except for a few years past, so as to have good company quarters, good storehouses and most excellent hospital, but the officers quarters have been neglected by General Pope, who seemed to take a fancy to *Cantonment* about fifty miles down the *Canadian River* which had not a military point about it, and which is now about to be abandoned. It is midway between Supply and Reno and cost something, but will be out in the spring. . . .
>
> It [Fort Supply] has been valuable heretofore strategically and as a supply camp, and is now valuable strategically for the protection of the Indian Territory, the Atlantic and Pacific RR and

[2] *Ibid.*; Haller to AAG, Dept. of Mo., May 12, 1880, Fort Supply, Letters Sent, Vol. 29½.

[3] G. M. Randall to Inspector General, Dept. of Mo., Sept. 1, 1881, Office of the Inspector General, Letters Received.

the cattle trail from Texas. I cannot give my approval to its abandonment.[4]

General Sheridan's intercession gave the fort new life. Defects at the post were remedied. The water system was improved by the installation of windmills and clay pipe. Mail deliveries were increased to six a week. The Fort Supply–Fort Dodge telegraph, begun in September, 1880, but temporarily discontinued, was completed. Fort Supply was destined to remain a fixture in western Indian Territory for another fourteen years.

The decision to continue the post increased the need for a military reservation. Questions of a reserve had first been discussed in 1870, but at that time the department commander, the division commander, and the general of the army had agreed that such action was premature, since the camp was only a temporary one. In March, 1881, Lieutenant Colonel John E. Yard, commanding Fort Supply, reopened the issue by petitioning headquarters for a military reservation. Action on the motion was delayed until the exact status of the lands in the Cherokee Outlet that were subject to reservation for military purposes could be determined.[5]

Fort Supply had been located on lands which two years previously had been granted in treaty to the Cherokee Indians. That agreement, arrived at in 1866, had made several divisions of the land. One provision of the treaty, Article 16, had even authorized the United States to settle friendly tribes in any part of the Outlet, the Cherokee Nation retaining possession until said occupation. The key provision was Article 27, which permitted the federal government to establish one or more military posts or

---

[4] Sheridan endorsement, Nov. 30, 1881, in Report of Inspector General D. B. Sacket, Oct. 22, 1881, Fort Supply, Reservation File, Records of the War Dept., National Archives, Washington, D. C.

[5] "Case of the Military Reservation for Fort Supply, I. T.," Mar. 28, 1881, in *ibid.*

stations in the outlet. It was a matter of interpretation whether or not that provision included a military reservation.[6]

The War Department took the matter under advisement, and under instructions of July 12, 1881, Colonel Joseph H. Potter examined the country surrounding the post with a view to laying out a reservation. On September 23, Potter recommended a reservation of thirty-six square miles with the post flagstaff as the center point. His recommendation was subsequently approved by the department commander.[7]

On May 10, 1882, Township 24 North, Range 22 West, embracing 23,040 acres, was proclaimed the Fort Supply Military Reservation in General Orders, No. 14, Department of Missouri. A subsequent survey established the need for additional timberlands and hayfields, and in January, 1883, the War Department, with the consent of the Indian Bureau, petitioned for an additional tract. Accordingly, the reservation was enlarged under an executive order of January 17, 1883, with the annexation of a portion of Township 25 North, Range 21 West. The addition of this tract of twenty-seven square miles brought the total reservation area to 40,320 acres. The reserve was surveyed by Lieutenant R. H. Hill, the boundaries were forwarded to the Office of the Chief Engineer, and a barbed-wire enclosure was erected.[8]

While legal technicalities were being worked out in western Indian Territory, Forts Dodge and Wallace and the Cantonment were abandoned by the Department of the Missouri, and their garrisons and equipment were transferred to Forts Reno,

[6] Report in K-File, Office of the Quartermaster General, Records of the War Dept., National Archives, Washington, D.C.

[7] J. C. Potter to AAG, Dept. of Mo., Sept. 23, 1881, Fort Supply, Letters Sent, Vol. 30; AAG, Dept. of Mo., to Commanding Officer, Fort Supply, Sept. 29, 1881, Fort Supply, Letters Received, Box 3.

[8] Petition of the War Dept., Jan., 1883, Fort Supply, Reservation File; Potter to Inspector General, Dept. of Mo., Sept. 3, 1884, Office of the Inspector General, Letters Received.

Supply, and Elliott.[9] The peaceable attitude of Indians in the region made the outposts no longer necessary, whereas the Apache wars in Arizona demanded additional troops which only the Southern Plains could spare.

Duty in those years was diversified. Timber thieves were particularly troublesome; Colonel Potter stated that the Cherokee Outlet was "swarming with these marauders." Scouts were frequently dispatched to remove the thieves, but the inability of the military to act on civilians within the Cherokee Outlet limited their effectiveness.[10] Except for an occasional murder or removal of an illegal hunting party, most of the action involved conflicts between Indians and cattlemen.

Beginning in 1866, large herds of Texas cattle streamed north to markets. In the next years nearly six million head of cattle were driven up Indian Territory trails to Kansas cow towns. The Indian country crossed by these north-to-south trails belonged to the Five Civilized Tribes in the east and to the Cheyennes, Arapahoes, Kiowas, and Comanches in the west. In time the cattle trade shifted to the Dodge City and Old Caldwell trails that pierced the Cheyenne and Arapaho Reservation.

Before long cattlemen were not content merely to trespass. Texas herds were frequently allowed to drift across the boundary line; "pilgrim cattle" lingered at length as their trail passed north through lush meadows; and there were some who knowingly kept stock on the reservation in direct violation of the laws.

In terms of acreage the Cheyenne and Arapaho Reservation was certainly large enough for both cattle trails and Indians. Indifference to Indian Bureau rules by drovers, however,

[9] *Cheyenne Transporter* (June 17, 1882) ; AAG, Dept. of Mo., to Commanding Officer, Fort Dodge, June 12, 1882 (copy), AAG, Dept. of Mo., to Commanding Officer, Cantonment, I.T., June 1, 1882, Fort Supply, Letters Received, Box 4; *Annual Report of the Secretary of War for the Year 1882*, 94.

[10] Potter to AAG, Dept. of Mo., Mar. 6, 1883, Fort Supply, Letters Sent, Vol. 31.

sparked trouble. Cattlemen refused to stay on the established trails, preferring to cut indiscriminately across Indian property without respect for herds, fences, or farms.

Under such circumstances it was easy for relations between the parties to deteriorate to a dangerous level. On August 1, 1880, "Doc" Day of Day Brothers Ranch had an encounter with Cheyennes that nearly resulted in bloodshed. Stone Calf and two friends approached the Day herd in friendly fashion and spent the night in camp with the cowboys. In the morning the Indians demanded a steer and, when refused, threatened the cattlemen with guns and stopped the herd. The timely arrival of Amos Chapman ended the confrontation with only harsh words, but the incident had foreboding implications. It was apparent to Captain Charles Wheaton at Cantonment that his greatest problem was to keep "Mr. Day and the cattle men out of the way of the Indians for [the ranchmen] are determined to come and go as they please, and allow none to interfere." Day remained adamant and stated that "no Indian Agent could fix any trail for him to drive cattle on, that he supported the government so he would drive his herd the way that seemed best."[11]

Attempts to put cattlemen off the reservation usually met with deception. When told to move from Cheyenne lands, ranchers demanded a survey to prove that they were not on property rented from Cherokees. Unsophisticated Cheyennes did not understand the ruse but quickly learned that setting fire to the ranges of unfriendly herders ended the argument. Others solicited a tax of one to three head of stock for each herd that passed.[12] Dissatisfaction on the part of Indians and ranchers alike made an immediate settlement vital.

[11] Dodge to Commanding Officer, Fort Elliott, Apr. 27, 1880, C. Wheaton to Miles, July 8, 1880, Wheaton to AAG, Dept. of Mo., Aug. 1, 1880, Cantonment, I.T., Letters Sent, Vol. 18.

[12] R. F. O'Bierne to Miles, Sept. 3, 1881, Charles C. Hood to Miles, May 27, 1882, in *ibid.*; Miles to H. Price, July 20, 1882, *Sen. Exec. Doc. No. 54*, 48 Cong., 1 sess., 72.

Agent John D. Miles proposed a system of leases as the most practical solution. The Department of the Interior rejected the proposal and then appealed to the War Department to curtail the infringement. Troops from Fort Reno made a token attempt, but then the War Department desisted, claiming it was an impossible task, and encouraged adoption of Miles's proposal.[13]

When the pressure of cattlemen on one side and short rations on the other became too great, Miles decided to proceed as he thought best and consult his superiors later. Accordingly, a council of chiefs met and concluded a leasing arrangement with seven cattlemen on January 8, 1883. The grant totaled nearly three million acres, ran for ten years, and brought approximately sixty thousand dollars a year to the Cheyennes and Arapahoes.[14]

Those ranchmen not included in the exclusive set of leases were understandably angry. B. H. Campbell protested to the Department of the Interior, but his claim went unheeded. The Dickey brothers, whose ranch straddled both the Cheyenne and Arapaho Reservation and the Cherokee Outlet, also demurred when they were ordered to move from the leased property.

Secretary of the Interior Henry M. Teller dictated department policy in the "Fenlon letter" of April 25, 1883. In substance Teller said that the department would not recognize the leases but "would endeavor to see to it that parties having no agreement are not allowed to interfere with those who have."[15] E. E. Dale concluded that the policy was absurd:

> It invited ranchmen to enter the Indian Territory and intrigue with savage tribesmen. It placed a premium upon bribery and

[13] Miles to Price, July 20, 1882, Randall to Pope, July 20, 1882, H. M. Teller to Secretary of War, Aug. 5, 1882, *Sen. Exec. Doc. No. 54*, 48 Cong., 1 sess., 72, 74–80; *Cheyenne Transporter* (Aug. 10, 1882).

[14] Miles to Price, Jan. 13, 15, 1883, *Sen. Exec. Doc. No. 54*, 48 Cong., 1 sess., 92–93; *Sen. Exec. Doc. No. 17*, 48 Cong., 2 sess., 21–29.

[15] Miles to Price, Apr. 6, 1883, Dickey Brothers to Price, July 30, 1883, Price to Miles, Aug. 7, 1883, Teller to E. Fenlon, Apr. 25, 1883, *Sen. Exec. Doc. No. 54*, 48 Cong., 1 sess., 89–92, 96–99, 110–12.

corruption and made of every agency employee a person to be flattered, cajoled, and, if possible, bribed by men with large investments at stake. Also, it could not be enforced. Men who had no agreements approved by the agent, but who were friendly with certain small bands of Indians, refused to remove, and their Indian friends, who were receiving more money from these ranchmen than their share of the lease money would amount to, refused to ratify the agreements made by their chiefs, and cut the fences and killed the cattle of the "approved lessees." The latter appealed to the agent for protection, demanding that men without leases be excluded; but the War Department, when called upon for troops, refused to furnish on the ground that leases had not been approved by the Department of the Interior.[16]

Nonleasing cattlemen banded together in an effort to break the contract. Encouraged by these men, six influential Cheyennes, including Stone Calf and Little Robe, in company with Amos Chapman and William Wells journeyed to Fort Supply to outline their grievances. Colonel Potter at first refused to enter into the squabble but at last heard the Indians on July 14. The Cheyennes insisted that Agent Miles had forced them to ratify the leases against their real wishes. Potter tended to believe the Indians, but Agent Miles demanded that they return to the agency, branding the chiefs tools of the cattlemen and Amos Chapman an unprincipled and irresponsible speaker for vested interests.[17] The Indians did return to the agency, and the Dickey brothers and others continued to exploit their influence over the Indians for their own purposes.

The lessees, now organized as the Cheyenne-Arapaho Live Stock Association, were dismayed to find their legal claims chal-

[16] "History of the Ranch Cattle Industry in Oklahoma," *Annual Report of the American Historical Association* (1920), 315.

[17] Potter to Miles, Potter to AAG, Dept. of Mo., July 18, 1883, Fort Supply, Letters Sent, Vol. 31; Miles to Potter, July 13, 16, 1883, *Sen. Exec. Doc. No. 54,* 48 Cong., 1 sess., 114–15; D. B. Dyer to Price, May 20, 1884, *Sen. Exec. Doc. No. 16,* 48 Cong., 2 sess., 11.

lenged by other tribes, in addition to the lessors, and by the whites. Kiowas stole cattle, cut fences, and exacted tolls on Cheyenne and Arapaho lands under the pretext that the stock was actually trespassing on the Kiowa-Comanche Reservation. Protests by the association were shifted from one federal department to another. Finally, in April, 1884, the secretary of the interior issued a statement that his department would offer no protection to lessees while they were on Indian lands.[18]

Disorder increased, and although Agent D. B. Dyer, who replaced Miles in April, 1884, appealed for troops six times, his requests were disregarded. Cheyenne and Arapaho bands, encouraged by cattlemen without leases, became increasingly hostile. In one instance E. M. Horton and three men were stopped by a small party of Cheyennes, who demanded ponies as toll for crossing their lands. Horton refused, and when Running Buffalo drew a gun, Horton shot him from his pony. When Running Buffalo tried to regain his feet, Horton coolly killed him. Only the arrival of troops from Fort Reno saved the whites from the enraged warriors. The *Cheyenne Transporter* deemed it the "most serious Indian affair for some time in the area."[19]

Little Robe's band, undaunted, continued bribery tactics on the Old Caldwell Trail throughout the summer. In August, Agent Dyer estimated the damage to cattlemen in the preceding year at not less than $100,000. When that loss was added to the more than $76,000 annual rent paid to the Cheyenne and Arapaho tribes, Dyer concluded that "the cattle business had other than bright sides." Even into December, 1884, Dyer knew of scarcely a week that passed "that does not bring notices of depredations, intimidations, etc."[20]

[18] E. E. Dale, "Ranching on the Cheyenne-Arapaho Reservation, 1880–85," *Chronicles of Oklahoma,* Vol. VI (Mar., 1928), 52–53; Teller to Robert T. Lincoln, Apr. 22, 1884, *Sen. Exec. Doc. No. 17,* 48 Cong., 2 sess., 11.

[19] (May 10, 1884).

[20] By this time additional leases brought the total revenue to about $76,000

Much the same conduct in the spring of 1885 made it apparent that Cheyenne opposition had not diminished over the winter. The shooting of Running Buffalo by Horton was serious, but the disappearance of Sitting Medicine, Little Robe's son, in late May, 1885, was incendiary to the Cheyennes.[21]

Rumors of a general outbreak resulted in orders for stronger measures against the Indians. Colorado and Kansas officials pleaded with government offices for protection, and state troops were put on a stand-by basis. Under such pressures Secretary of War William C. Endicott ordered General C. C. Augur to deploy those military forces at his command in a "prevent defense" against an Indian outburst. Some thirty-five hundred troops were quickly gathered as reinforcements for Fort Supply and Fort Reno, where they would take positions sealing the northern line of Indian Territory.

President Grover Cleveland was aware of the danger of a new Indian war and on July 10, 1885, ordered General Sheridan to meet with General Nelson A. Miles, now commanding officer of the Department of the Missouri, and with him visit the Cheyenne and Arapaho Reservation to examine the situation. The generals reached Fort Reno on July 15 and immediately initiated joint councils with the Cheyennes.[22]

After a series of interviews with the Indians, Agent Dyer, and two of the lessees, Sheridan made his recommendations to the President in a report of July 24. The Cheyenne tribe, he was certain, no longer approved the system of leases, although the agency employees favored them. Sheridan advocated rescinding

per year for some 4,000,000 leased acres. Dyer to Price, May 20, Dec. 24, 1884, *Sen. Exec. Doc. No. 16*, 48 Cong., 2 sess., 10, 21, 26.

[21] Sitting Medicine's body was found by Indian scouts twelve miles from Fort Supply on July 28, 1885. He had been shot in the back of the head. Potter to Sheridan, July 28, 1885, Fort Supply, Letters Sent, Vol. 34.

[22] Wright, "Fort Reno," *loc. cit.*, 100–103; *House Exec. Doc. No. 1*, 41 Cong., 2 Sess., 134.

the leases, removing unauthorized persons from the reservation, and replacing the civilian agent with an experienced army officer.

President Cleveland, however, acted on preliminary reports and one day before Sheridan wrote his report issued a proclamation voiding all leases on the Cheyenne and Arapaho Reservation. All persons and property were ordered to move within forty days. At the same time Captain Jesse M. Lee was ordered to the agency to relieve Agent Dyer. Two weeks later President Cleveland issued another proclamation, this time requiring the removal of all wire fences from Indian lands.[23]

Department Commander Miles contributed to the favorable government measures when he enlisted 130 of the most active young Cheyennes as scouts, 50 of whom were stationed with their families at Fort Supply.[24]

Troops from Fort Supply and Fort Reno shared the duty of visiting the members of the Cheyenne-Arapaho Live Stock Association to determine their progress in leaving the reservation. Colonel Potter, temporarily stationed at Cantonment to direct the removal of the estimated 210,000 head of cattle, called on Major Louis H. Carpenter and the Fifth Cavalry at Fort Supply to report on the three ranches south of the post.

Lieutenant E. P. Andrews, with a fourteen-man detachment, left Fort Supply on August 28. On the following day he reached the ranch of the Cheyenne and Arapaho Cattle Company, managed by Edward Fenlon. The personnel of the ranch, which covered some 570,000 acres on and around Commission Creek, had already abandoned or destroyed their buildings on Quartermaster Creek and were in the process of moving the headquar-

23 Sheridan Report, July 24, 1885, *Annual Report of the Secretary of War for the Year 1885*, 65–71; Presidential Proclamation, July 23, 1885 (copy), Fort Supply, Letters Received, Box 5; Kappler, *Indian Affairs*, I, 938–39.

24 *Report of the Secretary of War, 1885*, 133; Potter to J. E. Lee, Aug. 7, 1885, Fort Supply, Letters Sent, Vol. 34; Post Returns, Fort Supply, July, 1885.

ters ranch to Texas. Some forty-two hundred cattle had already started from the reservation, three thousand more were scheduled to start in a few days, and the remaining sixty-five hundred head would be driven out in herds of two thousand as fast as they could be gathered. Even the doubled work force, however, could not remove all the cattle by the September 4, 1885, deadline set by the executive proclamation, nor could they tear down the fences or dismantle the ranch equipment by that time. Lieutenant Andrews, satisfied that Fenlon was making every effort to carry out the proclamation, moved south to the next ranch.

Striking out across country, the detachment reached the roundup camp of the Taurus Cattle Company, directed by part owner A. S. C. Forbes. A crew three times normal size had driven forty-eight hundred head off the land, but there still remained forty-five hundred head. September 25 was considered the earliest possible completion date, and that did not include the time needed to remove ranch buildings and take down fences. Again Andrews was convinced that the Forbes outfit was doing its best to comply with the orders.

The Standard Cattle Company, managed by Richard Allen, was fortunate in having a favorable location for removal, a sixty-mile border on the Texas and Greer county lines. The herds were quickly driven from the leased pastures. About five thousand head had departed by August 30, but the remaining thirteen thousand could not be off the reservation by September 4. Ranch buildings were being moved one mile across the line to Texas, but it was estimated that it would take another six weeks' work to remove the fences. Again it appeared that the company was making an energetic attempt to comply with the proclamation, and Andrews could do no more.[25]

Since it was obvious that even the outfits closest to Texas

[25] E. P. Andrews to Post Adjutant, Fort Supply, Aug. 29, 31, Sept. 1, 3, 1885, Fort Supply, Letters Received, Box 5; L. H. Carpenter to AAG, Dept. of Mo., Sept. 4, 9, 1885, Fort Supply, Letters Sent, Vol. 34.

could not get all their stock off the Cheyenne and Arapaho Reservation by September 4, the deadline was extended to December. By that time all but one of the ranches had moved, and the process was carried out in a peaceful and organized manner. Only one cowman claimed Indian harassment during the removal period. J. V. Andrews asserted, in a letter of October 9, 1885, that the Cheyennes were killing his cattle, stealing his horses, and burning the grass as he moved his herds to newly leased ranges in the Cherokee Outlet. Colonel Potter investigated these reports at length and in January, 1886, determined that Andrews' allegations were not proved. Little Robe and his band did hold Andrews responsible for the death of Sitting Medicine, and they would have been prime suspects for harassment, but only one dead cow could be found, and that would hardly be retribution in Indian eyes.[26]

During the spring and summer of 1886 scouting parties from Forts Supply, Elliott, Sill, and Reno were frequently on duty expelling intruders, escorting cattle herds on the established trails, removing unauthorized cattle from the Indian reservations, and quelling trouble between cattlemen and Indians. Troops from Fort Supply operated in both the Cherokee Outlet and the Cheyenne and Arapaho Reservation.

Lieutenant John J. Brereton, Twenty-fourth Infantry, led several patrols during February and March, 1886, searching for unauthorized cattle on the Cheyenne and Arapaho Reservation. After a comprehensive search the lieutenant reported that about two thousand head of cattle belonging to various outfits had drifted from the Cherokee Outlet and were presently on Cheyenne and Arapaho lands. For the time being the stock was left alone, since burned-over ranges made it impossible to move them north.[27]

[26] Potter to Lee, Nov. 12, 1885, Potter to AAG, Dept. of Mo., Jan. 20, 1886, Fort Supply, Letters Sent, Vol. 35.

[27] Post Returns, Fort Supply, Feb., 1886; John J. Brereton to Potter, Mar. 26,

This activity was only a preview of the struggle in which Fort Supply would later take part when unauthorized herds were expelled from the Cherokee Outlet. For the time being, post forces were not as concerned about drift cattle as they were about wandering outfits on the Dodge City Trail and the Old Caldwell Trail, both of which crossed western Indian Territory.

The Dodge City Trail, also called the Western Cattle Trail,[28] was first used about 1876. It began near Bandera, Texas, ran north past Fort Griffin, and crossed the Red River into Indian Territory at Doan's Store. From there the trail passed through Greer County, crossed the North Fork of the Red River, and entered the Wichita Mountains between Soldier Mountain and Tepee Mountain. Passing east of Gyp Spring, the trail went north and then crossed the Washita, Canadian, and Cimarron rivers. After crossing the Cimarron, most herds were trailed on to Dodge City, although others were shifted eastward to follow the Dodge–Supply road. Millions of cattle and horses passed over the Dodge City Trail until it ceased to be used in 1889. The largest number of animals—over 300,000 head—moved northward in 1881.[29]

The Old Caldwell Trail, or Chisholm Trail, was established in 1868. It began near the southern tip of Texas, went through San Antonio, Austin, and Fort Worth, and entered Indian Territory at Red River Station. Heading due north, the trail crossed the Washita at Elm Springs and split at the Canadian, one part skirting Fort Reno, the other bearing farther east, up the valley of Kingfisher Creek. The trails rejoined near the Cimarron and

[1886], Fort Supply, Letters Received, Box 6; Potter to Lee, Apr. 21, 1886, in *ibid.*

[28] Other names for the Dodge City Trail were the Old Texas Trail, the Abilene and Fort Dodge Trail, and the Fort Griffin–Dodge Trail.

[29] A. L. Turner to J. Evetts Haley, July 2, 1926, Memoirs of E. A. Upfold as told to Robert Linder, June 30, 1939, C. F. Doan to J. Evetts Haley, Oct. 8, 1926, Division of Manuscripts Collection of the Panhandle-Plains Historical Society, Canyon, Texas.

continued through the Cherokee Outlet, ending at Caldwell, Kansas.[30]

In May, 1886, the Indians resumed their harassment of northbound herds through the reservation, and Fort Supply was ordered to detach a portion of its garrison to keep the trails open.[31] Colonel John E. Yard, commanding Fort Supply after Colonel Potter was attached to the Department of the Missouri, ordered Lieutenant C. H. Walls and a troop of the Fifth Cavalry to move south on the Dodge City Trail as far as the Washita River and from that vantage point observe all established cattle trails on the Cheyenne and Arapaho Reservation to see that they were kept clear.

Lieutenant Walls and fifteen enlisted men proceeded south on the Dodge City Trail to the point where it passed seven miles west of Fort Supply. The troopers met many herds, and each outfit complained of having lost two head of cattle as toll to Indians at the Washita. Before Walls could reach the Washita, word was received that a troop of cavalry from Fort Reno had arrived on the scene and that the tolls had ceased. The lieutenant then moved north on the Canadian to the point where the Old Caldwell Trail crossed the Fort Supply–Cantonment road. Finding the area around Cantonment patrolled by a detachment under Lieutenant E. P. Andrews, with a co-operating party of Indian scouts at Elm Creek, Walls returned to Fort Supply. With the Washita crossing under the control of troops from Reno and the Old Caldwell Trail protected by Cantonment and Elm Springs, Lieutenant Walls concluded that the established cattle trails through the Cheyenne and Arapaho Reservation were properly guarded.[32]

[30] H. S. Tennant, "The Texas Cattle Trails," *Chronicles of Oklahoma*, Vol. XIV (Mar., 1936), 86–122.

[31] AAG, Dept. of Mo., to Commanding Officer, Fort Supply, June 4, 1886, Dept. of Mo., Letters Sent, Vol. 125.

[32] Post Adjutant, Fort Supply, to C. H. Walls, June 4, 1886, Fort Supply,

Meanwhile, on June 5, Captain John B. Babcock had left Fort Supply under orders to check the Old Caldwell Trail as it passed west of Cantonment. Before much could be accomplished, however, a message of June 8 informed him that the company of the Fifth Cavalry under Lieutenant Andrews would take station for the summer at Cantonment and that he was to return to the post. But while camped at Deep Creek on the evening of the ninth, telegraphed orders summoned Babcock to inspect the Grimes cattle herd for stolen Indian ponies. Babcock moved to Eagle Chief Pool but reported that the herd had already passed him.[33] Thereupon, at midnight on June 12, Major Carpenter sent Lieutenant George W. Read and fifteen men of the Fifth Cavalry to Buffalo Creek Ranch to head off the Grimes herd and seize all Indian ponies and government cattle found in it.

Lieutenant Read overtook the herd at 11:00 A.M. on June 13 about six miles west of Grimes's ranch on the Cimarron River. A careful inspection was made of the fifty ponies with the herd, but only three were of questionable origin. The cattle herd of fifteen hundred head was also inspected, but no government brands were found. On June 19 the three ponies cut out by the Indian scouts were taken to Fort Supply, where a hearing determined the rightful owners.[34]

Persistent harassment by Indians in the early spring of 1886 offered a bleak preview of continued animosity. General Sheridan, therefore, upon the request of the Department of the Interior, directed the Department of the Missouri to station one

Letters Sent, Vol. 36; Walls to Post Adjutant, Fort Supply, June 13, 1886, Fort Supply, Letters Received, Box 6.

[33] Post Adjutant, Fort Supply, to John B. Babcock, June 5, 1886, Carpenter to Babcock, June 9, 1886, Carpenter to AAG, Dept. of Mo., June 10, 1886, Fort Supply, Letters Sent, Vol. 36; Babcock to Post Adjutant, Fort Supply, June 10, 15, 1886, Fort Supply, Letters Received, Box 6.

[34] Post Adjutant, Fort Supply, to G. W. Read, June 12, 1886, Fort Supply, Letters Sent, Vol. 36; Read to Post Adjutant, Fort Supply, June 13, 18, 19, 1886, Fort Supply, Letters Received, Box 6.

company of cavalry at Cantonment on the North Fork of the Canadian, with a backup detachment of Indian scouts at Elm Creek, for the duration of the summer. The objects of the move were (1) to arrest and expel from the reservation every unauthorized person, (2) to protect the Indians against molestation, (3) to patrol the northwestern frontier of the reservation, preventing the location of outsiders, (4) to remove all unauthorized cattle grazing on the reservation, (5) to supervise the northern half of the cattle trail, confining such herds to the trail, and (6) in general to promote peace and good order.[35]

On June 7, 1886, Lieutenant Andrews and several Indian scouts left Fort Supply for Cantonment in compliance with those orders. In the following weeks the troops diligently patrolled the northern boundary of the Cherokee Outlet and the Canadian River but failed to locate intruders or unauthorized cattle or learn of any depredations. Toward the end of July, Andrews was alerted to possible trouble with several bands of Indians in the region of Reno, Cantonment, and Supply, said to be killing steers pasturing on the Cherokee Outlet. Officers at Fort Supply immediately authorized the Cantonment detail to restrict the unguarded Cherokee Outlet area near the Canadian River. In addition, on August 6, Lieutenant William Black marched from Fort Supply, following the Canadian to Persimmon Creek, and sending small units into the sand hills and beyond.[36]

No depredations were observed by Lieutenant Black or Lieutenant Andrews, but Day Brothers' Turkey Track Ranch riders insisted that they had lost one hundred head of cattle to the Indians in the preceding six months. The Dickey brothers and J. V. Andrews complained of similar losses. Under the circum-

[35] AAG, Div. of Mo., to Commanding Officer, Dept. of Mo., June 4, 1886 (copy), Fort Supply, Letters Received, Box 6.

[36] AAG, Dept. of Mo., to Commanding Officer, Fort Supply, July 28, 1886, in *ibid.*; Post Adjutant, Fort Supply, to Andrews, Aug. 6, 1886, Fort Supply, Letters Sent, Vol. 36.

stances the best that could be done was to restrict Indian travel through the Outlet by use of passes and to continue the patrols. Andrews soon reported, "Everything has been quiet since the Troops have been here, and the Indians and cattlemen seem satisfied." In the next month, before the troops were released on September 15, three herds were escorted through the reservation, and only one Indian was arrested for horse stealing.[37]

A combination of many factors, including the removal of herds from the Cheyenne and Arapaho Reservation, the severe winters and dry summers, the overstocked ranges, and the invasion of portions of the cattle domain by homesteaders, caused a decline in the range-cattle industry.[38] The depression began in 1886 and was only one of several influences to link Fort Supply more closely with ranching in western Indian country.

The Old Caldwell Trail bore the largest cattle traffic in Indian Territory until 1883, when the Cherokee Strip Live Stock Association gave public notice that fences would close that portion of the trail passing over leased lands. Some outfits continued to pick their way across the Outlet, but most herds turned west to the Dodge City Trail.[39]

A meeting of cowmen from the associations in southern and northern Texas, Kansas, and Wyoming was held in Dallas in May, 1885, and several recommendations were made for solving the problems of trails, leases, and fences. Because of the increased use of barbed wire in Texas, the only safe and practical trail out of southern Texas was the one to Wichita Falls. It was suggested that herds then join the Dodge City Trail and cross Red River at Doan's Store, continuing north to the Washita. At

---

[37] Andrews to AAG, Dept. of Mo., Aug. 13, 1886 (copy), AAG, Dept. of Mo., to Commanding Officer, Fort Supply, Aug. 13, 1886, William Black to Post Adjutant, Fort Supply, Aug. 14, 1886, Fort Supply, Letters Received, Box 6.

[38] E. E. Dale, *The Range Cattle Industry*, 158.

[39] *Cheyenne Transporter* (May 28, 1883); Wayne Gard, *The Chisholm Trail*, 256–58.

that crossing herds heading for market would cut east to the Old Caldwell Trail, while stock for northern pastures would keep to the Dodge City Trail. At a point west of Fort Supply herds were encouraged to branch west to the Palo Duro, thence westerly to Coldwater and Buffalo Springs, and finally across the Cimarron into Colorado.[40]

Ranchers did not necessarily abide by these guidelines, but the use of the Washita as a separation point for herds from southern Texas became general. Many herds bound for market did not shift to the Old Caldwell Trail but simply continued up the Dodge City Trail to the Santa Fe Railroad. Those bound for the north country also used the Dodge City Trail, which was called the Colorado Trail north of the Washita. Other ranchers preferred connecting with the Jones-Plummer Trail, which passed fifty miles west of Fort Supply on a direct line over the old Dodge–Elliott road.[41]

With the cattle business increasingly dependent upon the Dodge City Trail, troops from Fort Supply correspondingly devoted more men to assuring proper conduct on the part of whites and Indians on the trail. From mid-May to early September the single most important duty of the post was service on the cattle trails. The reduced volume of herds that survived the elements of 1886 did not diminish the necessity to guard the established trails.

Troops from Fort Supply worked closely with the men at Fort Reno and Fort Elliott in keeping trail herds on the straight and narrow. In the spring of 1887 signs were posted at the Washita indicating the choice of trails for northbound herds.[42]

[40] *Kansas Cowboy* (May 30, 1885).

[41] Tennant, "Texas Cattle Trails," *loc. cit.*, 98; Bliss to AAG, Dept. of Mo., Jan. 2, May 29, 1887, Fort Supply, Letters Sent, Vol. 37; AAG, Dept. of Mo., to Commanding Officer, Fort Supply, Aug. 13, 1886, Fort Supply, Letters Received, Box 6.

[42] Bliss to AAG, Dept. of Mo., May 23, 1887, Fort Supply, Letters Sent, Vol. 37. Herds could (1) continue on the Dodge City Trail to (a) Dodge City or (b)

To help cattlemen make the correct choice, keep them on the trails, and prevent Indian intrusions, Fort Supply kept a small detachment at that point during the summer. Ordinarily a sergeant, ten privates, and half a dozen or so Indian scouts held the post for twenty-day periods before being relieved.

Such preparations had few rewards. As early as May, Indian authorities at Cantonment and Darlington informed Colonel Zenas R. Bliss at Fort Supply that cattlemen had reverted to the practice of cutting across Indian farms. In addition, the Indians, probably as much for retaliation as for simple larceny, were again extorting cattle from the drovers. A ninety-man force was requested from Fort Supply to keep herds on the trail and prevent Indian interference. Colonel Bliss was concerned but could spare only Lieutenant John Little with ten troopers and ten Indian scouts for a twenty-day station at Cantonment. Other detachments from Fort Supply relieved Lieutenant Little, and eventually troops from Fort Elliott took station at the Washita.[43]

Indian resentments persisted, and on June 24, Colonel Bliss directed the Cantonment detail to relocate the separation point of the Caldwell- and Dodge-bound cattle. The new division point at the Canadian crossing allowed herds to parallel Deep Creek before intersecting the North Canadian crossing of the Caldwell Trail. In this manner the heaviest concentration of Cheyenne farms—which had been deliberately trampled by herds on the Caldwell Trail south of the North Canadian—were protected. Amos Chapman directed the Cantonment detail in laying out the new route, appropriately called the Deep Creek Trail. Colonel Bliss described the changed system to his superior as follows:

> The main [Dodge City] trail crosses the Washita and South
> branch off for Colorado, or (2) they could shift to the Old Caldwell Trail for
> market at Caldwell, Kansas.

[43] Bliss to AAG, Dept. of Mo., May 21, 1887, Post Adjutant, Fort Supply, to W. E. Hawkins, June 20, 1887, in *ibid.*

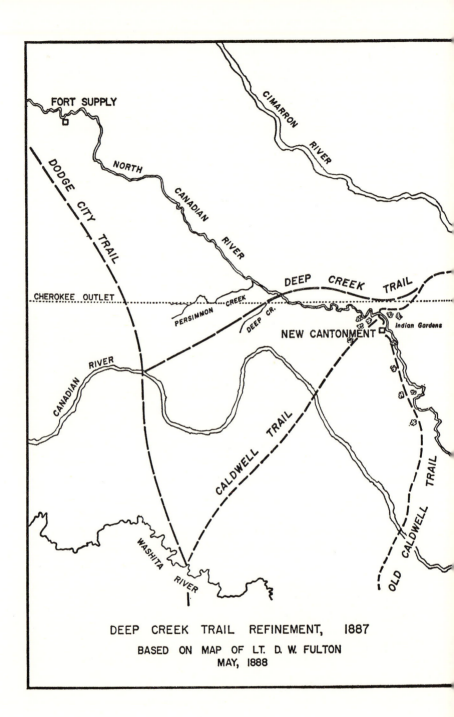

DEEP CREEK TRAIL REFINEMENT, 1887
BASED ON MAP OF LT. D. W. FULTON
MAY, 1888

Canadian near Deep Creek. The Colorado [branch of the Dodge City] Trail separates and goes to the west of Supply. The Caldwell Trail goes along Deep Creek and crosses North Fork of Canadian near mouth of Deep Creek and thence down North Fork to Sheridan's Roost where it comes into the old trail.[44]

Lieutenant Little was immediately posted to the Washita, where he directed oncoming herds north to the Canadian before they separated for their final destination. The detail from Fort Elliott proved particularly ineffective and was withdrawn, perhaps because the men, from a station more than one hundred miles on the west, were as unfamiliar with the new route as were the drovers. For the remainder of the season Fort Supply furnished escorts to trail herds from the Washita to the Canadian, while other Supply detachments continued the escort along Deep Creek Trail, frequently extending the service to the Cimarron.[45]

Deep Creek Trail proved to be a valuable link in the Indian Territory cattle-trail network, and the 1887 season was peaceful. Cattlemen who had once evaded the troops soon came to favor the presence of escorts, for they saved annoyance and loss as the herds passed through Indian lands. Some cattle companies even made a practice of writing ahead for escorts.

The 1888 drive was expected to operate on a modified plan of the preceding year. Fort Sill troops would pick up Texas herds at the Red River and lead them directly to the Washita, where a Fort Elliott detachment had jurisdiction. Proceeding over a now-worn trail, the herd would again be transferred, this time to a Fort Supply detail at the Canadian. Following precedent, the herds could proceed west on the Dodge City Trail or east on the Deep Creek Trail cutoff to the Old Caldwell Trail.[46]

Accordingly, on April 12, Sergeant John O'Toole and a de-

44 Bliss to AAG, Dept. of Mo., July 17, 1887, in *ibid.*

45 Bliss to Commanding Officer, Fort Elliott, July 1, 15, 1887, Bliss to AAG, Dept. of Mo., Aug. 30, 1887, in *ibid.*

46 Bliss to AAG, Dept. of Mo., Apr. 4, 1888, Fort Supply, Letters Sent, Vol. 38.

tachment of the Fifth Cavalry from Fort Supply were ordered to station themselves at the Canadian and from there escort herds to the North Canadian by way of the Deep Creek Trail. A week later it was reported that during the winter a fence had been built across the Deep Creek Trail where it crossed the Cherokee Outlet lease of William Lazarus.[47] Amos Chapman investigated and confirmed the report. Temporarily the Deep Creek Trail was closed.

For the time being, three herds, numbering seventy-three hundred head, were allowed to separate for Dodge City or Caldwell at Dead Man Creek, ten miles north of the Washita. Under emergency circumstances that portion of the Old Caldwell Trail between Dead Man Creek and the North Canadian was reinstated. Lieutenant David W. Fulton gathered the detachment at the Canadian crossing on May 4 and moved to the new headquarters, where they divided into parties, some to escort herds and others to signal oncoming outfits.[48]

The Cheyennes did not approve of this new maneuver by the military, for once again Texas herds were gathering in their stock and trampling their farms. At first there were only murmurs of resentment, but in time several influential Cheyennes near Cantonment were threatening trouble unless another solution was found.[49]

[47] William Lazarus of Sherman, Texas, leased his range in the Outlet from the Cherokee Nation, and others had no authority to trespass on his property. Post Adjutant, Fort Supply, to John O'Toole, Apr. 20, 1888, in *ibid.*

[48] Bliss to AAG, Dept. of Mo., May 1, 1888, Bliss to David W. Fulton, May 1, 3, 1888, in *ibid.*; AAG, Dept. of Mo., to Commanding Officer, Fort Elliott, May 2, 1888, Dept. of Mo., Letters Sent, Vol. 129; Fulton to Post Adjutant, Fort Supply, May 26, 1888, Fort Supply, Letters Received, Box 7.

[49] *Ibid.*; Fulton to Post Adjutant, Fort Supply, May 3, 8, 11, 12, 13, 15, 1888, Fort Supply, Letters Received, Box 7; Bliss to AAG, Dept. of Mo., May 12, 13, 1888, Fort Supply, Letters Sent, Vol. 39. In an effort to lift the complications created by the closing of the Deep Creek Trail, the agency informally suggested a new trail to run north and east of Cantonment on the lands of the Arapahoes, under the supposition that they were more peaceful than the Cheyennes and

In response, on May 15, Lieutenant Lester W. Cornish and a detail of the Fifth Cavalry reinforced the men on trail duty. Before relieving Lieutenant Fulton, however, Cornish was under post orders to investigate carefully the conflict involved in conducting trail herds.[50]

The lieutenant began his inquiry by following the Deep Creek Trail through the Lazarus pasture. He then considered the possibility of a trail passing on the outside—the south side—of the fence. The idea appeared encouraging, but not one of the three North Canadian entrances to the Old Caldwell Trail was feasible. After serious consideration Cornish concluded that, even though the Deep Creek Trail passed through twenty-six miles of the Lazarus lands, it was an indispensable cattle route to Caldwell.[51]

Upon receipt of this information, Colonel Bliss proposed to the adjutant general of the Department of the Missouri that permission should be sought from the Department of the Interior or the Department of War to reopen Deep Creek Trail through the Lazarus lease.[52] In the interest of justice to the Indians, Colonel Bliss asked for immediate action.

Before word on Bliss's proposal could be received, the Twenty-fourth Infantry, which had been stationed at Fort Supply since December, 1880, was transferred to New Mexico Territory and was replaced by the Thirteenth Infantry. The combined garrison

would not complain if they understood that the trail was laid out by the agent and the military authorities. No action was taken.

[50] Post Adjutant, Fort Supply, to Lester W. Cornish, May 15, 1888, Fort Supply, Letters Sent, Vol. 39.

[51] Lieutenant Cornish further recommended that the Deep Creek Trail, once through the Lazarus pasture, keep to the mouth of the Deep Creek, turn north to the Cimarron, and there rejoin the Old Caldwell Trail. This was a small refinement of the Deep Creek Trail of 1887 which rejoined the Old Caldwell Trail near the North Canadian. The suggestion was not approved. Cornish to Post Adjutant, Fort Supply, May 24, 1888, Fort Supply, Letters Received, Box 7.

[52] Bliss to AAG, Dept. of Mo., May 28, 1888, Fort Supply, Letters Sent, Vol. 39.

of the Thirteenth Infantry and the Fifth Cavalry, which had been stationed at Fort Supply since July, 1885, numbered about three hundred men and officers for the rest of the summer.[53]

On June 23, the Department of the Missouri, with the consent of the Interior Department, directed the Indian inspector at the Ponca Agency to proceed along Deep Creek Trail and open it for the passage of cattle. Faced with higher authority than his Cherokee lease, Lazarus stood aside, and the trail that had brought peace to the ranchers and the Indians in 1887 was reopened.[54]

Deep Creek Trail continued to serve ranchmen for several more years. In the trail drives of 1889, Fort Elliott and Fort Sill assumed responsibility for conducting herds to Deep Creek, where Fort Supply detachments took over, and there were only a few unpleasant experiences. The abandonment of Fort Elliott in 1890 forced Fort Supply to assume a larger share of the cattle-escort details until the Cheyenne and Arapaho Reservation lands were opened to settlement in 1892. After April 23, 1892, Fort Sill troops accompanied all herds on established trails through the former Cheyenne and Arapaho Reservation, and Fort Supply details then escorted the herds through the Cherokee Outlet.[55]

In the decade of the 1880's several new trails were opened, linking Fort Supply in a vast frontier transportation and communication network. The north-south road to Dodge City, the Dodge–Supply road, and the road from Fort Supply southwest to Fort Elliott remained well traveled and in good repair. In the

[53] Headquarters, Field Staff, Band, and Companies B, H, and D of the Thirteenth Infantry left Fort Wingate, New Mexico Territory, at 5:00 P.M., June 1, 1888, and marched three miles to the railroad which transported them to Woodward. A march of fifteen miles brought the regiment to Fort Supply on June 4. Post Returns, Fort Supply, June, 1888.

[54] AAG, Dept. of Mo., to Commanding Officer, Fort Supply, June 23, 1888, Fort Supply, Letters Received, Box 7.

[55] AAG, Dept. of Mo., to Commanding Officer, Fort Sill, Apr. 23, 1892 (copy), Fort Supply, Letters Received, Box 9.

spring and summer of 1885, Fort Supply troops laid a new road northwest to New Kiowa, Kansas, and the Southern Kansas Railroad. In addition, because Fort Supply stationed troopers at Cantonment in the spring and summer of 1886 to 1889, the seventy-mile southeastern Cantonment–Supply road was reopened.

By 1887 telegraphic communication included connection with Dodge City, Fort Elliott, Cantonment, Fort Reno, and Fort Sill. In 1886 the Southern Kansas Railroad arrived at New Kiowa, thus cutting twenty miles off the earlier supply route from Dodge to Supply. In June, 1887, the same railroad line reached Woodward, about sixteen miles south of the post. Ashland, Kansas—with a population of about one thousand in 1887—fifty miles north on the Dodge–Supply road, was now the closest settlement to Fort Supply.

In spite of its cattle-escort responsibilities Fort Supply was not too busy to lend a hand in opening the Oklahoma lands. Troops from Fort Sill and Fort Reno had patrolled those lands for many months, but as the time for the April 22, 1889, opening neared, fears were entertained for the peace of the country, and additional troops were gathered. Fort Elliott and Fort Supply each furnished several companies of the Thirteenth Infantry, while Forts Reno, Sill, and Leavenworth offered all available cavalry troops. Companies B and H of the Thirteenth Infantry, an aggregate of eighty-two men and officers, left Fort Supply on April 17 and from their stations in Guthrie and Kingfisher helped supervise the run into the Unassigned Lands. Other detachments from Fort Supply patrolled the established highways, military roads, and cattle trails, aiding the homeseekers as they moved through the Cherokee Outlet to the northern border of the Oklahoma lands.[56]

[56] *House Exec. Doc. No. 1*, 51 Cong., 1 sess., 163–64; AAG, Dept. of Mo., to Commanding Officer, Fort Supply, Apr. 13, 1889, Dept. of Mo., Letters Sent, Vol. 131.

Chapter VIII

Cattle, the Outlet, and Leases
1880–92

THE cattlemen of the 1880's were as much interested in grazing rights in the Cherokee Outlet as they were in those in the Cheyenne and Arapaho Reservation, but unusual circumstances affected their entrance to the Outlet. In 1828 the Cherokee Indians had left their lands in Arkansas for a new grant of seven million acres in northeastern Indian Territory and an outlet one degree in width extending west from their reservation as far as the western boundary of the United States, at that time the one hundredth meridian. The status of these lands remained unchanged for more than three decades until 1861, when the unfortunate Cherokee alliance with the Confederate States of America forced the federal government to dictate a new treaty. The Treaty of Washington of 1866 permitted the Cherokee Nation to retain possession of the Outlet, but only until other tribes, to be designated by the government, were authorized to share this western reserve. Several tribes, including Osages, Kaws, Poncas, Otos, and Tonkawas, were located in the eastern portion of the Outlet, but the western section remained unassigned.[1]

Cattlemen from Kansas soon found the area a perfect place to graze their herds. In addition, drovers heading north on the Old Caldwell Trail frequently stopped to fatten their cattle on Cherokee pastures, and by 1880 considerable numbers of cattle were using the Outlet. At first the Cherokees were unconcerned

---

[1] E. E. Dale, "The Cherokee Strip Live Stock Association," *Chronicles of Oklahoma*, Vol. V (Mar., 1927), 58–62.

about the use of their land, but about 1879 they began to demand payment. Tribute was ordinarily paid to individual Cherokees who came to the Outlet and took up ranges under assumed headrights and then charged ranchers a tax on the newly obtained grasslands.

In the spring of 1880 cattlemen with an interest in the Outlet met at Caldwell, Kansas, to discuss the tax, as well as other problems of common grazing. A loosely organized association was formed for mutual protection, scheduling of roundups, and settlement of disputes. In the same year the Cherokee Council levied a forty-cent head tax on all cattle in the Outlet and collected nearly eight thousand dollars.[2]

The position of the Department of the Interior was not clear on the taxing system. It was admitted that the Cherokees had possession of the unoccupied Outlet and that they sometimes gave permission to graze, but it was not known whether they themselves could legally settle on the land and then charge for use of their headrights. It was only a matter of time until those Cherokees privately leasing range in the Outlet found themselves contradicting permits issued by the Cherokee Council. Double-taxed ranchers brought the matter to the attention of the commissioner of Indian affairs. In 1882, after due consultation, a ruling of the United States attorney general denied the Cherokee Nation the right to settle its citizens in the Outlet. The commissioner then asked the War Department to clear all improvements and fences from the Outlet.[3] Ranchmen violently protested. They were willing to pay a single assessment for use of the tribal grounds and felt that, given time, they could make a mutually satisfactory agreement with the Cherokees. The arbitrary action of the commissioner was rescinded, primarily

---

[2] *Ibid.*; George Rainey, *The Cherokee Strip*, 163.

[3] Price to J. W. Strong, Oct. 11, 1881, Price to J. Q. Tufts, Dec. 30, 1882, *Sen. Exec. Doc. No. 54*, 48 Cong., 1 sess., 129, 131.

because of the disinclination of the secretary of war to dispatch troops, not because of the cattlemen's arguments.

In the meantime, other ranchers' meetings had been held at Caldwell in March, 1882, and again in 1883. At the latter conference the Cherokee Strip Live Stock Association was incorporated under the laws of Kansas. Dale has described this peculiar organization:

> It was not a corporation in the ordinary sense of the term, since it had no capital stock, and, in consequence, no stockholders. It was an association with a membership composed of individuals, partnerships, and corporations, many of the last named with a heavy capitalization with numerous stockholders. Operating in a region without law or courts, it had little authority for its acts except the general consent of its members and yet for seven years or more this great association, with no property except such as it obtained from assessments of its members was one of the most powerful factors in the history of the development of Indian Territory.[4]

The ultimate objective of this pool was reached in May, 1883, when the Cherokee Council passed a bill leasing the entire Outlet to the Cherokee Strip Live Stock Association for a five-year term in consideration of an annual payment of $100,000. The lease was signed in July and went into effect on October 1. Outlet lands were surveyed, space was left for trails and quarantine lands, and about one hundred individuals and firms divided the remaining five million acres of grazing land.

Until 1886, Fort Supply troops seldom patrolled the leased portions of the Cherokee Outlet, believing that the Cherokee police or the lessees themselves were responsible for the region. In 1886, however, post jurisdiction was expanded to include protection of the Cherokee Outlet west of a line from Cantonment to Kiowa, Kansas. In co-operation with Fort Reno and a

[4] "Cherokee Strip Live Stock Association," *loc. cit.*, 68.

detachment at Chilocco Camp, Fort Supply troops were under orders to remove all persons from the Outlet who did not have authority from the Cherokee Live Stock Association. The secretary of the association, the principal chief of the Cherokee Nation, and the agent for the Cherokees based their claim for military removal of nonassociation outfits upon Article 27 of the 1866 treaty, whereby the United States guaranteed the protection of Cherokee property from trespass and, upon the recommendation of the Cherokee agent, removal of persons who had entered the Outlet unlawfully.[5]

Timber cutters in the Outlet were also considered to be illegally trespassing on Indian property, and details from Fort Supply scouted that portion of the Outlet under post jurisdiction, with particular attention to the cedar-filled canyons near the Cimarron. Kansans usually slipped into the wooded section of the Outlet by the Kiowa road or by the Cimarron crossing below the Salt Plains. The numbers of intruders were ordinarily light, although in late July, 1886, one scout stopped twenty-one violators, ten of whom had cedar logs in their wagons. From that time regular reconnaissance of the Outlet was ordered by the Department of the Missouri.[6]

Constant patrols of the Cimarron country in 1886 and 1887 indicated that the timber thieves had business ties with the Southern Kansas Railroad, which was working its way from Kiowa, Kansas, to Woodward, Indian Territory. Freighters hauling supplies to the construction crews frequently returned to Kansas with wagons loaded with logs. In March, 1887, sev-

[5] AAG, Dept. of Mo., to Commanding Officer, Fort Supply, Jan. 28, 1886, Dept. of Mo., Letters Sent, Vol. 125; Robert L. Owen to Commanding Officer, Fort Supply, Oct. 23, 1886, May 24, 1887, Fort Supply, Letters Received, Box 6; Kappler, *Indian Affairs*, II, 942.

[6] Read to Post Adjutant, Fort Supply, Aug. 5, 1886, Fort Supply, Letters Received, Box 6; AAG, Dept. of Mo., to Commanding Officer, Fort Supply, Aug. 12, 1886, Dept. of Mo., Letters Sent, Vol. 125.

eral thieves were arrested, relieved of their contraband, and escorted up the Dodge–Supply road to Kansas. Only after the railroad announced that employees who cut Indian Territory timber would be discharged did the practice cease. Small-scale individual cutting continued for some years, and railroad box-cars were sometimes used to transport the stolen wood, but such violations were not widespread.[7]

The expulsion of timber cutters and hunters from the Outlet was of questionable legality. The Department of the Interior was not clear in its policy regarding the Cherokee Outlet in 1887, and as a result the War Department was not consistent in its actions against trespassers. A self-defeating round of arrests, confiscations, and acquittals developed.

The practice of Fort Supply personnel regarding intruders in the Outlet was merely to arrest them, take their lumber or game, and release them outside Indian Territory. When timber viola-tions increased in late 1886, Colonel Zenas R. Bliss asked for a clarification of the law regarding the ejections. According to officials of the Department of the Missouri, military forces could be employed to apprehend intruders in Indian Territory, who were to be brought before the nearest civil authority—in this case the United States commissioner at Ashland, Kansas.

At Ashland hunters and timber cutters were usually freed for lack of evidence on the plea that there was no clear law for-bidding trespass on the Indian lands or that there was no spe-cific prohibition against wood gathering, as there was, for example, against the manufacture of liquor. In addition, hunters could be arrested only when they were found with game in their possession, and protests were made that the fence at the Kansas line was not accurately placed and that a man arrested inside the

---

[7] Post Returns, Fort Supply, Feb., Mar., 1887; Bliss to AAG, Dept. of Mo., Mar. 5, 1887, Fort Supply, Letters Sent, Vol. 37; Montgomery Bryant to U. S. District Attorney, Mar. 6, 1890, Fort Supply, Letters Sent, Vol. 39.

Outlet fence might actually be within Kansas boundaries. The vagueness of the statutes caused the United States commissioner to agree with the defendants that they were no more "foreigners" to Indian Territory than were employees of ranchers on leased property, travelers, or any of the hundreds of railroad employees coming and going in the Outlet.[8]

No official reaction to these events was received at Fort Supply, and the post continued scouring the countryside for hunters and timber cutters, arresting them, and turning them over to the commissioner, who usually acquitted them. Hunters, too, shipped their evidence out of Indian Territory on the railroad, returning to Kansas disguised as travelers. Even after the closing of the Outlet in 1890, hunters continued to poach in Indian Territory, knowing that the United States district attorney at Topeka disapproved of taking their cases to court, since it cost the government more to try them than could be obtained from a conviction.[9]

In 1888 a new five-year lease was negotiated between the Cherokee Strip Live Stock Association and the Cherokee Nation, this time for $200,000 a year. On the surface it appeared that the association had a bright future, but in Washington events were taking place that would put an end to the organization within two years.

In March, 1889, Congress set up a commission of three persons to negotiate with the Cherokees and other tribes for the cession of the Outlet. The act that created the Cherokee Commission offered $1.25 an acre for the Outlet. If the offer was accepted, the area would be opened to settlement, just as the Okla-

[8] AAG, Dept. of Mo., to Commanding Officer, Fort Supply, Dec. 2, 1886, Fort Supply, Letters Received, Box 6; Bliss to AAG, Dept. of Mo., Jan. 17, 19, 1887, Fort Supply, Letters Sent, Vol. 37.

[9] H. Soper to Bryant, Dec. 6, 1889, Fort Supply, Letters Received, Box 7; Bryant to AAG, Dept. of Mo., Dec. 20, 1890; Bryant to Horace Speed, Feb. 8, 1892, Fort Supply, Letters Sent, Vol. 40.

homa lands would be opened the following month. The commission understandably made little progress, for as early as 1886 a syndicate of cattlemen had offered $3.00 an acre for the Outlet.[10] The government, however, was determined to make the settlement. Secretary of the Interior John W. Noble believed that the Cherokees' title to the lands they were then leasing was void and that the offer of $1.25 an acre was therefore munificent. He recommended that the government cancel the leases in the Outlet and take the lands.[11]

The policy of Secretary Noble was clear. If the Cherokees refused to sell the Outlet lands at his price, they would be deprived of any benefit from them until they accepted the offer. Meanwhile, the department threatened to take the lands by force.

Caught between the stubborn Cherokees and the relentless federal government, the Cherokee Strip Live Stock Association was the immediate loser. The Department of the Interior, yielding to the demands of homeseekers and encouraged by the Run of 1889, was determined to open the Outlet to settlement. President Benjamin Harrison, advised by the attorney general that leasing in the Outlet was without legal force, issued a presidential proclamation on February 17, 1890, forbidding all grazing in the Outlet and ordering all cattle removed by October 1, 1890.[12] According to Dale, the proclamation was calculated injustice:

> When we consider that these lands were not opened to settlement until September, 1893, or almost three years later, it must be obvious that the purpose here was not to prepare the lands for settlement but that this was a political move directed against the Cherokees to force a cession of the lands.[13]

[10] Dale, "Cherokee Strip Live Stock Association," *loc. cit.*, 71–72.
[11] John W. Noble to Lucius Fairchild, Oct. 26, 1889, *House Rep. No. 3,768*, 51 Cong., 2 sess., 9–16.
[12] Kappler, *Indian Affairs*, II, 946.
[13] Dale, *Range Cattle Industry*, 144.

Fair or not, the presidential proclamation was presented to the secretary of war, and troops were ordered to clear the Cherokee Outlet. The first step was to halt herds bound for pasture. Detachments from Fort Supply and Fort Elliott promptly began guarding the Dodge City Trail, the Deep Creek Trail, and all routes leading to the Outlet from the Texas Panhandle. Fort Sill closed the Dodge City Trail at Doan's Store, and Fort Reno troops patrolled the Old Caldwell Trail and all its approaches from Texas.[14]

The public misunderstood the situation, and settlers began to move toward the Outlet expecting another land opening. President Harrison issued another proclamation on March 15, 1890, stating that the Cherokee Outlet was not open for settlement and that entrance into the lands was unlawful. Troops from Fort Supply and Reno were ordered to take the field and remove all herds in the Outlet, as well as intruding settlers. Two separate squads of the Fifth Cavalry left Fort Supply on March 17 under Captain George H. Paddock and Lieutenant E. P. Andrews to operate west of Medicine Lodge Creek, north and south through the Outlet. Fort Reno similarly sent two troops of cavalry to clear the Outlet east of Medicine Lodge Creek.[15]

Ten days after the return of Captain Paddock's troop on April 8, Captain Jacob A. Augur took Troop A, Fifth Cavalry, into the field as a replacement. Little time was spent searching for intruders or cattlemen; the escort of several trail herds required immediate attention. The understanding by Department of the Missouri officials was that the President's proclamation of

---

[14] Indian scouts were used to patrol the lines of the Outlet but only troopers could turn back herds. AAG, Dept. of Mo., to Commanding Officer, Fort Supply, Feb. 28, 1890, Dept. of Mo., Letters Sent, Vol. 133; *House Exec. Doc. No. 1,* 51 Cong., 2 sess., 196–97.

[15] Presidential Proclamation, Mar. 15, 1890 (copy), AAG, Dept. of Mo., to Commanding Officer, Fort Supply, Mar. 16, 1890, Fort Supply, Letters Received, Box 8.

mid-February did not forbid driving cattle through the Outlet, and herds were therefore allowed to pass into Kansas. Fort Sill troops accompanied outfits to the Washita crossing of the Dodge City Trail, where they were met by a detachment from Fort Supply, who accompanied them to the northern limit of the Outlet.[16]

Providing security details on established trails was a large order in itself, but Augur's duties were further extended. Some outfits in the Outlet headed for Oklahoma City, others chose to use the Colorado Trail west of Supply, and in both cases the captain was ordered to furnish escorts.[17] Augur's troop returned to Fort Supply on May 31, leaving Lieutenant Andrews alone in the field.

Ranchers in the Outlet secured an extension of the withdrawal date to December 1, 1890, but even then there was doubt about their complete removal.[18] In the summer of 1890, Fort Supply and Fort Reno personnel were too busy escorting herds through the Outlet to have time to inspect the ranches. As a result, complaints were directed to the secretary of the interior that large numbers of cattle had not been removed from the Outlet. J. M. Larison, of Caldwell, reported in a letter of May 18, 1891, that several thousand head of cattle removed in 1890 had shortly returned to winter in the Outlet, followed in the spring by Texas herds, mostly owned by men who had formerly rented lands in the Outlet. "I feel safe in saying," wrote Larison, "that there are more cattle immediately South, between here and Oklahoma [Territory] than have been there at any time for two years, and more coming." The concern of the Kansas farmers and ranchers

[16] Memorandum "B," "Papers Relating to the Cattle Business," Fort Supply, Letters Received, Box 9.

[17] Augur to Post Adjutant, Fort Supply, Apr. 30, May 5, 9, 15, 1890, Fort Supply, Letters Received, Box 8; Post Adjutant, Fort Supply, to Augur, May 1, 15, 1890, Fort Supply, Letters Sent, Vol. 39.

[18] Presidential Proclamation, Sept. 19, 1890 (copy), Fort Supply, Letters Received, Box 9.

was that the marketable Texas and Indian Territory cattle, being lower in price because they paid no Kansas tax or Cherokee rent, were the main cause of hard times in Kansas.[19]

Robert B. Ross, treasurer of the Cherokee Nation, and L. B. Bell, president of the Cherokee Senate, were equally concerned. Unable to lease their lands by presidential order, yet unwilling to sell to the government for some ten million dollars less than the cattle syndicate was willing to pay, the Cherokees now watched ranchers using their lands free of charge. Investigating the matter in person, Ross estimated that in early June, 1891, intruders were grazing upward of fifty thousand head of cattle in the Outlet south of Arkansas City, Caldwell, Kiowa, and Hunnewell, Kansas.

William Grimes, United States marshal at Guthrie, Oklahoma Territory, substantiated Ross's claim and even suggested that the estimate was low. Apparently the cattlemen had not yet exhausted their resources. Leases were acquired on the Ponca Reserve, east of the disputed property, and not included in the government's action against the Cherokees, and train after train unloaded thousands of head of cattle at Ponca Switch. The underlying intention was to allow the herds to drift into the Outlet.[20]

Fort Supply troops continued to scout the Outlet in February, March, and April, 1891, but with no great success since most herds were on the far-eastern side near the Ponca Reserve. In March orders were received to continue escorting herds through the Outlet under the 1890 agreement with Fort Sill, and Captain Augur and Troop A, Fifth Cavalry, proceeded to take stations on the established trails, while Captain George Paddock with Company F, Fifth Cavalry, performed removal duty in co-

[19] J. M. Larison to Secretary of Interior, May 18, 1891 (copy), R. V. Belt to Secretary of Interior, June 4, 1891 (copy), Fort Supply, Letters Received, Box 9.

[20] Robert B. Ross to Noble, June 15, 1891 (copy), William Grimes to W.H.H. Miller, June 8, 1891 (copy), Fort Supply, Letters Received, Box 9.

operation with Fort Reno. Paddock was able to divert only slightly more than two thousand head into the Oklahoma Panhandle before dropping south to the Canadian country.[21]

Cattlemen were not easily removed from the Outlet. At one point Jacob Guthrie brought suit in a United States district court for an injunction against Captain William P. Hall to restrain him from performing orders of the secretary of war regarding the removal of cattle and people from the Cherokee Outlet. The injunction was denied in July, 1891, and Captain Hall proceeded out of Kingfisher, Oklahoma Territory, to continue the removal.[22]

The Cherokee Nation then brought suit against the Cherokee Strip Live Stock Association for full payment of the lease money, in an effort to compel the cattlemen to stand with them. Horace Speed, United States attorney at Guthrie, advised the United States attorney general that, "if it is possible, I think the Government should order these suits discontinued as we do not want cattlemen to act in connection with the Cherokees at all, and do not want the Cherokees to obtain one cent of lease money from the Strip hereafter or have any hope that they can do so."

Speed further observed that, since the quarantine laws of Kansas and Oklahoma Territory, of the Osage Reservation, and of tribes east of the Outlet would not permit driving cattle into their areas, Texas lands were the only remaining grazing areas. In that case, he suggested, cattlemen should be notified "that every steer that cannot be driven out legally and quietly will be killed."[23]

[21] AAG, Dept. of Mo., to Commanding Officer, Fort Supply, Mar. 27, 1891, Fort Supply, Letters Received, Box 8; Paddock to Post Adjutant, Fort Supply, July 13, 26, Aug. 5, 1891, Fort Supply, Letters Received, Box 9; Bryant to AAG, Dept. of Mo., July 26, 1891, Fort Supply, Letters Sent, Vol. 40.

[22] Speed to U. S. Attorney General, July 7, 1891 (copy), Fort Supply, Letters Received, Box 9.

[23] *Ibid.* No Man's Land was an alternative which Speed did not acknowledge.

More pressure to sell was placed on the Cherokees when Acting Secretary of the Interior George Chandler asked the secretary of war for help in removing Cherokee Indians and their property from the Outlet. Interior Department policy held that the Cherokees had only an easement to the Outlet and that occupation by any tribesmen of the Outlet without the consent of the United States therefore constituted trespass. Only the humanitarian intercession of President Harrison on behalf of the Cherokees who had permanent settlements or farms in the Outlet prevented the Indians from being driven away.[24]

By August the Department of the Interior had redoubled its campaign to clear the Outlet of an estimated 150,000 head of cattle.[25] Captain Paddock was ordered to enlist the aid of nearby Fort Reno troops and move from the Canadian to Kiowa, Kansas, where he would find several large herds. Merely putting the cattle into Kansas was not enough, he was warned, for herds had the habit of shortly reappearing. If necessary, the troops were to remain until the herds had been shipped to market.[26]

Paddock worked his way around Kiowa and not far from Supply found several large herds totaling about nine thousand head. Owners were forced either to push their stock into Kansas or to ship them at Woodward. If cattlemen insisted upon going back to Texas, they were not allowed to cut across the Outlet into the Panhandle, but rather paid a penalty and followed the Dodge City Trail south to the Washita, where Fort Sill troops picked them up and escorted them to the Red River.[27]

[24] George Chandler to Secretary of War, Aug. 4, 1891 (copy), Benjamin Harrison to Secretary of Interior, Aug. 12, 1891 (copy), Fort Supply, Letters Received, Box 9.

[25] Chandler to Secretary of War, Aug. 4, 1891 (copy), Fort Supply, Letters Received, Box 9.

[26] AAG, Dept. of Mo., to Commanding Officer, Fort Reno, Aug. 7, 1891 (copy), Fort Supply, Letters Received, Box 9; Bryant to Paddock, Aug. 5, 1891, Fort Supply, Letters Sent, Vol. 40.

[27] Paddock to Post Adjutant, Fort Supply, Aug. 10, 11, 14, 1891, AAG, Dept.

Later Captain Augur was released from escort duty and moved to Pond Creek. From there he sent scouts west, southwest, and south. On August 9 two troops of the Fifth Cavalry out of Fort Reno met Augur at Enid, Indian Territory, and the combined force policed the countryside. Within a week six herds, totaling about fifteen thousand head, had been ordered to ship from Enid or head for Kiowa. Splitting his command into an advance party, scouts, and the main body, Augur successfully cleared the Kiowa region of another thirty-five hundred head by August 25.[28]

Several more herds were located before the end of the month. Their drovers pleaded that they were heading for Kansas but were temporarily detained by quarantine laws. Augur found this excuse insufficient and thought it a subterfuge to pasture "through" cattle on the Outlet until they were ready for shipment. After inspecting the cattle, he ordered the Grimes and Ewing herds to the Kiowa stockyards, but the Wilson and the Short brothers' animals were found to be sick and were allowed to remain.[29]

Captain Augur's judgment on the infected herds was secretly contested by Atchison, Topeka and Santa Fe Live Stock Agent F. P. Morgan in a letter of September 2 to Colonel Montgomery Bryant:

> After making a thorough investigation of cattle at and near Kiowa on the Cherokee Strip, I find that there are two herds

---

of Mo., to Commanding Officer, Fort Supply, Aug. 17, 1891, Fort Supply, Letters Received, Box 9. The Fort Sill troops were not holding station at the Washita, but would be informed in advance of the herd by telegraph.

[28] Augur to Post Adjutant, Fort Supply, Aug. 15, 17, 18, 25, 1891, Fort Supply, Letters Received, Box 9; Post Adjutant, Fort Supply, to Augur, Aug. 20, 1891, Fort Supply, Letters Sent, Vol. 40.

[29] Augur to Post Adjutant, Fort Supply, Aug. 26, 29, 1891, Fort Supply, Letters Received, Box 9.

held on account of quarantine, claiming they are sick. Stock men in that vicinity are really laughing over the matter on the grounds above mentioned. Captain Augur is doing good work in getting cattle all out of the country as fast as possible, unless it is this exception. . . . The cattle mentioned belong to Abner Wilson, Young Short, and a man by the name of Goodly. I am perfectly satisfied that there is no sickness among these herds.[30]

Upon orders from Fort Supply, Augur checked the herds once more and again concluded that they should not be moved because of sickness. Just before pulling out of his camp on Medicine Lodge Creek, near Kiowa, on September 8, he allowed a third herd to remain temporarily in the Outlet because of diseased animals. Captain Augur was satisfied that all other intruders were gone.[31]

The struggle by cattlemen to remain inside the Outlet caused Fort Supply Commander Bryant to seek a clarification of quarantine regulations from the secretary of agriculture. The policy of the Department of Agriculture was reported as follows:

Cattle from south the quarantine line can not be driven to any point north [and then shipped by rail] whether . . . for immediate slaughter or otherwise. [But] the cattle south of the quarantine line may be shipped for immediate slaughter provided they are loaded on cars within the infected area.[32]

In essence, Fort Supply troops acted without authority when

---

[30] F. P. Morgan to Bryant, Sept. 2, 1891, Fort Supply, Letters Received, Box 9. Morgan concluded his letter: "I will kindly ask you to make this a strictly personal matter, as it would not do for the cattlemen to get hold of this, as it would injure our line, and I wish to give you all the information I can in order to help you out."

[31] Augur to Post Adjutant, Fort Supply, Sept. 1, 5, 1891, Fort Supply, Letters Received, Box 9.

[32] Instructions of Secretary of Agriculture, Sept. 4, 1891, Memorandum "G," "Papers Relating to the Cattle Business," Fort Supply, Letters Received, Box 9.

they ordered market cattle shipped from Caldwell or Kiowa, because both towns were across the quarantine line. Rail stations at Woodward, Pond Creek, and Enid were within their jurisdiction. Legally or not, however, Augur and Paddock cleared the Outlet from south, north, and west of Fort Supply to the satisfaction of Colonel Bryant.

Captain Paddock remained in the field throughout August and split his Fifth Cavalry command into three parts, one operating on the Washita, another patrolling on Persimmon Creek, and a third scouting between Fort Supply and the one hundredth meridian. Both Augur and Paddock returned to the post in mid-September, and a final scout by a junior officer two weeks later assured Colonel Bryant that all herds within his post jurisdiction had been removed.[33]

The year closed with news that the Cherokee Nation had given in to the inevitable and sold the Outlet to the federal government for slightly more than $8,500,000, or about $1.40 an acre. The Indians could no longer resist government pressure.

Fort Supply troops continued their patrol of the Cherokee Outlet in the spring of 1892, except for a month-long detached service during the opening of the Cheyenne and Arapaho lands in April. Captain Paddock and Troop F, Fifth Cavalry, began their reconnaissance on May 19. The nearly five thousand head of cattle belonging to Wilson, Short, and others allowed to remain in the Outlet by Augur the previous September were the first order of business. After inspecting the situation, Paddock referred an unusual problem to his senior officer. Colonel Bryant, in turn, reported to his superior on May 31:

Since these cattle were driven to the [Kansas] line, J. C. Guthrie has bought them. The purchase is probably fictitious, but, as the

[33] E. B. Winans, Jr., to Post Adjutant, Fort Supply, Sept. 27, 1891, Fort Supply, Letters Received, Box 9; Post Returns, Fort Supply, Sept., 1891.

articles of agreement are duly executed, I am powerless to do anything more toward their removal from the Outlet.[34]

Jacob Guthrie, a Cherokee, had held land in the Outlet for eight years and was grazing about three thousand head of cattle. Although he had been evicted by Fort Supply troops more than once, Guthrie was permitted to remain on the Outlet after August, 1891, because after that date President Harrison allowed Cherokees with permanent settlements to stay. It was well known that the cattlemen were being hard pressed by the Department of the Interior and would pay handsomely to keep their herds in the Outlet. Apparently Guthrie made agreements with the ranchers to hold their cattle as his property.

Kansas stock raisers continued to blame the Outlet cattle for keeping beef prices low, and Congressman Jerry Simpson charged the Department of the Interior and the War Department with conspiracy. On July 18, Simpson introduced a letter from Henry S. Landis, of Medicine Lodge, Kansas, before the United States House of Representatives. According to Landis, Guthrie arrived at Kiowa with letters of reference from persons in high government positions, including the secretary of the interior, and promised protection of herds in the Outlet until December 1, 1892. For his services Guthrie accepted payment of twenty-five cents a head cash, and notes for twenty-five cents a head payable on December 1—for the Kansas quarantine was applicable only from March 1 to December 1—a total of near sixteen thousand dollars. The letter further charged:

> While the troops under Captain Paddock were trying to get the cattle out this man Guthrie interfered so that Capt. Paddock telegraphed the Department about his, Guthrie's, claims of authority and his importance, and received a telegram in reply telling him, Capt. Paddock, that Guthrie had full authority and that

[34] Bryant to AAG, Dept. of Mo., May 31, 1892, Fort Supply, Letters Sent, Vol. 40.

he must recognize Guthrie's wishes. All the cattle on the Strip were transferred to this man Guthrie, and within an hour were transferred back to the actual owners. The one transfer to be used with the Department and the other for the protection of the owners in case Guthrie should be disposed to act unfairly.[35]

Incensed by the adverse publicity, Secretary of the Interior Noble and Secretary of War Samuel B. Elkins waged an unyielding war on the cattlemen. Troops from Forts Reno and Supply were ordered to redouble their efforts to prevent the invasion of the Outlet by cattlemen and, if necessary, to call upon Fort Riley, Kansas, for additional cavalry. Nearly sixteen thousand head of cattle were found in the Outlet near Kiowa, and cattlemen were presented with the option of shipping their cattle by August 31 or having them sent to No Man's Land. In order to avoid conflict with the quarantine laws established by the Department of Agriculture, herds were moved only to the Kansas line and were then pushed west.[36]

Officials in the Department of the Missouri, eager to clear the Outlet before Guthrie's so-called protection date of December 1, pushed their officers hard. By September 4 all the cattle in the Kiowa district had been shipped, put to pasture in Kansas, or started for Texas. In addition, that portion of the Outlet immediately south of Fort Supply—another troubled area—was rapidly being cleared of herds, which were being shipped at Woodward. Colonel Bryant assured his superiors that "the portion of the Outlet assigned to this post for police has been thoroughly cleared of cattle."[37]

[35] *Congressional Record*, 52 Cong., 1 sess., Vol. XXIII, 6,341. Secretary of Interior Noble naturally refuted the charges, and his argument is carried in Noble to S. B. Elkins, July 21, 1892 (copy), Fort Supply, Letters Received, Box 9.

[36] AAG, Dept. of Mo., to Commanding Officer, Fort Reno, July 29, 1892, Dept. of Mo., Letters Sent, Vol. 138; Post Returns, Fort Supply, Aug., 1892; Bryant to AAG, Dept. of Mo., Aug. 27, 1892, Fort Supply, Letters Sent, Vol. 40.

[37] Augur to Post Adjutant, Fort Supply, Sept. 4, 1892, Fort Supply, Letters

Persistent reports of new invasions near the old Day Brothers Ranch, however, caused Bryant to send several more patrols into the field. The Pond Creek and Alva areas yielded several small herds, and all two-time offenders were brought to Fort Supply, where they were released. Others were warned that if they were caught again they too would be sent to Supply and then forced to ship at Woodward. On November 16 the Fifth Cavalry at Fort Supply was able to report that no cattle were grazing on the Outlet within scouting distance of the post.[38]

Fort Supply troops continued to block trespassers on the Outlet, with varying degrees of success. Some ranchmen ignored the presidential proclamation, and their outfits continued to play hide-and-seek with military patrols, especially in the Kiowa area. In a midwinter scout in January, 1893, Captain Paddock once again located boundary violators. Sixteen miles west of Kiowa a herd of three thousand head was found scattered twenty-five miles along the creeks flowing into the Cimarron. Captain Paddock drove the steers until dark as a means of convincing the owners that if they attempted to evade the restricting orders their cattle would have to suffer. Later the cattle were gathered and driven across the Outlet boundary by the owners.

Leaving two detachments in the area to track and observe, Captain Paddock and the remaining troops proceeded to a point near Alva, established a camp, and scouted the country as far south and east as was usual in Fort Supply patrols. No cattle were found on the east, but one herd of four thousand head was found south of Alva. The cattle were moved by the owner on January 19 and crossed into Kansas pursued by troopers. Paddock believed that this patrol had been accomplished with heavy

Received, Box 9; Bryant to AAG, Dept. of Mo., Sept. 5, 1892, Fort Supply, Letters Sent, Vol. 40.

[38] Augur to Post Adjutant, Fort Supply, Nov. 1, 6, 1892, Fort Supply, Letters Received, Box 9; Francis Moore to AAG, Dept. of Mo., Nov. 16, 1892, Fort Supply, Letters Sent, Vol. 41.

loss to the owners; the animals were already worn and in poor condition from continuous storms and cold weather. On January 22, having completed his duties, Paddock started for Fort Supply, arriving on January 26.[39]

[39] Paddock to Post Adjutant, Fort Supply, Jan. 26, 1893, Fort Supply, Letters Received, Box 10.

Chapter IX

Opening the Outlet
and Closing the Post
1893–94

AFTER the preliminary agreement to sell the Cherokee
Outlet was made in December, 1891, negotiations between the
Cherokee Council and the Cherokee Commission faltered. It
was not until March 3, 1893, that final sale was approved by the
United States Congress. Included in the agreement was the ex-
pressed intent of the federal government to open the Outlet for
settlement within six months after approval by the Cherokee
Nation.[1]

At this point potential settlers began protesting the cattlemen's use of the government-owned Outlet and demanding equal
access to the lands. When officials in the Department of the Missouri recognized the possibility of illegal colonization, they ordered Colonel James P. Wade, commanding Fort Reno, to use
military measures to prevent further unauthorized occupation
of the Outlet.[2] Captain Jacob Augur was temporarily detached
with a troop from Fort Supply and ordered to aid Colonel Wade
throughout March.

Although the tide of sodbusters was temporarily stemmed, by
May, Secretary of the Interior Hoke Smith was again being

[1] *Annual Report of the Commissioner of Indian Affairs for the Year 1893*, 33;
Berlin B. Chapman, "Opening the Cherokee Outlet: An Archival Study," *Chronicles of Oklahoma*, Vol. XL (Summer, 1962), 158–63.

[2] AAG, Dept. of Mo., to Commanding Officer, Fort Reno, Feb. 24, 1893
(copy), Fort Supply, Letters Received, Box 10; AAG, Dept. of Mo., to Commanding Officer, Fort Reno, Mar. 1, 1893, AAG, Dept. of Mo., to Commanding
Officer, Fort Supply, Mar. 1, 1893, Dept. of Mo., Letters Sent, Vol. 139.

deluged with reports of cattle grazing in the Outlet. That portion below Kiowa, the headquarters of the never-say-die cattlemen, was rumored to be supporting ten thousand head.[3] The secretary of war was charged anew with removal procedures.

Ever since learning of the accusations in the Landis letter of July, 1892, the General Land Office and the Department of the Interior had suspected an unsavory alliance between the military and the ranchers. Now, when great herds were reported in the Outlet just as the department was preparing to release it, General Land Office Inspector George W. Andrews filed a letter of dissatisfaction:

> It seems quite common talk among the few interested in cattle, that the cattlemen will have the benefit until Fall. They have continually herded this strip for two years. The soldiers were one year ago directed to drive out the cattlemen, and would only drive them toward the border and the cattlemen immediately follow them back. From what I learn of their carrying orders there is a tacit understanding between the cow-boys and the soldiers that these orders from the Department will not be rigidly enforced and the soldiers or their officers in charge have, it is believed, received some benefits from the owners of herds to immediately retrace their steps when nearing the borders in order to let the cow-boys return at once to the strip with their herds.[4]

Colonel Dangerfield Parker, who had been placed in command of Fort Supply in January, 1893, denied any conspiracy. He asked whether the Department of the Interior was aware of the legal handicaps which troopers faced in the performance of their duties. Differing state and territorial quarantine laws, he

---

[3] Silas W. Lamoreaux to Secretary of Interior, May 26, 1893 (copy), Fort Supply, Letters Received, Box 10.

[4] George W. Andrews to Commissioner of the General Land Office, May 25, 1893 (copy), E. A. Bowes to Secretary of Interior, June 2, 1893 (copy), Fort Supply, Letters Received, Box 10.

said, added to the policing problem by making officers liable to civil suit when they put herds across the Outlet.[5]

Drought conditions on the plains in the spring and summer of 1893 made it easy for detachments from Fort Supply to patrol the Outlet. Since there were only a few areas with enough water to hold cattle, the infantry was pressed into patrol duty. Lieutenant Marion B. Saffold and a company of the Thirteenth Infantry left Fort Supply on June 11 and proceeded to a camp near Alva, from which regular scouts were performed twenty-five miles west along the Kansas line. Two herds were found the first week; one was shipped out because it had nowhere to go, and the other was forced back into Kansas.

Several small herds belonging to Kansas stockmen were discovered in the days following. Most herds contained fifty head or thereabouts, but no herds as large as the ten thousand reported by Inspector Andrews were found. Kansas ranchers, not easily discouraged, boldly ran herds into the Outlet even with the knowledge that troops were nearby. When confronted by Lieutenant Saffold, they usually agreed to return to Kansas but used a lack of drovers as an excuse for failure to make speedy withdrawals. Saffold recommended that "it would be well if authority could be obtained to, in such cases, kill several head of cattle" to indicate the determination of the military.[6]

After these incidents only a few cattle were found along the Kansas border, and Saffold departed for Fort Supply, leaving Lieutenant H. L. Thelkeld and a company of the Thirteenth Infantry to keep watch after July 19. Large herds were temporarily restrained from crossing into the Outlet, but it was impossible to keep out the Kiowa town herd and small groups of horses and cattle. Realizing that it was a job for cavalry, on July 20, Colonel

5 Dangerfield Parker to AAG, Dept. of Mo., June 19, 1893, Fort Supply, Letters Sent, Vol. 41.

6 M. B. Saffold to Post Adjutant, Fort Supply, June 19, 26, 1893, Fort Supply, Letters Received, Box 10.

Parker positioned a small detachment of the Third Cavalry near Kiowa Creek to remove any elusive intruders or cattle. No trespassers were found, but two herds of cattle—one of about fifteen hundred head, the other near nine hundred head—were located and dispatched. The party returned to post four days later. In the meantime, Lieutenant Thelkeld was not idle. He himself found and drove out one small herd each day of the week prior to July 24. Some ranchers decided to ship their herds rather than continually move them back and forth across the line, but those who could not sell out during that period of abnormally low market prices found entering the Outlet a necessary risk because it appeared to be the only place their herds could water.[7]

Thelkeld and the infantry withdrew on August 1, and Lieutenant Kirby Walker, Third Cavalry, assumed control of the Kiowa area. Several herds of about 150 head were tended, but dozens of small herds crossed the Outlet lines daily to water and graze for a day or two, and there was almost no way to stop them.[8]

About July 1, the Interior Department suddenly realized that thousands of homesteaders were crowding the Kansas line waiting for word of the exact date of the opening. Acting quickly, on July 6, Secretary of the Interior Smith appointed Alfred P. Swineford, former governor of Alaska, to the post of inspector of surveys general and district land offices. His instructions were to proceed to Oklahoma Territory and set up land offices and county seats for the Outlet.[9]

Before the end of the month the Department of the Missouri

[7] H. L. Thelkeld to Post Adjutant, Fort Supply, July 17, 24, 1893, E. P. Kraus to Commanding Officer, Fort Supply, July 24, 1893, Fort Supply, Letters Received, Box 10.

[8] Kirby Walker to Post Adjutant, Fort Supply, Aug. 8, 1893, Fort Supply, Letters Received, Box 10.

[9] Joe B. Milam, "The Opening of the Cherokee Outlet," *Chronicles of Oklahoma*, Vol. IX (Sept., 1931), 280; Chapman, "Opening the Cherokee Outlet," *loc. cit.*, 169.

had become concerned about the small number of troops available near the Outlet to keep peace. Upon the request of General Nelson A. Miles the cavalry troops at Forts Supply and Reno were reinforced by four troops of the Third Cavalry from Fort Riley. At the same time Colonel Parker was placed in command of the force, which was to remove all unauthorized persons and open the Cherokee Outlet in an orderly manner. With these details arranged, on August 19, President Cleveland affixed his signature to the official proclamation opening the Cherokee Outlet at noon on September 16, 1893.[10]

The proclamation divided the Cherokee Outlet into seven counties, lettered *K* through *Q*, each of which was open to settlement. The only reserved lands in the Outlet were certain assignments belonging to the Osage, Kaw, Ponca, Oto-Missouri, Tonkawa, and Pawnee tribes, the Chilocco School Reservation, and the Fort Supply Military Reservation. Four land offices representing land districts set up by Swineford were provided within the Outlet at Alva, Enid, Woodward, and Perry.

Almost every conceivable detail of registering and running for a claim was outlined in the President's orders. A strip of land one hundred feet wide all around and immediately within the Outlet at nine points on the Outlet boundary line was reserved for registration booths.[11] At these places perhaps 115,000 persons completed one of three forms, one for a homestead entry, one for a town lot, or a soldier's declaratory statement.

The task of ejecting sooners from nine thousand square miles of territory with four hundred miles of northern and southern border, plus that of guarding four land offices and nine registra-

[10] Miles to Secretary of War, Aug. 7, 1893, AAG, Dept. of Mo., to Parker, Aug. 12, 28, 1893, Dept. of Mo., Letters Sent, Vol. 139; James D. Richardson, *Messages and Papers of the Presidents*, IX, 406–27.

[11] Booths were placed in Kansas on the northern border at Arkansas City, Hunnewell, Caldwell, Cameron, and Kiowa City; and in Oklahoma Territory at Stillwater, Orlando, Hennessey, and Goodwin.

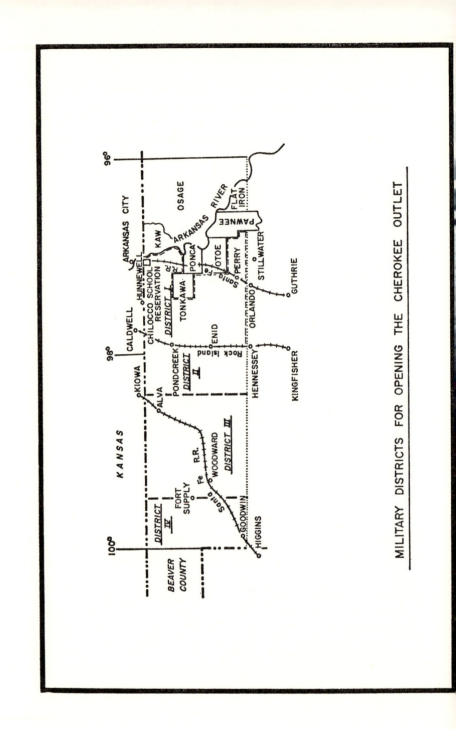

MILITARY DISTRICTS FOR OPENING THE CHEROKEE OUTLET

tion booths, fell to Colonel Parker. After receiving a copy of the proclamation of August 19, Parker began to assemble his force. Forts Supply, Reno, and Riley furnished eight troops of the Third Cavalry, and Forts Supply, Reno, and Sill provided four companies of the Thirteenth Infantry. The objectives of the military, as Parker understood them, were to preserve the peace, protect government property and mails, and guard the people from lawlessness and disorder. Four military districts, distinct from the land districts, were laid out to aid the scouting details in reaching these objectives.[12]

Securing the First District on the east was Lieutenant F. M. Caldwell and Troop C, Third Cavalry, at Chilocco; on the west, Captain O. Elting, Troop E, Third Cavalry, near Bluff Creek; and on the south, Captain J. B. Johnson, Troop B, Third Cavalry, at Orlando. District Two was guarded north to south by Captain G. A. Dodd, Troop F, Third Cavalry, at Pond Creek, and by Captain C. A. Hedekin, Troop A, Third Cavalry, at Enid. The Third District was patrolled by Captain F. H. Hardie and Troop G, from Alva, and by Captain G. Hunter, Troop K, near Woodward, both of the Third Cavalry. Lieutenant Kirby Walker, Troop D, Third Cavalry, cleared District Four, the Clear Creek area.

Lieutenant Frank M. Caldwell and forty men of Troop C, Third Cavalry, traveled on the Santa Fe Railroad from Fort Riley and arrived in the First District on August 31. The following day Caldwell's men camped within five miles of Arkansas City, Kansas. In accordance with orders from Colonel Parker, Caldwell directed his men in patrolling nearly seventy miles of Outlet border: fifteen miles on the north along the Kansas line; thirty-two miles on the east, following the Arkansas River;

[12] Medical History of Fort Supply, Vol. 170, 14; AAG, Dept. of Mo., to Parker, Sept. 5, 1893, Dept. of Mo., Letters Sent, Vol. 139; E. M. Heyl to AAG, Dept. of Mo., Oct. 19, 1893, *House Exec. Doc. No. 27*, 53 Cong., 1 sess., 4. (Hereinafter this government document will be referred to as *House Doc. 27*, with appropriate pages.)

and twelve miles along both the northern and the western boundaries of the Ponca Reservation.[13]

On September 5 guards were directed to the registration booth at Arkansas City to control about ten thousand impatient registrants. After the booth opened on September 10, crowds and troublemakers several times threatened the use of force.[14]

Scouts continued between September 5 and 13, and some thirty families were conducted to the northern line of the Outlet. Twenty-five or thirty teams were also turned back at the northern end of the Ponca Reservation. In spite of these efforts Lieutenant Caldwell was convinced that there were many sooners in the Outlet at the time of the opening, mostly from the Kaw, Osage, and Ponca lands.[15]

The western part of the First District[16] was likewise intensely scouted after September 2. Two herds of cattle and several sooners were ejected by Captain Oscar Elting, Troop E, Third Cavalry, also from Fort Riley. Patrols moved along nineteen miles of northern Outlet border, and in addition Troop E guarded registration booths at Caldwell and Hunnewell. On the morning of the opening Elting's mounted sentinels were stationed eight hundred to one thousand yards apart, holding back more than twenty-six thousand registered homeseekers.[17]

---

13 F. M. Caldwell to Parker, Sept. 24, 1893, Fort Supply, Letters Received, Box 10; Heyl to AAG, Dept. of Mo., Oct. 19, 1893, Caldwell to J. M. Lee, Oct. 11, 1893, *House Doc. 27*, 5, 13.

14 *Ibid.*; Statements of Louis P. Conway, Edward Murphy, and George Morris, Oct. 2, 1893, *House Doc. 27*, 36–39.

15 Caldwell to Parker, Sept. 18, 24, 1893, Fort Supply, Letters Received, Box 10; Caldwell to Lee, Oct. 11, 1893, *House Doc. 27*, 13.

16 The First District consisted of that portion of the Outlet bounded on the east by the Arkansas River, on the west by the Rock Island Railroad, on the south by the Oklahoma Territory line, and on the north by the northern boundary of the Outlet.

17 O. Elting to Parker, [Sept. 20, 1893], Fort Supply, Letters Received, Box 10; Heyl to AAG, Dept. of Mo., Oct. 19, 1893, Statements of Elting and T. R. Rivers, Oct. 2, 1893, *House Doc. 27*, 6, 46–48.

The remaining section of the First District, "that portion of the Cherokee Outlet east of Rock Island RR and south of the continuation of the line dividing the Otoe and Ponca reservations," was protected by Captain John B. Johnson and Troop B, Third Cavalry. Captain Johnson's command entered the Outlet after June 26, pursuant to orders from Fort Reno, and joined the command for the opening when Colonel Parker took authority. Johnson's force made camp on September 1 about three miles north of Orlando, Oklahoma Territory, and patrols continued to remove violators through September 14. During this period about nineteen thousand head of cattle, horses, and mules, as well as 154 men, were driven out of the Outlet into Oklahoma and Kansas.

Detachments also guarded the Perry Land Office and the Stillwater and Orlando registration booths, where troopers succeeded in controlling immense crowds, including ruffians, as well as serious homeseekers, without riots or bloodshed. On September 14, Captain B. H. Rogers and a company of infantry assumed command of the Perry Land Office and townsite. Johnson then withdrew to Orlando and Stillwater, where he effected the opening two days later.[18]

The Second Military District of the Cherokee Outlet was commanded by Captain George A. Dodd and Lieutenant Charles A. Hedekin. Patrol of the northern half of that district was perhaps the busiest and most far-reaching assignment, in view of the past history of the region of the Outlet below Kiowa. Captain Dodd, commanding Troop F, Third Cavalry, out of Fort Riley, took station at Pond Creek, within the Outlet, on August 29. Immediately lookouts were stationed on hills armed with field glasses to spy out intruders. When a trespass was sighted, troopers, riding bareback for greater speed, sped out to make

18 Statements of J. B. Johnson, Oct. 7, 1893, Harry Colt and E. E. Westervelt, Oct. 5, 1893, *House Doc. 27*, 48–49, 64–65; Johnson to Parker, Sept. 23, 1893, Fort Supply, Letters Received, Box 10.

the arrest. Captain Dodd's patrol district was "bounded on north (56 miles) by southern line of Kansas; on east (32 miles) by Chicago, Rock Island and Pacific Railway; south (36 miles) by sixth standard parallel; west (29 miles) by north and south line passing through Kiowa." Covering 153 miles of border and an area of 1,624 square miles, Troop F was remarkably successful in removing 59 intruders, about 1,600 cattle, 121 horses and mules, and 40 wagons.

Before September 16 dawned, the forty-five men under Dodd had constantly scouted four major trails between the Kansas border and Hennessey, Oklahoma Territory, and had cleared their jurisdiction of sooners in marches totaling 1,626 miles. On the morning of the run the command stood guard over three Rock Island Railroad bridges, the townsites of Pond Creek and Round Pond, a registration booth at Cameron, Kansas, and the Outlet border between Caldwell and Kiowa.[19]

The southern portion of the Second District—the portion of the Outlet south of the sixth standard parallel between the Rock Island tracks and the Kiowa line—was supervised by Lieutenant Charles A. Hedekin, Troop A, Third Cavalry, from Fort Reno. Every effort was made to clear the sooners near Enid, but fifteen thousand homeseekers on the southern line of the Outlet kept most of the troopers busy at the Hennessey registration booth. Enid Townsite was later protected by Captain William W. Waterbury and the infantry, and Hedekin stretched his command at three-quarter-mile intervals along thirty miles of border west of Hennessey.[20]

On August 31, Captain Francis H. Hardie and forty-three men of Troop G, Third Cavalry, out of Fort Riley, took station

[19] Statement of George A. Dodd, Oct. 8, 1893, *House Doc. 27*, 49; Dodd to Parker, Oct. 5, 1893, Fort Supply, Letters Received, Box 10.

[20] Heyl to AAG, Dept. of Mo., Oct. 19, 1893, Statement of C. A. Hedekin, Oct. 6, 1893, *House Doc. 27*, 51; Hedekin to Parker, Sept. 19, 1893, Fort Supply, Letters Received, Box 10.

at Alva, eighteen miles south of the Kansas line. District Three comprised a large area, but the property was less valuable than the first two areas, and consequently there were fewer entrants. Hardie patrolled the northern half of a section of the Outlet bounded on the east by a line running north and south through Fort Supply. The townsite at Alva was policed only until the arrival of Lieutenant Marion B. Saffold and the Thirteenth Infantry. Troop G also took a position at the Kiowa registration booth, but the main duty was regular patrols of the Outlet border twenty-five miles west of Kiowa.[21]

The southern half of the Third District was patrolled by Captain George K. Hunter and Troop K of the Third Cavalry. Leaving Fort Reno on August 29, Captain Hunter entered the Outlet near Hennessey on September 2 and proceeded west to the Third District. Three intruders were discovered and ejected, two on September 3 and one on September 10. After taking station near Waynoka, scouts found several Texans in the Outlet, ejected them, and continued to police a six-mile length of southern border. On September 13 the command moved to Woodward to watch the northern portion of the southern half of the district and there met Captain Henry G. Cavenaugh and the infantry stationed at the Land Office. Captain Hunter started one thousand persons into the Outlet from the Oklahoma Territory border at noon on September 16.[22]

As part of Fort Supply's regular patrol of the Cherokee Outlet, Lieutenant Kirby Walker and a ten-man detachment of the Third Cavalry policed the Alva area from late July until the arrival of Captain Hardie. The detail then joined the remainder of Troop D, Third Cavalry, from Fort Supply, who had been in

[21] Heyl to AAG, Dept. of Mo., Oct. 19, 1893, Statement of F. H. Hardie, Oct. 2, 1893, *House Doc. 27*, 7–8, 52–53; Hardie to Parker, Sept. 4, 19, 23, 1893, Fort Supply, Letters Received, Box 10.

[22] G. K. Hunter to Parker, Sept. 14, 1893, Fort Supply, Letters Received, Box 10; Statement of Hunter, Oct. 7, 1893, *House Doc. 27*, 57.

the field since September 1, to maintain the booth in Goodwin, Indian Territory. Scouting and escorting the Clear Creek vicinity for more than one thousand miles in the weeks preceding the opening, the troop completely cleared their section of the Outlet. The run on September 16 was made by thirty men on horses and about three hundred persons on Santa Fe cars out of Higgins, Texas.[23]

Land offices were operated by government officials but guarded by the officers and men of the Thirteenth Infantry. On September 14, Captain Henry G. Cavenaugh and Troop B marched from Fort Supply to take station at Woodward and remained on the townsite guarding government property until September 23. Lieutenant Marion B. Saffold and Company E followed Troop B to Woodward on September 14 and then took the Santa Fe to Alva, where they performed like duty.[24]

Fort Reno officers stationed Company C, Thirteenth Infantry, at Enid under Captain William Waterbury, and Fort Sill sent Company G, Thirteenth Infantry, under command of Captain Benjamin H. Rogers to the Perry Land Office and townsite. On only one occasion, on the morning of the opening at Perry, did any of the troops have trouble. Apparently most of the rowdyism occurred at the registration booths, for when the homesteaders reached the four townsites to file their claims, no disturbances occurred. Soldiers remained at the land offices until September 28, when they returned to their posts.[25]

Because of the small numbers of homeseekers in the southern part of the Third District and the entire Fourth District, the

[23] Post Returns, Fort Supply, July–Sept., 1893; Heyl to AAG, Dept. of Mo., Oct. 19, 1893, Statements of J. Walker, I. Ware, Oct. 13, 1893, Henry Holden, Oct. 10, 1893, *House Doc. 27*, 57–59.

[24] Statements of H. G. Cavenaugh, Oct. 10, 1893, Saffold, Oct. 18, 1893, *House Doc. 27*, 59–61.

[25] Statements of William Waterbury, Oct. 8, 1893, Benjamin H. Rogers, Oct. 4, 1893, in *ibid.*

runs in those areas were orderly and easily controlled. Each of the remaining six cavalry officers, however, had his share of trouble. Lieutenant Caldwell, in the eastern portion of the First District, posted troops along all railroad crossings and the west bank of the Arkansas River to prevent settlers from running onto the Osage Reservation.[26] The approximately thirty thousand persons along the Kansas state line east and west of the Chilocco Reservation and the southern line of the School Reservation moved out in orderly fashion, but the line of settlers west of the Chilocco Reservation on the Kansas border stampeded about 11:56 A.M. at the sound of a false shot. J. R. Hill, of Keansburg, New Jersey, was shot and killed by troopers for breaking the line, but he was so closely followed by eager thousands that the start was uneven.[27]

Captain Elting guarded the Rock Island crossing into the Outlet south of Caldwell from his position in the First District. Promptly at noon fifteen thousand or more persons below Caldwell were sent on their mad way by Captain Elting, but Lieutenant Tyree R. Rivers, acting for Elting at the start below Hunnewell, could not stop one man, who broke through the line at full gallop one minute before twelve, and thousands followed. Recognizing the hopelessness of the situation, Rivers fired his pistol to start the others.[28]

Captain Johnson, at the south end of the First District, spread his troops along the Oklahoma Territory border, confidently holding an estimated twenty-two thousand persons between Orlando and Stillwater. Two men started out just before noon, but

[26] In this manner persons along the south line of the reservation were actually three miles below those along the Kansas border.

[27] Caldwell to Parker, Sept. 18, 1893, Fort Supply, Letters Received, Box 10. Twenty-nine eyewitness statements regarding the killing of J. R. Hill may be found in *House Doc. 27*, 12–40.

[28] Elting to Parker, [Sept. 20, 1893], in *ibid.*; Statements of Elting and Rivers, Oct. 2, 1893, *House Doc. 27*, 46–48.

were immediately cut off and arrested. The spirit of the crowd was not broken, however, and about three minutes before twelve o'clock someone fired a shot, and the rush was on.[29] Thus in each of the three commands of the First District there was some mishap at the start.

Farther west, along the southern Outlet boundary at Hennessey, fifteen thousand homesteaders assembled near the Rock Island tracks. About eleven thousand rushed into the Outlet at 11:55 A.M., but Lieutenant Hedekin, although unable to restrain the break, refused to give the signal early. Approximately four thousand citizens stood fast until the proper sign was given at precisely noon.[30]

Of the first two military districts only Captain Dodd, in the northern half of District Two, was able to provide an absolutely fair start for the homesteaders. Because Dodd had to extend his force between Caldwell and Kiowa to command a registration booth, two townsites, and three railroad bridges, he sought aid from Captain Hardie in the northern portion of District Three. Hardie obliged by pulling his command ten miles east of Kiowa, thus allowing Dodd to close ranks. Dodd's signal was given at exactly high noon from watches set by telegraphic communication, and every homesteader had an equal chance for land.[31]

Captain Hardie, in District Three, initially spread his troops fifteen miles west of Kiowa and later ten miles east. The run was allowed to begin, however, at only one four-mile section. About four minutes before the starting time someone among the assembled horsemen discharged a pistol, and five thousand persons leaped forward. Hardie, seeing that it was impossible to stop the rush, fired his pistol, which was promptly answered along the line, so that the start was practically simultaneous. The first

---

29 Statement of Johnson, Oct. 7, 1893, *House Doc. 27*, 48–49.
30 Statement of Hedekin, Oct. 6, 1893, in *ibid.*, 51–52.
31 Dodd to Parker, Oct. 5, 1893, Fort Supply, Letters Received, Box 10.

man to break was captured by a trooper, but Captain Hardie said, "The killing of three or four would not have stopped the avalanche of people in their mad rush."[32] In the final count only three of the eight sections, in four districts, had fair starts, and the opening was marred by false and premature starts in five of six portions with crowds larger than five thousand.

Colonel Parker reviewed the Outlet opening from the Chilocco School Reservation, returning to Fort Supply on September 17. Newspapers charged malfeasance by the military, indicating that bribes were accepted, that drunkenness was common among officers and men, and that soonerism was rampant everywhere. Public officials, local and federal, for the most part disagreed, and in the end Colonel Parker and his officers were congratulated for directing such a large land rush with so small a command.[33] Parker retained command of the troops in the field until October 5, when all but Captain Dodd's troop returned to their posts. Captain Dodd lingered in the Pond Creek area through the first week of October in an effort to avert trouble between the townsites of Round Pond and Pond Creek.

The opening of the Cherokee Outlet lands to occupation ended nearly three years of patrol duty for Fort Supply. The men at the post subsequently led less active lives, performing only the usual garrison duties. The monotony of practice marches and visitor escorts was finally broken on November 26, when a letter was received from the citizens of Cheyenne, Oklahoma Territory, asking for immediate protection. On November 20, Wolf Hair, a Cheyenne, had gone to town to buy provisions and had met Tom O'Hare, a drunken Texan, who had amused himself by drawing his gun to frighten the Indian. Wolf Hair left town in his wagon to avoid trouble, but O'Hare mounted his horse and

[32] Hardie to Parker, Sept. 23, 1893, in *ibid.*

[33] The action of the eight cavalry and four infantry officers in the opening of the Cherokee Outlet is evaluated by citizens and officials in testimony collected in *House Doc. 27*, 1–86.

followed. Schoolchildren saw him, gun in hand, stalking the Indian past the hills southeast of town until the men were lost to view. Two shots were heard from that direction, and shortly afterward O'Hare reappeared to turn himself in to the sheriff, admitting he had killed the Indian. Townsmen grew angry over the crime, and O'Hare was ordered brought to trial before a coroner's jury. The next day, before he could be summoned, eighty-five Indians rode into town, went to the jail, and demanded the prisoner. The sheriff refused to release him, and the Indians fired their guns in the air before reluctantly returning to their camps.

Colonel Parker immediately dispatched Lieutenant Walker with Troop D, Third Cavalry, and scout Amos Chapman to the scene of the trouble. Chapman's arrival at the Cheyenne camp was more important than the arrival of the cavalry, for the Indians by that time had no fear of troops.[34]

Lieutenant Walker stationed his troops at Cheyenne and with an interpreter rejoined Chapman at the Indian village. Walker spent the night with the Indians, holding long talks with three chiefs, Spotted Horse, Red Moon, and White Shield. It soon became clear that the disturbance involved more than the murder of one Indian by a white man. The chiefs made several complaints to Lieutenant Walker, and he believed that they spoke the truth:

> First in regard their lands, they complain that for years the whites have been closing in on them from all sides and now although their lands are small they are pressed further and further. The whites pasture cattle and horses on their lands and the Indian can get no redress. They feel that although they are citizens they do not obtain the same rights as white citizens. Again, they

[34] Amos Chapman to Commanding Officer, Fort Supply, Nov. 25, 1893, Memorandum of Citizens of Cheyenne, O.T., to Amos Chapman, Nov. 26, 1893, Fort Supply, Letters Received, Box 10; Parker to AAG, Dept. of Mo., Nov. 29, 1893, Fort Supply, Letters Sent, Vol. 41.

are hungry and half naked. They do not get their full ration and what they do get is of inferior quality and often times not fit for dogs to eat. The issue of blankets and clothing heretofore has not been made at the beginning of the winter when needed, but in the spring. They feel they are unjustly treated in these and other ways.[35]

The good influence of Chapman, the understanding of Lieutenant Walker, and prompt and just action by the citizens of Cheyenne averted trouble. Colonel Parker remained concerned about the dissatisfaction among the Cheyennes but felt powerless to act without approval from his less sympathetic superiors.

The sudden rush of white settlement around Fort Supply in September, 1893, brought renegades as well as pioneers. Before the end of the year two men named McDonald and Hall had established a saloon, brothel, and gambling establishment three miles northeast of the Fort Supply Reservation boundary. The almost two hundred men of the Third Cavalry and Thirteenth Infantry stationed at the post found the ranch all too attractive, and the number of men absent without leave rose rapidly.

Woodward authorities closed the brothel and the gambling house, but since the proprietors had obtained the necessary liquor license, the saloon remained open. Colonel Parker unsuccessfully sought to dispossess the owners of the saloon by proving that they had taken up a claim with a declaration that the land would be used for agricultural or grazing purposes. At last, in March, 1894, Colonel Parker decided that only a general court-martial with a view to dishonorable discharge would stop the flight of enlisted men. Punishment, he said, had not worked, "there being no 'privileges' etc. at this Post of which to deprive the men."[36]

[35] Walker to Post Adjutant, Fort Supply, Dec. 6, 1893, Fort Supply, Letters Received, Box 10.

[36] Parker to County Attorney, Woodward, O.T., Jan. 22, 1894, Parker to AAG, Dept. of Mo., Mar. 23, 1894, Fort Supply, Letters Sent, Vol. 41.

Summer of 1894 was the last season in which Fort Supply served the citizens of Oklahoma Territory. Before the opening of the Cherokee Outlet the secretary of the interior, in accordance with the acts of Congress, had laid out two county-seat towns, Round Pond and Enid, on the Chicago, Rock Island and Pacific Railroad line. From almost the first day of settlement in September, 1893, the two towns had bitterly vied with each other for an exclusive railroad depot. It was the need to control those animosities that had kept Captain George Dodd in that vicinity for several weeks after his portion of District Two was opened.

In the following year the battle continued, with complications involving seven Cherokee allotments and Rock Island ownership of land at Round Pond and Enid. In an effort to restore peace, the secretary of the interior established two new townsites three miles south of the old stations, at Pond Creek and South Enid. There citizens brought great pressure against the Rock Island to establish depots at their towns by actions in Congress, in the Oklahoma territorial government, and in the courts.[37]

When they failed to secure results, Pond Creek and South Enid passed city ordinances attempting to force trains to slow down to "walking speed" as they passed, but the engineers refused, saying that if they did so they would be dragged from their cabs. Citizens used red lanterns, fired guns, and placed dynamite caps, a frame house, and even a stuffed effigy on the tracks to stop the locomotives, but all without success. By the end of June, 1894, stronger measures were taken, and citizens of Pond Creek blew up several bridges, tore up about one hundred yards of track, derailed a freight express, and stopped two mail and passenger trains.

[37] Berlin B. Chapman, "The Enid 'Railroad War': An Archival Study," *Chronicles of Oklahoma*, Vol. XLIII (Summer, 1965), 126–27; Rainey, *The Cherokee Strip*, 366–86.

When on July 12, 1894, the final legal appeal of the two towns to stop the trains was rebuffed by the Supreme Court of Oklahoma Territory, the towns resorted to even more violent efforts. Trestle-bridge supports, weakened by sawing, wrecked a fifteen-car train at dawn on Friday, July 13, and Marshal E. D. Nix at Guthrie was dispatched to the scene to protect government mail and interstate commerce. In addition to Marshal Nix, who went alone to Pond Creek, troops of the Third Cavalry from Fort Reno were sent by train directly to Pond Creek and Enid. Railroad employees patrolled tracks and bridges, but, undaunted, citizens burned two bridges near Pond Creek on July 16 and attempted to dynamite the Enid bridge.[38]

At that point Company H, Thirteenth Infantry, from Fort Supply was ordered out. Forty-eight men under Captain William Aurman and Lieutenant Abraham P. Buffington left Fort Supply at 7:00 A.M. on July 18 and moved fifteen miles by wagon to the Santa Fe station at Woodward. From there they were transported to Enid, arriving at mid-morning. Lieutenant Buffington and eighteen men were detached at Pond Creek while en route to guard bridges between that point and Enid. The rest of the company camped near Enid to guard the bridges and rails to South Enid. In all, the Thirteenth Infantry patrolled a twenty-mile strip.

Co-operating with the staff of the commander of the Department of the Missouri, on July 22 the force from Fort Supply proceeded to Round Pond, where they supported deputy marshals in arresting citizens who had acted against the railroad. After returning to their posts later that day, the troopers continued to guard the railroad bridges until July 28, when Captain Frank D. Baldwin of General Miles's staff reassembled

---

[38] Chapman, "Enid 'Railroad War,'" *loc. cit.*, 170, 178; Evett Dumas Nix, *Oklahombres*, 159–60.

them at Pond Creek. They left that station for Fort Supply on July 30.[39]

In the following weeks Congress stepped into the "Railroad War," and both South Enid and Pond Creek won depots on the Rock Island line. The Cherokee Outlet was far from tamed, but that series of incidents had demonstrated the great mobility which railroads provided troops in the Outlet. Distant posts either inside or outside Oklahoma Territory could rush troops to trouble spots in a very short time. It was no longer necessary, it seemed, to keep a post in the most isolated and sparsely settled part of Oklahoma Territory. The War Department talked of abandoning Fort Supply, and this time there was no reprieve.

Under orders of the Headquarters of the Army dated September 15, 1894, the garrison of Fort Supply—first the Third Cavalry and then the Thirteenth Infantry—left the post in October, 1894. A skeleton crew remained to forward equipment to Fort Sill until February 26, 1895, when Lieutenant F. E. Lacy, Tenth Infantry, placed Fort Supply in the custody of the Department of the Interior.[40]

[39] Post Returns, Fort Supply, July, 1894.

[40] General Orders No. 45, Headquarters of the Army, Sept. 15, 1894, AAG, Dept. of Mo., to Commanding Officer, Fort Supply, Nov. 23, Dec. 14, 1894, Fort Supply, Letters Received, Box 11; Post Returns, Fort Supply, Oct.–Dec., 1894, Feb., 1895.

Bibliography

I. MANUSCRIPTS

Duke University, Division of Manuscripts, Durham, North Carolina.
Seymour Kitching Papers.
Fort Sill Museum, Division of Manuscripts, Fort Sill, Oklahoma.
Medical History of Fort Sill, 1873–80.
Fort Sill, Letters Received, 1875–76, 1894–95.
Fort Sill, Letters Sent, 1875–76, 1886–90.
Kansas State Historical Society, Division of Manuscripts, Topeka, Kansas.
Joseph G. Masters Collection.
Henry H. Raymond Collection.
National Archives, Washington, D. C.
Records of the War Department.
Office of the Adjutant General, Record Group 94.
Post Returns, Fort Supply, I.T., 1868–95.
Medical History of Fort Supply, I.T., 1868–94.
Fort Supply, Reservation File.
United States Army Commands, Record Group 98.
Fort Supply, I.T., Letters Sent, 1868–95.
Camp Supply, I.T., Letters Received, 1868–75.
Fort Supply, I.T., Letters Received, 1868–95.
Organizational Returns.
Third Infantry, 1868–71.
Sixth Infantry, 1871–75.
Thirteenth Infantry, 1888.
Nineteenth Infantry, 1874–79.
Twenty-Fourth Infantry, 1880–88.
Twenty-Fifth Infantry, 1879–80.
Fourth Cavalry, 1877–81.

Fifth Cavalry, 1875–76, 1882–85.

Ninth Cavalry, 1882–85.

Tenth Cavalry, 1869–73.

Department of the Missouri, Letters Sent, 1873–94.

Department of the Missouri, Letters Received, 1870.

Cantonment, I.T., Letters Sent, 1879–82.

Cantonment, I.T., Letters Received, 1879–82.

Office of the Quartermaster General, Record Group 92.

Consolidated Quartermaster Correspondence.

K-File, Fort Supply.

Office of the Inspector General, Record Group 159.

Index to Inspection Reports, 1878–89.

Letters Received, 1869, 1878–89.

Office of the Commissary General, Record Group 192.

List of Military Posts in the United States and How Supplied with Subsistence, 1872–76.

Records of the Office of Indian Affairs, Record Group 75.

Central Superintendency, Field Office Files, Letters Received, 1869–77.

Central Superintendency, Field Office Files, Letters Sent, 1869–77.

Central Superintendency, Letters Received, 1869–75.

Central Superintendency, Letters Sent, 1879.

Cheyenne and Arapaho Agency, Letters Received, 1875.

Upper Arkansas Agency, Letters Received, 1869–75.

Records of the Department of the Interior, Record Group 49.

Federal Land Office, Abandoned Military Reservation File.

Commissioner of Indian Affairs, Letters Sent.

Oklahoma Historical Society, Indian Archives Division, Oklahoma City, Oklahoma.

Cheyenne and Arapaho Files.

Panhandle-Plains Historical Society, Division of Manuscripts, Canyon, Texas.

Laura V. Hamner Collection.

Division of Manuscripts Collection.

Interviews by J. Evetts Haley.

University of Oklahoma, Western History Collections, Norman, Oklahoma.

Donald J. Berthrong Collection.

Copies of Department of the Missouri, Selected Letters Sent, 1868–75.

Copies of Department of the Missouri, Selected Letters Received, 1873.

Copies of Headquarters of the Army, Selected Letters Received, 1868.

Copies of Military Division of the Missouri, Selected Letters Sent, 1868, 1874–75.

Copies of Military Division of the Missouri, Selected Letters Received, 1868–69.

Copies of Office of the Adjutant General, Selected Letters Received, 1868.

Walter S. Campbell Collection.

Typescript copies of Department of the Missouri, Selected Letters Received, 1878–79.

Typescript copies of Department of the Missouri, Selected Letters Sent, 1878.

Typescript copies of Military Division of the Missouri, Selected Letters Received, 1878.

Medical History of Fort Dodge, Kansas, 1868–69.

Reports and Journals of Scouts and Marches, Fort Dodge, Kansas, 1873–79.

Typescript of J. Wright Moor Interview.

Camp Supply Collection.

Camp Supply Letter Book.

Ben Clark Collection.

Dill's Indian Museum and Trading Post Collection.

Indian-Pioneer Papers.

William H. Leckie Collection.

Post Returns, Fort Dodge, Kansas, 1868–82.

Carl Coke Rister Collection.

Sherman-Sheridan Typescripts.

Phillips Collection Photostats on Cherokee Strip Live Stock Association.

II. GOVERNMENT PUBLICATIONS

Annual Report of the Commissioner of Indian Affairs for the Years 1868–94.

Annual Report of the Secretary of War for the Years 1868–94.

Congressional Record, 52 Cong., 1 sess.

Heitman, Francis B. *Historical Register and Dictionary of the United States Army.* 2 vols. Washington, Government Printing Office, 1903.

Hill, Edward E. *Preliminary Inventory of the Records of the Bureau of Indian Affairs.* 2 vols. Washington, The National Archives, 1965.

Hodge, Frederick W. *Handbook of American Indians North of Mexico.* Bulletin 30, Bureau of American Ethnology. Washington, Government Printing Office, 1912.

Kappler, Charles J. *Indian Affairs: Laws and Treaties.* 3 vols. Washington, Government Printing Office, 1903.

List of Military Posts, etc. Established in the United States from Its Earliest Settlement to the Present Time. War Department, Adjutant General's Office, Returns Division. Washington, Government Printing Office, 1902.

Mooney, James. "Calendar History of the Kiowa," *Seventeenth Annual Report of the Bureau of American Ethnology, 1895–96.* Washington, Government Printing Office, 1899.

Murphy, Kathryn M. *Oklahoma History and the National Archives.* N.p., n.d. [Box 286, Library of the National Archives, Washington, D. C.]

Pendell, Lucille H., and Elizabeth Bethel (comps.). *Preliminary Inventory of the Records of the Adjutant General's Office.* Washington, The National Archives, 1949.

Richardson, James D. *A Compilation of the Messages and Papers of the Presidents, 1789–1897.* 10 vols. Washington, Government Printing Office, 1896–99.

Thian, Raphael P. (comp.). *Notes Illustrating the Military Geography of the United States.* Adjutant General's Office. Washington, Government Printing Office, 1881.

U. S. Army, Military Division of the Missouri. *Record of Engagements with Hostile Indians within the Military Division of the Missouri, from 1868 to 1882.* Washington, Government Printing Office, 1882.

U. S. Congress, House. *House Exec. Doc. No. 1,* 41 Cong., 2 sess.; *No. 43,* 42 Cong., 3 sess.; *No. 32,* 43 Cong., 1 sess.; *No. 145,* 47 Cong., 1 sess.; *No. 17,* 48 Cong., 1 sess.; *No. 7,* 48 Cong., 2 sess.; *No. 240,* 49 Cong., 2 sess.; *No. 1,* 51 Cong., 1 sess.; *No. 27,* 53 Cong., 1 sess. *House Rep. No. 799,* 44 Cong., 1 sess.; *No. 3,768,* 51 Cong., 2 sess. *House Misc. Doc. No. 156,* 49 Cong., 2 sess.

U. S. Congress, Senate. *Sen. Exec. Doc. No. 13,* 40 Cong., 1 sess.; *No. 6,* 46 Cong., 2 sess.; *No. 111,* 47 Cong., 1 sess.; *No. 54,* 48 Cong., 1 sess.; *No. 16,* 48 Cong., 2 sess.; *No. 17,* 48 Cong., 2 sess.; *No. 41,* 50 Cong., 1 sess.; *No. 56,* 52 Cong., 1 sess.; *No. 63,* 52 Cong., 2 sess. *Sen. Rep. No. 708,* 48 Cong., 2 sess.

War Department, Circular No. 4, Surgeon General's Office. *A Report on Barracks and Hospitals, with Descriptions of Military Posts.* Washington, Government Printing Office, 1870.

War Department, Circular No. 8, Surgeon General's Office. *A Report on the Hygiene of the United States Army with Descriptions of Military Posts.* Washington, Government Printing Office, 1872.

III. ARTICLES

Archambeau, Ernest R. (ed.). "The Battle of Lyman's Wagon Train," *Panhandle-Plains Historical Review,* Vol. XXXVI (1963).

Bailey, Mahon. "Medical Sketch of the Nineteenth Regiment of Kansas Cavalry Volunteers," *Kansas Historical Quarterly,* Vol. VI (Nov., 1937).

Barteau, A. W. "Indian Raid Items," *Collections of the Kansas State Historical Society,* Vol. II (1879–80).

Breck, T. E. "When the Territory Was Young," *Chronicles of Oklahoma,* Vol. XIV (Sept., 1936).

Buntin, Martha. "Difficulties Encountered in Issuing Cheyenne and Arapaho Subsistence, 1861–70," *Chronicles of Oklahoma,* Vol. XIII (Mar., 1935).

Byers, O. P. "Personal Recollections of the Terrible Blizzard of 1886," *Collections of the Kansas State Historical Society*, Vol. XII (1912).

Campbell, Charles E. "Down Among the Red Men," *Collections of the Kansas State Historical Society*, Vol. XVII (1926–28).

Cassal, Hillary. "Missionary Tour in the Chickasaw Nation and Western Indian Territory," *Chronicles of Oklahoma*, Vol. XXXIV (Winter, 1956).

Chapman, Berlin B. "The Enid 'Railroad War': An Archival Study," *Chronicles of Oklahoma*, Vol. XLIII (Summer, 1965).

———. "How the Cherokees Acquired and Disposed of the Outlet," *Chronicles of Oklahoma*, Vol. XV (Mar., June, Sept., 1937).

———. "The Land Run of 1893, as Seen at Kiowa," *Kansas Historical Quarterly*, Vol. XXXI (Spring, 1965).

———. "Opening the Cherokee Outlet: An Archival Study," *Chronicles of Oklahoma*, Vol. XL (Summer, Autumn, 1962).

Collins, Herbert E. "Edwin Williams, Engineer," *Chronicles of Oklahoma*, Vol. X (Sept., 1932).

Connelley, William E. "John McBee's Account of the Expedition of the Nineteenth Kansas," *Collections of the Kansas State Historical Society*, Vol. XVII (1928).

Covington, James W. "Causes of the Dull Knife Raid," *Chronicles of Oklahoma*, Vol. V (Mar., 1927).

Dale, Edward E. "The Cherokee Strip Live Stock Association," *Chronicles of Oklahoma*, Vol. V (Mar., 1927).

———. "The Cheyenne-Arapaho Country," *Chronicles of Oklahoma*, Vol. XX (Dec., 1942).

———. "History of the Ranch Cattle Industry in Oklahoma," *Annual Report of the American Historical Association* (1920).

———. "Ranching on the Cheyenne-Arapaho Reservation, 1880–85," *Chronicles of Oklahoma*, Vol. VI (Mar., 1928).

———. "The Ranchman's Last Frontier," *Mississippi Valley Historical Review*, Vol. X (June, 1923).

Garfield, Marvin. "Defense of the Kansas Frontier, 1866–67," *Kansas Historical Quarterly*, Vol. I (Nov., 1932).

————. "Defense of the Kansas Frontier, 1868–69," *Kansas Historical Quarterly*, Vol. I (Aug., 1932).

————. "The Military Post as a Factor in the Frontier Defense of Kansas," *Kansas Historical Quarterly*, Vol. I (Nov., 1931).

Godfrey, E. S. "Some Reminiscences, Including an Account of General Sully's Expedition against the Southern Plains Indians," *Cavalry Journal*, Vol. XXXVI (July, 1927).

Hadley, James A. "The Kansas Cavalry and the Conquest of the Plains Indians," *Collections of the Kansas State Historical Society*, Vol. X (1908).

Harrel, Melvin (ed.). "My Life in the Indian Territory of Oklahoma —The Story of Augusta Corson Metcalf," *Chronicles of Oklahoma*. Vol. XXXIII (Spring, 1955).

Hastings, James K. "The Opening of Oklahoma," *Chronicles of Oklahoma*, Vol. XXVII (Spring, 1949).

Hazen, William B. "Some Corrections to Custer's *Life on the Plains*," *Chronicles of Oklahoma*, Vol. III (Dec., 1925).

Hollon, W. E. "Rushing for Land: Oklahoma, 1889," *The American West*, Vol. III (Fall, 1966).

Jacobs, Richard T. "Military Reminiscences of Captain Richard T. Jacobs," *Chronicles of Oklahoma*, Vol. II (Mar., 1924).

Kahn, Herman. "Records in the National Archives Relating to Range Cattle Industry, 1865–95," *Agricultural History*, Vol. XX (July, 1946).

Keeling, Henry C. "My Experiences with the Cheyenne Indians," *Collections of the Kansas State Historical Society*, Vol. XI (1909–10).

Kennan, Clara B. "Neighbors in the Cherokee Strip," *Chronicles of Oklahoma*, Vol. XXVIII (Spring, 1949).

Lemon, G. E. "Reminiscences of Pioneer Days in the Cherokee Strip," *Chronicles of Oklahoma*, Vol. XXII (Winter, 1944).

McKinley, J. W. "J. W. McKinley's Narrative," *Panhandle-Plains Historical Review*, Vol. XXXVI (1963).

Milam, Joe B. "The Opening of the Cherokee Outlet," *Chronicles of Oklahoma*, Vol. IX (Sept., Dec., 1931); Vol. X (Mar., 1932).

Montgomery, Mrs. Frank C. "Fort Wallace and Its Relation to the Frontier," *Collections of the Kansas State Historical Society*, Vol. XVII (1928).

Moore, Horace L. "The Nineteenth Kansas Cavalry," *Collections of the Kansas State Historical Society*, Vol. VI (1897–1900).

Murphy, John. "Reminiscences of the Washita Campaign and of the Darlington Indian Agency," *Chronicles of Oklahoma*, Vol. I (June, 1923).

Nicholson, William. "A Tour of Indian Agencies in Kansas and the Indian Territory in 1870," *Kansas Historical Quarterly*, Vol. III (Aug., Nov., 1934).

Records, Ralph H. "Recollections of April 19, 1892," *Chronicles of Oklahoma*, Vol. XXI (Mar., 1943).

Rister, Carl Coke. "Colonel A. W. Evans' Christmas Day Indian Fight (1868)," *Chronicles of Oklahoma*, Vol. XVI (Sept., 1938).

Runyon, A. L. "A. L. Runyon's Letters, from the Nineteenth Kansas Regiment," *Kansas Historical Quarterly*, Vol. IX (Feb., 1940).

Shirk, George H. "Campaigning with Sheridan: A Farrier's Diary," *Chronicles of Oklahoma*, Vol. XXXVII (Spring, 1939).

Snell, Joseph W. (ed.). "Diary of a Dodge City Buffalo Hunter, 1872–73," *Kansas Historical Quarterly*, Vol. XXXI (Winter, 1965).

Steele, Aubrey L. "The Beginning of Quaker Administration of Indian Affairs in Oklahoma," *Chronicles of Oklahoma*, Vol. XVII (Dec., 1939).

———. "Lawrie Tatum's Indian Policy," *Chronicles of Oklahoma*, Vol. XXII (Spring, 1944).

Taylor, Joe E. (ed.). "The Indian Campaign on the Staked Plains, 1874–75," *Panhandle-Plains Historical Review*, Vol. XXXIV (1961).

Tennant, H. S. "The Texas Cattle Trails," *Chronicles of Oklahoma*, Vol. XIV (Mar., 1936).

Wade, J. S. "Uncle Sam's Horse-Race for Land: The Opening of the 'Cherokee Strip,'" *Chronicles of Oklahoma*, Vol. XXXV (Summer, 1957).

Wardell, Morris L. "The History of No-Man's Land or Old Beaver County," *Chronicles of Oklahoma*, Vol. I (Jan., 1921).

Welty, Raymond L. "The Policing of the Frontier by the Army, 1860–70," *Kansas Historical Quarterly*, Vol. VII (Aug., 1938).

———. "Supplying the Frontier Military Posts," *Kansas Historical Quarterly*, Vol. VII (May, 1938).

White, Lonnie J. "Indian Battles in the Texas Panhandle, 1874," *Journal of the West*, Vol. VI (Apr., 1967).

———. "Winter Campaigning with Sheridan and Custer," *Journal of the West*, Vol. VI (Jan., 1967).

Wright, R. M. "Personal Reminiscences of Frontier Life in Southwest Kansas," *Collections of the Kansas State Historical Society*, Vol. VII (1902).

IV. NEWSPAPERS AND MAGAZINES

Army and Navy Journal.
Caldwell (Kansas) *Messenger.*
Coldwater (Kansas) *Enterprise.*
Darlington (Oklahoma Territory) *Cheyenne Transporter.*
Dodge City, Kansas, *Kansas Cowboy.*
Dodge City (Kansas) *Times.*
El Reno (Oklahoma) *Herald.*
Ford City (Kansas) *Gazette.*
Ford County (Kansas) *Globe.*
Harper's Weekly Magazine.
Leavenworth (Kansas) *Daily Commercial.*
New York Herald.
Oklahoma City, Oklahoma, *Daily Oklahoman.*
Ryansville (Kansas) *Boomer.*
Supply (Oklahoma) *Republican.*
Winners of the West.

V. BOOKS

Adams, Andy. *The Log of a Cowboy.* Boston, Houghton Mifflin Co., 1931.

Adams, E. Lee. *The Stripper.* N.p., 1954.

Armes, George A. *Ups and Downs of an Army Officer*. Washington, D. C., 1900.

Armor, T. H. *Tactics and Techniques of Cavalry*. Harrisburg, Military Service Publishing Co., 1939.

Ashburn, Percy M. *A History of the Medical Department of the United States Army*. Boston, Houghton Mifflin Co., 1929.

Athearn, Robert G. *William Tecumseh Sherman and the Settlement of the West*. Norman, University of Oklahoma Press, 1956.

Baldwin, Alice Blackwood (ed.). *Memoirs of the Late Frank D. Baldwin*. Los Angeles, Wetzel Publishers Co., Inc., 1929.

Berthrong, Donald J. *The Southern Cheyennes*. Norman, University of Oklahoma Press, 1963.

Biddle, Ellen McGowan. *Reminiscences of a Soldier's Wife*. Philadelphia, J. B. Lippincott Co., 1907.

Boyd, Mrs. Orsemus Bronson. *Cavalry Life in Tent and Field*. New York, J. Selwin Tait and Sons, 1894.

Brill, Charles J. *Conquest of the Southern Plains*. Oklahoma City, Golden Saga Publishers, 1938.

Brininstool, E. A. *Dull Knife*. Hollywood, privately printed, 1935.

Carter, William Harding. *The Life of Lieutenant General Chaffee*. Chicago, University of Chicago Press, 1917.

Chandler, Melbourne C. (comp.). *Of Garry Owen in Glory: The History of the Seventh United States Cavalry Regiment*. Annadale, Va., The Turnpike Press, 1960.

Collins, Dennis. *The Indians' Last Stand or the Dull Knife Raid*. Girard, Kan., The Appeal to Reason Press, 1915.

Conover, G. W. *Sixty Years in Southwest Oklahoma*. Anadarko, Okla., N. T. Plummer, 1927.

Croy, Homer. *Trigger Marshal: The Story of Chris Madsen*. New York, Duell, Sloan and Pearce, 1958.

Custer, George A. *My Life on the Plains*. Norman, University of Oklahoma Press, 1962.

Custer, Mrs. Elizabeth. *Tenting on the Plains*. New York, C. L. Webster and Co., 1887.

Dale, Edward E. *Cow Country*. Norman, University of Oklahoma Press, 1942.

————. *The Range Cattle Industry.* Norman, University of Oklahoma Press, 1960.

Dixon, Olive. *The Life of Billy Dixon.* Dallas, Tex., P. L. Turner Co., 1927.

Dyer, Mrs. D. B. *Fort Reno.* New York, G. W. Dillingham, 1896.

Forsyth, George A. *Thrilling Days in Army Life.* New York, Harper and Brothers, 1902.

Frazer, Robert W. *Forts of the West.* Norman, University of Oklahoma Press, 1965.

Freeman, G. D. *Midnight and Noonday: Or the Incidental History of Southern Kansas and the Indian Territory.* Caldwell, Kan., 1892.

Gard, Wayne. *The Chisholm Trail.* Norman, University of Oklahoma Press, 1954.

Gould, Charles N. *Covered Wagon Geologist.* Norman, University of Oklahoma Press, 1959.

Grinnell, George B. *The Fighting Cheyennes.* Norman, University of Oklahoma Press, 1956.

Hamner, Laura V. *Short Grass and Longhorns.* Norman, University of Oklahoma Press, 1943.

Herr, John K., and Edward S. Wallace. *The Story of the United States Cavalry, 1775–1942.* Boston, Little, Brown and Co., 1953.

Hudson, Wilson M. *Andy Adams: His Life and Writings.* Dallas, Southern Methodist University Press, 1964.

Hunter, John M. *The Bloody Trail in Texas: Sketches and Narratives of Indian Raids and Atrocities on Our Frontier.* Bandera, Tex., J. M. Hunter, 1931.

Johnson, Virginia W. *The Unregimented General: A Biography of Nelson A. Miles.* Boston, Houghton Mifflin Co., 1962.

Kansas State Historical Society and Department of Archives. *History of Kansas Newspapers, 1854–1916.* Topeka, Kansas State Printing Plant, 1916.

Keim, De B. Randolph. *Sheridan's Troopers on the Borders: A Winter Campaign on the Plains.* Philadelphia, Claxton, Remsen and Haffelflinger, 1870.

Knight, Oliver H. *Following the Indian Wars.* Norman, University of Oklahoma Press, 1960.

Lackey, Vinson. *The Forts of Oklahoma*. Tulsa, Tulsa Printing Co., 1963.

Leckie, William H. *The Buffalo Soldiers*. Norman, University of Oklahoma Press, 1967.

———. *Military Conquest of the Southern Plains*. Norman, University of Oklahoma Press, 1963.

Miles, Nelson A. *Personal Recollections of General Nelson A. Miles*. Chicago, Werner Co., 1896.

Morris, John W., and Edwin C. McReynolds. *Historical Atlas of Oklahoma*. Norman, University of Oklahoma Press, 1965.

Morrison, William B. *Military Posts and Camps in Oklahoma*. Oklahoma City, Harlow Publishing Co., 1936.

Nix, Evett Dumas. *Oklahombres*. N.p., 1929.

Nye, Wilbur S. *Carbine and Lance: The Story of Old Fort Sill*. Norman, University of Oklahoma Press, 1937.

Price, George F. (comp.). *Across the Continent with the Fifth Cavalry*. New York, D. Van Nostrand, 1883.

Prucha, Francis Paul. *A Guide to the Military Posts of the United States, 1789–1895*. Madison, Wisconsin State Historical Society, 1964.

Rainey, George. *The Cherokee Strip*. Guthrie, Okla., Co-operative Publishing Co., 1933.

Rickey, Don, Jr. *Forty Miles a Day on Beans and Hay: The Enlisted Soldier Fighting the Indian Wars*. Norman, University of Oklahoma Press, 1963.

Rister, Carl Coke. *Border Command: General Phil Sheridan in the West*. Norman, University of Oklahoma Press, 1944.

———. *Land Hunger: David L. Payne and the Oklahoma Boomers*. Norman, University of Oklahoma Press, 1942.

———. *No Man's Land*. Norman, University of Oklahoma Press, 1948.

Roe, Frances M. A. *Army Letters from an Officer's Wife, 1871–88*. New York, D. Appleton and Co., 1909.

Sandoz, Mari. *Cheyenne Autumn*. New York, McGraw-Hill, 1953.

Scanlan, Tom (ed.). *Army Times Guide to Army Posts*. Harrisburg, Military Service Division, The Stackpole Co., 1963.

Sheridan, Philip H. *Personal Memoirs*. 2 vols. New York, Chester L. Webster and Co., 1888.

Sherman, William T. *Memoirs of General W. T. Sherman*. 2 vols. New York, Chester L. Webster and Co., 1892.

Spotts, David L. *Campaigning with Custer and the Nineteenth Kansas Volunteer Cavalry on the Washita Campaign, 1868–69*. Los Angeles, Wetzel Publishing Co., 1928.

Whitman, S. E. *The Troopers: An Informal History of the Plains Cavalry, 1865–90*. New York, Hastings House, 1962.

VI. Unpublished Materials

Fowler, Arlen L. "The Negro Infantry in the West, 1869–91." Unpublished Ph.D. dissertation, Department of History, Washington State University, 1968.

Kroeker, Marvin E. "William B. Hazen: A Military Career in the Frontier West, 1855–80." Unpublished Ph.D. dissertation, Department of History, University of Oklahoma, 1966.

Monahan, Forrest D., Jr. "Trade Goods on the Prairie: The Kiowa Tribe and White Trade Goods, 1794–1875." Unpublished Ph.D. dissertation, Department of History, University of Oklahoma, 1965.

Oswald, James. "Fort Elliott, Texas: Frontier Post." Unpublished M.A. thesis, Department of History, West Texas State College, 1958.

Wright, Peter M. "Fort Reno, Indian Territory, 1874–85." Unpublished M.A. thesis, Department of History, University of Oklahoma, 1965.

Index

Adobe Walls, Texas: 88ff., 102, 118

Allen, Richard: 167

Alva, Indian Territory: 199, 203, 205, 207, 211, 212

Amick, Lt. Myron J.: 38, 50, 52

Andrews, George: 202

Andrews, J. V.: 168, 172

Andrews, Lt. E. P.: 166, 167, 170ff., 189–90

Arapaho Indians: 3, 11, 14, 28, 30–31, 34–35, 39–40, 42–43, 45–46, 49, 53, 54, 57, 59, 61ff., 72ff., 82, 86, 108–11, 116ff., 131–32, 160, 162, 164, 178n.

Arkansas City, Kans.: 134, 135, 191, 205n., 207, 208

Arkansas River: 4, 15, 34n., 42, 45, 70, 78, 91, 126, 127, 207, 208n., 213

Armes, Capt. George W.: 49

Ashland, Kans.: 186

Atchison, Topeka and Santa Fe Railroad: 64, 91, 130, 131, 144, 145, 174, 194–95&n., 207, 212, 219

Atlantic and Pacific Railroad: 60, 64, 157

Augur, Capt. Jacob A.: 189–91, 194–96, 201

Augur, Gen. C. C.: 92, 165

Aurman, Capt. William: 219

Babcock, Capt. John B.: 171

Baker's Ranch (Indian Territory): 79

Baldwin, Lt. Frank D.: 93–94, 96–97, 100, 219

Barrett, Theodore H.: 76

Battle of Camp Supply (1870): 52–53

Battle of Lyman's Wagon Train (1874): 97–98

Battle of Punished Woman's Fork (1878): 127–28

Battle of Sand Creek (1878): 126–27

Battle of Turkey Springs (1878): 122–23

Battle of the Washita (1868): 23–24

Bear Creek Mail Station, Kans.: 43–44, 49–50, 54, 57, 66–67, 71, 89; see also Upper Bear Creek Station, Kans.

Beaver River: 11–12, 14, 17n., 20, 34, 39, 46ff., 52, 53, 58, 59, 64, 71, 93, 109, 131, 146

Belknap, William: 148

Bell, L. B. (Cherokee): 191

Biddle, Maj. James: 92, 102, 104, 107

Big Bow (Kiowa): 84

Big Horse (Cheyenne): 46

Big Jake (Cheyenne): 55–56

Big Mouth (Arapaho): 51, 117

Bishop, Lt. Horace S.: 109

Black, Lt. William: 172

Black Beaver (Deleware): 73

Black Horse (Cheyenne): 105

Black Kettle (Cheyenne): 23, 25

Bliss, Col. Zenas R.: 175, 179, 186

Bodamer, Lt. John A.: 50–52

Bonney, Seth: 32–36

Boomers: 133–34

Bradford, Capt. James: 110, 127

Brereton, Lt. John J.: 168

Bristol, Capt. H. B.: 92

Broadhead, Maj. A. J.: 151

Brooke, Lt. Col. John R., commander of Fort Supply: 77–90

Brown, John F. (Seminole): 73

Bryant, Col. Montgomery, commander of Fort Supply: 194–99
Budd, Lt. Otho W.: 118
Buell, Lt. Col. George P.: 92, 104
Buffalo hunters: 85, 88, 90, 107–108&n., 109
Buffington, Lt. Abraham P.: 219
Bull Bear (Cheyenne): 40, 43, 45, 46, 77, 86

Caldwell, Kans.: 85, 87, 89, 90, 170, 175, 178, 183, 184, 190, 191, 205, 208, 210, 213ff.
Caldwell, Lt. F. M.: 207, 213
Caldwell Cattle Trail: 175, 177; *see also* Old Caldwell Cattle Trail
"California Joe" (Moses E. Milner): 23, 24
Cameron, Kans.: 205n., 210
Campbell, B. H.: 162
Campo, Joe: 149–50&n.
Camp Supply: *see* Fort Supply
Camp Supply Social Club: 154
Canadian River: 61, 64, 71, 82, 89, 94ff., 101ff., 119, 147, 157, 169ff., 177, 193
Cantonment (on North Fork of Canadian River, Indian Territory): 129–30, 132ff., 144, 157, 159, 161, 166, 171, 172, 175, 178&n., 181, 184
Cantonment (on Sweetwater River, Texas): 103–104, 107; *see also* Fort Elliott, Texas
Cantonment–Supply road: 181
Carpenter, Capt. Louis H.: 48, 166, 171
Carr, Maj. Eugene A.: 14, 15, 28, 30, 45
Cavenaugh, Capt. Henry G.: 211, 212
Chaffee, Capt. Adna R.: 78, 106
Chalk (Arapaho): 123
Chandler, George: 193
Chapman, Amos: 11, 79, 98–99&n., 100n., 116, 120, 131–32, 161, 163, 175, 178, 216–17
Cherokee Commission: 87, 201
Cherokee Indians: 157, 158, 161ff., 182, 185ff., 191, 201; acquire Cherokee Outlet, 182–83; dispute title to Out-

let, 188; sell Outlet, 196; sue Cherokee Strip Live Stock Association, 192; *see also* Cherokee Outlet
Cherokee Outlet: 34n., 36, 157, 160, 162, 168ff., 180ff.; grazing forbidden in, 188; illegal trespass in, 187; patroled by military, 185, 189–204; preparations to open for settlement in, 204; *see also* Cherokee Indians
Cherokee Strip Live Stock Association: 173, 185, 188, 192; incorporation of and leases by, 184, 187
Cheyenne and Arapaho Agency: 32n., 38, 45–46, 51, 53, 56, 60, 64, 67, 87ff., 102ff., 110–11, 113, 115, 175
Cheyenne and Arapaho Cattle Company: 166
Cheyenne and Arapaho Reservation: 25, 35, 36, 160, 162, 165ff., 170, 173, 180, 182, 196
Cheyenne-Arapaho Live Stock Association: 164, 166
Cheyenne Indians: 3–4, 10–11, 14, 28–31, 34, 37–38, 40, 42–43, 45–46, 51, 53ff., 60–61, 67–71, 74ff., 82, 86ff., 107ff., 129ff., 151, 160ff., 175, 178&n.
Cheyenne Medicine Lodge Reservation: 31, 34&n., 35–36
Chicago, Rock Island and Pacific Railway: 208n., 209, 210, 213, 214, 218–20
Chilocco School Reservation: 175, 205, 207, 213, 215
Chisholm Trail: 90, 169
Cimarron Redoubt, Kans.: 57–58, 70, 71, 73, 107, 145&n.
Cimarron River: 5, 10–11, 16, 18, 34n., 57, 58, 70ff., 82, 85ff., 105, 112, 119, 125, 131, 133, 145, 146n., 152, 169, 174, 177, 179n., 185, 199
Clark, Ben: 11, 34, 40, 47, 73, 81, 129
Clark, Sidney: 44
Clarke, Red: 145
Cleary, Peter J. A.: 141
Cleveland, Pres. Grover: 165, 166, 205
Cody, William (Buffalo Bill): 28
Coffeyville, Kans.: 134
Colcord, Charles: 122

Coleman, Lt. L. H.: 49
Colorado Cattle Trail: 174, 190
Comanche Indians: 3ff., 11, 14, 27,
  42–43, 46–47, 52, 57, 59, 62, 81, 89ff.
Compton, Maj. Charles E.: 89, 90, 92,
  93
Coons, Harry: 124
Corbin, Joe: 23
Cornish, Lt. Lester W.: 179
Council Grove, Kans.: 5, 42
Crawford, Gov. Samuel J.: 4, 9, 19&n.
Curtis, Dick: 47, 49, 52
Custer, Col. George A.: 16, 18, 23ff.,
  100
Custer Trail: 40

Dallas, Maj. Alexander J.: 131, 132,
  135
Darlington, Brinton: 31–32&n., 34, 38–
  39, 44–46, 56, 61, 72
Darlington Agency: see Cheyenne and
  Arapaho Agency
Davidson, Col. John: 92, 104, 122, 156;
  commander of Fort Supply, 56–77
Davis, Capt. Wirt: 113–14
Davis, Col. Jefferson C.: 53, 130
Davis, Lt. William: 20, 51
Day Brothers' Turkey Track Ranch:
  161, 172, 199
Deep Creek Cattle Trail: 175, 177–
  80&n., 189
Deming, E. N.: 76
Department of Agriculture, U.S.: 195,
  198
Department of the Interior, U.S.: 9,
  91, 119, 162, 171, 179, 180, 183, 186,
  188, 193, 197, 202, 204, 220
Department of the Missouri (U.S.
  Army): 5, 8, 45, 65, 68, 78, 91ff., 100,
  107, 121–22, 129, 131, 133–34, 147,
  157, 159, 165, 170, 171, 179, 180, 185,
  186, 189, 197ff., 219
Department of Texas: 78, 92
Department of War, U.S.: 5, 9, 91, 159,
  162, 163, 179, 183, 186, 197
Desertion: 142
Dickey brothers' ranch (in Cherokee
  Outlet): 162, 163, 172

Dilsey, Jacob: 83
District of the Upper Arkansas (U.S.
  Army): 8, 10, 15, 16
Division of the Missouri (U.S. Army):
  5, 24, 79
Dixson, Billy: 98–100&n.
Doan's Store (on Red River): 169, 173
Dodge, Lt. Col. Richard I.: 130, 132
Dodge City, Kan.: 15, 64, 73, 117, 118,
  126, 130, 141–48&n., 160, 169, 178,
  181
Dodge City Cattle Trail: 169, 170, 173,
  174, 189, 190, 193
Dodge City (Kans.) *Times*: 143
Dodge–Elliott Road: 146&n., 174
Dodge–Supply Road: 18n., 40, 43–44,
  49, 51, 57ff., 63, 70ff., 89ff., 106, 108,
  120–21, 130, 131, 145, 146, 169, 180,
  181, 186
Dog Soldiers (Cheyenne): 3, 11, 30,
  40, 43, 61
Driskill, J. W.: 125&n.
Dull Knife (Northern Cheyenne):
  116–17, 119–28, 131
Dyer, D. B.: 164–66

Edmonson, Will: 52
Eighth Cavalry, U.S.: 92, 104
Eleventh Infantry, U.S.: 92
Elkins, Samuel B.: 198
Elliott (or Elliot), Maj. Joel H.: 10,
  12, 13, 27
Elting, Capt. Oscar: 207, 208, 213
Enid, Indian Territory: 194, 196, 205,
  207, 210, 212, 218–19
Evans, Col. Andrew W.: 15, 27–28
Evans, J. S.: 148
Ewers, Capt. Ezra P.: 79

Farnsworth, Lt. Henry J.: 104
Fenlon, Edward: 162, 166, 167
Fifth Cavalry, U.S.: 108, 110, 111,
  166, 170, 171, 178ff., 189, 191, 196,
  199
Fifth Infantry, U.S.: 79, 90, 92
Forbes, A. S. C.: 167
Ford County Globe (Dodge City):
  143–44

Fort Arbuckle, Indian Territory: 8, 13&n., 28
Fort Bascom, New Mexico Territory: 8, 14, 15, 27–28, 63, 76, 77, 82, 84
Fort Bayard, New Mexico Territory: 8
Fort Cobb, Indian Territory: 4n., 15, 18, 27ff.
Fort Dodge, Kans.: 8, 10ff., 26, 27, 29, 38, 40, 44, 49, 50, 57, 58, 62ff., 77, 78, 80, 89ff., 102, 104, 122ff., 133, 144, 145, 151, 159
Fort Elliott, Texas: 103–104, 111ff., 125, 129ff., 144, 146&n., 160, 174, 175, 180, 181, 189; *see also* Cantonment (on Sweetwater River, Texas)
Fort Gibson, Indian Territory: 8, 13n., 135
Fort Griffin, Texas: 169
Fort Griffin–Dodge Cattle Trail: 169n.
Fort Harker, Kans.: 8, 35
Fort Hays, Kans.: 8, 15, 17, 42, 44, 64, 66, 122, 144
Fort Larned, Kans.: 8, 38, 64, 77
Fort Leavenworth, Kans.: 8, 13n., 64, 96
Fort Lyon, Colorado Territory: 8, 13ff., 28, 72, 83, 91, 122, 131
Fort Reno, Indian Territory: 107, 111, 112, 119ff., 129ff., 150, 157, 159, 162, 164ff., 174, 181, 184, 189ff., 198, 201, 205, 207, 209ff., 219
Fort Riley, Kans.: 8, 125, 198, 205ff.
Fort Sill, Indian Territory: 27ff., 35, 54, 65, 79, 84, 87, 91ff., 104–105, 113–14, 122, 144, 148, 177, 180, 181, 189, 193, 207, 212
"Fort Sitting Bull" (at Springer whisky ranch): 151
Fort Smith, Ark.: 8, 74
Fort Sumner, New Mexico Territory: 82
Fort Supply, Indian Territory: location of, 13, 16, 35–37, 67–68, 156; supply duty of, to military, 13, 26, 63–64, 93–104, 107; building program of, 17, 20, 39, 63–64, 137–38; as temporary Cheyenne and Arapaho Agency, 31–45; supply duty of, to

Indians, 32–34, 45, 54, 117–18; and horse thieves, 42, 79–80, 108–109, 112, 114–15; and whisky peddlers, 44, 60, 64–65, 73–75, 80; Indian attacks on, 47–53; legal restrictions on duties of, 60, 73–74, 157, 160, 186, 195, 202–203; and Kiowa raids, 62, 66–71; patrol and escort duty of, 70–71, 78–79, 82, 184–87; and illegal buffalo hunters, 85–86; and Indian Territory Expedition, 93–104; and Dull Knife Raid, 120–28; in Enid Railroad War, 128–30; cattle removal by, from Cheyenne-Arapaho Reservation, 166; cattle-trail duty of, 170–74; cattle removal by, from Cherokee Outlet, 189–204; and opening of Cherokee Outlet to settlement, 205–15; abandonment of, 220; *see also* Fort Supply Military Reservation
Fort Supply Military Reservation: 157–59, 205, 217; *see also* Fort Supply, Indian Territory
Fort Union, New Mexico Territory: 8, 83, 92
Fort Wallace, Kans.: 8, 106, 109, 122, 159
Fort Wingate, New Mexico Territory: 8, 180n.
Fourth Cavalry, U.S.: 92, 108, 113, 115ff., 120–29, 131, 134
"Frenchy" (horse thief): 75, 79, 86–87&n.
Fulton, Lt. David W.: 178, 179

Gageby, Capt. James J.: 75
Gallagher, "Slippery Jack": 75, 79–80, 86–87, 89
Gardner, Lt. Cornelius: 94
Garfield, Rep. James A.: 148
Gibbs, Bill: 149, 150
Grant, Pres. Ulysses S.: 29
Gregg, Col. J. Irwin: 81
Grey Beard (Cheyenne): 61, 69, 77, 89
Grimes, William: 191, 194
Guerrier, Edmond: 81

237

Gunther, Capt. Sebastian: 116, 125–
28&n.
Guthrie, Jacob (Cherokee): 192, 196–
98
Guthrie, Oklahoma Territory: 181, 191,
219

Hale, Lt. Joseph: 45, 51, 53
Hall, Capt. William P.: 192
Haller, Col. Granville O.: 156
Hambright, Maj. Henry A.: 115,
119ff., 123, 128
Hamilton, Capt. John M.: 110
Hamilton, Capt. Louis M.: 25
Harbers, H.: 137, 142
Hardie, Capt. Francis H.: 207, 210,
211, 214
Harper, Lt. William: 70, 78
Harriman, Joseph: 112
Harrington, John: 98–99&n.
Harrison, Pres. Benjamin: 188, 189,
193, 197
Hays, Lt. Edward M.: 110–11
Hazen, Gen. William B.: 14, 27, 29, 30,
148
Head, Capt. George B.: 68, 70
Heaps of Birds (Arapaho): 63
Hedekin, Capt. Charles A.: 207, 209,
210, 214
Hemphill, Capt. William A.: 120–21,
124–25, 128–29, 134–35
Henley, Lt. Austin: 106
Hennessey, Oklahoma Territory:
205n., 210, 211, 214
Hennessey, Patrick: 89
Hershfield, Jacob: 42–43
Hill, J. R.: 213&n.
Hill, Lt. R. H.: 159
Hoag, Enoch: 45, 90
Hoag, J. J.: 74
Hollis, Bob: 79–80, 86–87
Holloway, John F.: 88
Hollsenfrillen, Capt. Charles W.: 95
Horse thieves: 42, 79–80, 86–88, 90,
107–109, 111–15, 118–19
Horton, E. M.: 164, 165
Hughes, Capt. Robert: 58
Hunnewell, Kans.: 191, 205n., 208, 213

Hunter, Capt. George K.: 207, 211
Hunting: 22, 152; illegal, 186–87

Indian Territory Expedition: 92–104
Inman, Maj. Henry: 19, 26

Jefferson, Johnny: 114
Jenkins, Maj. R. W.: 19
"Jerry," letter from, to *Ford County
Globe*: 143
Johnson, Capt. J. B.: 207, 209, 213
Jones, Chummy: 113–14
Jones-Plummer Cattle Trail: 146n.,
174
Jordan, Richard: 72

Kansas Pacific Railroad: 64, 110, 122
Kaw Indians: 42, 182, 205, 208
Keim, De B. Randolph: 17, 19ff.
Kelley, Lt. Joseph M.: 70, 75
Kennedy, Capt. William B.: 57, 61, 65,
70
Kerrigan, Sgt. Patrick: 151
Keyes, Lt. Edward L.: 108
Kickingbird (Kiowa): 42–43, 46
Kidd, Maj. Milo: 38–39, 43, 49–50
Kingfisher, Oklahoma Territory: 192
Kingsbury, Lt. Henry P.: 85, 98, 99
Kiowa, Kans.: 184, 185, 191, 193ff.,
202ff., 205n., 209ff., 214
Kiowa-Apache Indians: 3ff., 14, 27, 46,
48, 57, 62
Kiowa-Comanche Reservation: 4n., 27,
164
Kiowa Indians: 3ff., 11, 14, 27, 42–43,
46–47, 48ff., 57ff., 66–71, 81ff., 88ff.,
160, 164
Kiowa road (in Cherokee Outlet): 185
Kollar's Ranch (near Fort Supply):
124&n.

Landis, Henry S.: 197, 202
Larison, J. M.: 190
Lawton, Lt. Gerry W.: 113
Lazarus, William: 178–80&n.
Ledbetter, Tom: 150
Lee, Capt. Jesse M.: 166
Lee and Reynolds Company (post

238

traders): 59–60, 65, 104, 114, 141, 147, 149, 153, 154
Lee, W. M. D.: 80, 148, 149n.
Leeper, Lt. William: 132
Lefebvre, E. C.: 88, 109
Left Hand (Arapaho): 61, 119
Lewis, Lt. Granville: 97
Lewis, Lt. Col. William H.: 112, 124, 127–28; commander of Fort Supply, 90–108
Little, Lt. John: 175, 177
Little Beaver (Osage): 24
Little Chief (Northern Cheyenne): 131, 133
Little Heart (Kiowa): 47, 53–54
Little Raven (Arapaho): 28, 57, 60, 64, 69, 116, 119
Little Robe (Cheyenne): 29, 30, 42, 46–47, 71, 76, 81, 86–88, 118, 129, 163ff., 168
Little Wolf (Northern Cheyenne): 120–28
Lone Wolf (Kiowa): 4, 5, 27, 86
Lyman, Capt. Wyllys: 94–95, 97–98, 100, 101
Lyster, Capt. William J.: 128–29, 138

McCarlow, Charles: 115
Mackenzie, Col. Ranald S.: 92, 102, 104
Malaley, William: 112
Maley, Silas: 145
Marshall, Nate: 20&n.
Martin, Hurricane Bill: 86–87&n.
Maxson, Lt. Mason M.: 48, 52–53
Mauck, Lt. Clarence: 125, 128, 129
Medicine Arrow (Cheyenne): 31, 37, 40, 44ff., 89
Medicine Lodge Treaty: 4, 27, 74; *see also* Cheyenne Medicine Lodge Reservation
Medicine Water (Cheyenne): 89
Mescalero Apache Indians: 62
Miles, Col. Nelson A.: 92–104, 165, 166, 205, 219
Miles, John D.: 72ff., 81, 86, 88–90, 111–13, 120, 162ff.

Milner, Moses E. ("California Joe"): 23, 24
Mizner, Maj. John K.: 120
Moore, Capt. Orlando H.: 65–67, 69
Moore, Col. Horace L.: 18
Morrow, Charlie: 113–14
Morse, Capt. Charles E.: 126–27
Murray, James: 49–50

Neill, Lt. Col. Thomas H.: 92, 105, 107
Nelson, Lt. Col. Anderson D.: 142, 148; commander of Fort Supply, 31–56
Nichols, W. A.: 23, 54
Nicholson, William: 112
Nineteenth Infantry, U.S.: 90, 94–95, 106, 108, 111, 122, 126, 127, 151, 153
Nineteenth Kansas Volunteer Cavalry: 15, 17&n., 18ff., 21, 24, 26, 28
Ninth Cavalry, U.S.: 92
Nix, E. D.: 219
Noble, John W.: 188, 198&n.
Nolan, Capt. Nicholas: 47–48, 52–53, 59, 62, 63
No Man's Land (Oklahoma Panhandle): 112, 192n., 198
North Canadian River: 12, 17n., 27, 34, 35, 62, 64, 78, 80, 130, 133, 172, 175ff., 179n.
Northern Arapaho Indians: 86–87
Northern Cheyenne Indians: 72, 113, 116–17, 119–28, 131–33, 135

O'Hare, Tom: 215
Oklahoma Territory: 187–88, 192, 204, 205n., 208n., 211, 213, 218
Old Cactus (of *Dodge City Times*): 117, 143, 154
Old Caldwell Cattle Trail: 160, 164, 169, 170ff., 178, 179&n., 182, 189; *see also* Caldwell Cattle Trail
Old Texas Trail: 169n.
Orlando, Oklahoma Territory: 205n., 207, 209, 213
Osage Indians: 24–25, 34, 38, 71, 82, 182, 192, 205, 208, 213

Oto-Missouri Reservation: 182, 205, 209

Paddock, Capt. George H.: 189, 191–93, 196–200
Page, Capt. John H.: 10, 13, 26, 28, 38, 51, 57
Parker, Col. Dangerfield, commander of Fort Supply: 202–17
Parker, Eli S.: 36, 56
Parker, Samuel: 44
Pawnee Indians: 115–18, 119, 134, 135, 205
Payne, E. W.: 122
Penrose, Gen. William W.: 28
Pepoon, Lt. Silas: 17n., 24, 33, 35–37
Perry Land Office: 205, 209, 212
Piley, Capt. A. J.: 18
Ponca Indian Reservation: 180, 182, 191, 205, 208, 209
Pond Creek, Indian Territory: 32, 34ff., 194, 196, 199, 207, 209, 210, 215, 218ff.
Pope, Gen. John: 46, 56, 69, 77, 79, 90, 91, 93ff., 108ff., 157
Potter, Col. (U.S. Army): 160, 163, 168, 170
Powder Face (Arapaho): 117
Pratt, Lt. R. B.: 74
Price, Maj. William: 92ff., 101–102

Quarantine laws: 194, 195, 197, 198, 202–203

Rafferty, Capt. William A.: 106
Railroad survey crews: 60, 63, 76–79, 88
Randall, Capt. George M.: 157
Rankin, W. A.: 38, 44
Rath, Peter: 98–99&n.
Raulston, Capt. George F.: 44, 52
Read, Lt. George W.: 171
Remington, Capt. Philip H.: 108, 122
Remington, Frederick: 99n.
Rendlebrock, Capt. Joseph: 120–28&n.
Reno–Wichita Road: 134
Reynolds, Albert E.: 148, 149n.
Rife, Capt. Joseph B.: 58

Ripley, Capt. H. I.: 33
Rivers, Lt. Tyree R.: 213
Rock Island Railroad: see Chicago, Rock Island and Pacific Railway
Roe, Frances M.: 137
Rogers, Capt. B. H.: 209, 212
Ross, Robert B. (Cherokee): 191
Round Mound (on Santa Fe Trail): 59
Round Pond, Oklahoma Territory: 210, 215, 218, 219
Running Buffalo (Cheyenne): 164, 165
Ryan, Pat: 145

Safford, Lt. Marion B.: 203, 211, 212
Sand Creek Massacre: 3, 65
Santa Fe Trail: 5, 59
Satanta (Kiowa): 4, 27, 42–43, 46, 84
Schindel, Capt. Jeremiah S.: 60
Schmalse, William F.: 98
Seventh Cavalry, U.S.: 11, 15, 18, 24ff.
Sheedy, D.: 117, 122, 133
Sheridan, Gen. Philip H.: 5, 8ff., 28, 29, 37, 130, 157, 165, 166, 171; at Fort Supply, 17–25
Sheridan's Roost, Indian Territory: 81, 130, 177
Sherman, Gen. William T.: 5, 9, 90–91, 93
Short brothers (cattlemen): 194–96
Simpson, Jerry: 197
Sitting Medicine (Cheyenne): 165&n., 168
Sixteenth Infantry, U.S.: 125, 127
Sixth Cavalry, U.S.: 62, 65ff., 78, 80, 85, 89ff., 102, 106, 108
Smith, Col. C. H.: 126
Smith, George W.: 98–99&n.
Smith, Hoke: 201, 204
Smith, John: 11, 13
Smith, Lt. Abiel L.: 131–32, 134–35
Smithers, Lt. Robert G.: 49–51, 53
South Enid, Oklahoma Territory: 218ff.
Southern Kansas Railroad: 181, 185
Speed, Horace: 192

Spotted Horse (Pawnee): 119
Springer, A. G.: 147, 150, 151, 152&n.
Standard Cattle Company: 167
Stillwater, Oklahoma Territory: 205n., 209, 213
Stone Calf (Cheyenne): 117, 132, 161, 163
Stone Wolf (Kiowa): 88
Sully, Gen. Alfred: 13ff., 68, 146; expedition of, against Indians, 10–12
Sully trail (near Fort Supply): 10, 16, 40, 71
Supply–Agency road: 83
Supply–Elliott road: 146n., 150, 180
Supply–Kiowa road: 181
Swineford, Alfred P.: 204, 205

Tall Bull (Cheyenne): 30, 40
Talley, William: 85, 88
Tappan, John F.: 148
Tatum, Lawrie: 90
Taurus Cattle Company: 167
Telegraph: 158, 181
Teller, Henry M.: 162
Tenth Cavalry, U.S.: 17n., 21, 30, 35, 38, 43, 47ff., 59ff., 74–75, 106, 138
Thelkeld, Lt. H. L.: 203–204
Third Cavalry, U.S.: 204, 205, 207, 217, 219
Third Infantry, U.S.: 10, 21, 26, 40, 45, 49, 52–53, 57–58, 75, 90
Thirteenth Infantry, U.S.: 179–81&n., 203, 207, 217, 219
Thomas, George: 150
Thompson, Lt. James: 108
Timber thieves: 160, 185–87
Tonkawa Reservation: 182, 205
Tracy, Charles F.: 48
Treaty of Little Arkansas River (1865): 3
Treaty of Washington (1866): 182, 185
Tupper, Capt. Tullius C.: 62
Twenty-fourth Infantry, U.S.: 153, 157, 168, 179

Twenty-third Infantry, U.S.: 130, 153, 156

Upper Arkansas Indian Agency: 31&n., 32n., 34
Upper Bear Creek Station, Kans.: 57, 58, 70, 143&n.; *see also* Bear Creek Mail Station, Kans.
Ute Indians: 61, 63, 72, 75, 82–83

Viele, Capt. Charles D.: 60, 63, 65, 66, 70

Wade, Col. James P.: 210
Walker, Lt. Kirby: 204, 207, 211, 216–17
Wallace, Lt. I.: 40
Walls, Lt. C. H.: 170
Washita River: 4&n., 46, 57, 61, 62, 80, 94, 96–97, 147, 169, 170, 174, 175, 177, 190, 193, 196
Waterbury, Capt. William: 210, 212
Watkins, William: 89
Wells, William: 132–33, 163
Wenie, Lt. Thomas M.: 152
West, Lt. Frank: 83, 96, 97
Western Cattle Trail: 169
Wheaton, Capt. Charles: 161
Whirlwind (Cheyenne): 46, 118
Whisky traders: 44, 59–60, 64–65, 73–75, 80–81, 86, 88, 90, 107–108
White Horse (Kiowa): 46
Williams, Benjamin: 85, 108, 109
Williams, John F.: 77
Wilson, Abner: 194–96
Wolf Hair (Cheyenne): 215
Wood, Lt. Abraham E.: 126–27
Woodall, Capt. Zachariah T.: 98–99&n.
Woodward, Indian Territory: 180n., 181, 185, 196, 198, 205, 207, 211, 212, 217, 219
Wynkoop, Edward W.: 3

Yard, Lt. Col. John E.: 158, 170
Yellow Bear (Arapaho): 61, 119

FORT SUPPLY, INDIAN TERRITORY was printed on paper which bears the watermark of the University of Oklahoma Press and has an effective life of at least three hundred years.

UNIVERSITY OF OKLAHOMA PRESS

NORMAN